DR. CAROL J. EAGLE
AND CAROL COLMAN

A FIRESIDE BOOK

PUBLISHED BY SIMON & SCHUSTER

NEW YORK   LONDON   TORONTO   SYDNEY   TOKYO   SINGAPORE

ALL

THAT

HELPING YOUR DAUGHTER

SHE

MAINTAIN HER SELF-ESTEEM

CAN

BE

FIRESIDE
ROCKEFELLER CENTER
1230 AVENUE OF THE AMERICAS
NEW YORK, NEW YORK 10020

FIRST FIRESIDE EDITION 1994

FIRESIDE AND COLOPHON ARE REGISTERED TRADEMARKS
OF SIMON & SCHUSTER INC.

DESIGNED BY KAROLINA HARRIS
MANUFACTURED IN THE UNITED STATES OF AMERICA

5   7   9   10   8   6   4

LIBRARY OF CONGRESS
CATALOGING-IN-PUBLICATION DATA
EAGLE, CAROL K.
ALL THAT SHE CAN BE : HELPING YOUR DAUGHTER
MAINTAIN HER SELF-ESTEEM /
CAROL J. EAGLE AND CAROL COLMAN.
P.   CM.
INCLUDES BIBLIOGRAPHICAL REFERENCES AND INDEX.
1. PARENT AND TEENAGER—UNITED STATES.
2. TEENAGE GIRLS—UNITED STATES—PSYCHOLOGY.
3. TEENAGE GIRLS—UNITED STATES—GROWTH.
4. SELF-ESTEEM IN ADOLESCENCE—UNITED STATES.
5. SELF-PERCEPTION IN ADOLESCENCE—UNITED STATES.
I. COLMAN, CAROL.   II. TITLE.
HQ799.15.E34   1993
305.23'5—DC20   93-6791   CIP
ISBN: 0-671-78948-1
ISBN: 0-671-88554-5 (PBK)

ACKNOWLEDGMENTS

Many people helped us with this book. We would like to thank Meg Schneider for her excellent advice. We owe a special debt of gratitude to our editors at Simon & Schuster, Marilyn Abraham and Bob Bender, for helping to make this project a reality. We also want to thank our agent Richard Curtis for his support.

Many thanks to Jane Simon, M.D., for sharing her thoughts and insights with Carol Colman early on in this project.

A special mention to Lillian Schwartz, Ph.D., my coauthor for *Psychological Portraits of Adolescents* (Lexington Books, in press), a colleague and dear friend who has contributed much to my knowledge.

Many thanks to Rebecca Fleischer for her thorough research and Sebastian Bliffield and Amy Schiff for their secretarial help.

I would like to thank all of the many cotherapists and students who have worked with me in the psychotherapy group for young adolescent girls at Montefiore Medical Center. Through the years, I have learned a great deal from our collaborative efforts. Finally, I would like to thank the girls themselves—those in the clinic group and those in my private practice—who have shared their thoughts, feelings, and opinions with me. *All That She Can Be* is a tribute to these very special girls.

To Susan: the best of all daughters
Carol J. Eagle

To my mother—with love always
Carol Colman

CONTENTS

I YOUR DAUGHTER'S ADOLESCENCE

1 IS YOUR DAUGHTER AT RISK?   13
2 STILL ANGRY AFTER ALL THESE YEARS?   32
3 HER CHANGING BODY   46
4 HER INTELLECTUAL AND EMOTIONAL GROWTH   60

II YOUR DAUGHTER'S WORLD

5 THE FAMILY DYNAMIC   81
6 "WHO AM I NOW?"   107
7 PEERS, PRESSURE, AND FRIENDSHIP   130
8 THE ACADEMIC SLIDE   148
9 DATING AND SEXUALITY   170

III SPECIAL SITUATIONS

10 SELF-DESTRUCTIVE BEHAVIORS   199
11 DIVORCE AND STEPFAMILIES   220

    RESOURCES   237
    SELECT BIBLIOGRAPHY   239
    INDEX   243

I

YOUR DAUGHTER'S ADOLESCENCE

ONE: IS YOUR DAUGHTER AT RISK?

Jennifer, who has just turned 13, was always a good student and enthusiastic about school. In fact, she was such a good student that she was placed in a special honors program at her junior high school. Within the past year, however, her grades have slipped to B's and C's in two subjects—math and science. Now Jennifer wants to drop out of the advanced classes in these subjects, because, she says, they are "too hard" and she doesn't have any time to have fun. On the one hand, her parents are convinced that she can do better, on the other hand, they're not sure that she needs to.

Although 14-year-old Chris is slim and attractive, she is constantly dieting and has recently become a vegetarian. Chris loves to cook gourmet feasts for her family, but she rarely joins them for dinner. Chris's parents know that their daughter's mood on any particular day is directly correlated to whether the scale has gone up or down. Although Chris's parents can understand her desire to be thin, they've noticed that her clothes are beginning to hang loose on her.

Karen's parents had always thought of their 12-year-old daughter as a self-assured girl with a mind of her own. Much to their chagrin, however, ever since Karen started junior high school, she has been dressing, talking, and even walking exactly like her best friend. Karen's parents can't wait for their daughter to grow out of it.

The parents of these teenagers have noticed a dramatic change in their daughters' behavior, which they are quick to dismiss as a "teenage phase." To the untrained eye, these girls do appear to be perfectly normal teenagers who are experiencing perfectly normal "growing pains." Jennifer's lack of interest in school, Chris's obsession with her looks, and Karen's desire to be just like her best friend are not unusual for girls their age. However, by dismissing the girls' behavior as "typical," these parents are overlooking important warning signs that their daughters may be headed for trouble.

In reality, Jennifer may not want to drop out of the math and science classes because the work is too hard—she may have lost confidence in her ability to compete, particularly in "male" bastions such as math and science. Chris's zealous dieting and newfound vegetarianism may signal the onset of one of the eating disorders that are epidemic among teenage girls. Karen's copycat tendencies may be a sign that she is losing confidence in her ability to make her own decisions.

If these girls are having difficulty coping with adolescence, they are not alone. Adolescence—traditionally defined as the transitional years between childhood and adulthood—is marked by turmoil and confusion for both sexes. However, it exacts a far greater toll on girls.

In the early 1970s, shortly after I was appointed head of the Division of Child and Adolescent Psychology at Montefiore Medical Center, I started a psychotherapy group for young adolescent girls. What these girls had to say about themselves and their perception of the world around them was at once fascinating and somewhat alarming. Like so many adults, I had forgotten what monumental emotional and physical changes occur during the early adolescent years —especially for girls—and what a vulnerable time this is for them. For many girls, puberty is a negative turning point in their lives. It marks the beginning of a downward spiral that profoundly affects their growth and development, and one that could severely hamper their prospects for the future.

A girl with low self-esteem and a poor sense of herself is going to be an insecure, unhappy teenager. Throughout her adolescence and early adulthood

- She will be at greater risk of developing emotional problems, such as depression and eating disorders, that can have serious long-term consequences.
- Her lack of confidence will prevent her from being able to master the skills she will need to participate fully in the high-tech world of the next century.

- She will be more likely to put her health at risk by smoking, by not practicing safe sex, by becoming pregnant before she is ready to become a parent, and by abusing drugs and alcohol.

If she does not overcome her negative feelings about herself

- She is likely to grow up to be a woman with low self-esteem who is unable to fulfill herself in any number of important ways.
- She is more likely to enter into destructive personal and professional relationships, and she is less likely to assert her rights in the workplace or in social situations.
- She is at greater risk of ending up in a dead-end, low-paying job or having her aspirations thwarted by "glass ceilings" and wage gaps.
- She is at greater risk of becoming a victim of crimes such as date rape and sexual harassment. (Although any woman may be a victim of these crimes, studies show that a woman who has a poor self-image and a poor sense of herself is a more likely victim.)

THE PARENTING DILEMMA

Adolescence is a time of strained communication between parents and their daughters. Girls in particular are not good at articulating their own needs. Most girls lack the clarity of thought and self-confidence needed to clearly state what is on their minds. Although boys also may have difficulty putting their thoughts into words, they manage to get their point across through their actions and behavior. Girls, however, who are typically less aggressive and more inner-directed, do not.

In my private practice, where I meet with patients one on one, weeks or months can go by before a girl finally reveals what is really bothering her. As a therapist, I know that there are few tasks as frustrating as working with a teenage girl. You can feel the intensity of her pain and her anguish, yet, when you try to draw her out, she will sit there in stony silence. Thus it's not surprising that even the most sensitive parents may fail to notice that their daughter is having a difficult time and may be at risk of developing a serious problem that could hamper her growth and development.

When it comes to remembering adolescence, I have noticed that parents, for many reasons, seem to experience a kind of "temporary amnesia." If parents had a troubled adolescence, they may prefer to leave the pain behind. Even parents nearing middle age may find the turmoil of adolescence too close for comfort. Indeed, many psychologists call middle age "middlescence" because, like adolescence, it is a time of growth and self-discovery that can also be a time of awkwardness and self-doubt. For parents grappling with their own "mid-life crises," their daughters' adolescent angst may be a dark mirror of their own insecurities. As a result, in many cases, parents avoid dealing with these problems by withdrawing at precisely the time when their daughters need them the most.

In my practice, I have also been struck by the fact that although most of the parents of the girls in my group knew that their daughters were unhappy—in fact most of these girls had been referred to the clinic because of depression—they didn't have the foggiest notion why. The transition from childhood to adulthood can be a very confusing one, both for girls and their parents. Today's girls appear to be maturing earlier than ever before, but looks can be very deceiving. By age 12½, the typical girl is already menstruating and may be very physically developed. Thanks in part to television and movies, young girls these days use a very sophisticated, adult vocabulary that they often do not fully understand. Yet, because they look so much like women, often dress like women, and may at times even talk like women, their parents expect them to think like, behave like, and indeed *be* women. But they are not women, and no matter how mature they may appear, they are still developing children.

The typical adolescent girl will swing from independence to dependence in the blink of an eye. Although this can be puzzling and exasperating, it is perfectly normal. As one mother put it, "One minute she's telling me that I'm the worst mother in the world. The next minute all one hundred pounds of her crawls into my lap and wants to be babied. *I never know what to expect.*"

It became apparent to me that parents are as thrown by adolescence as their daughters are: They are totally unprepared for this stage of parenting. Ironically, being a parent to an adolescent is in many ways a lot tougher than parenting a younger child. Adolescents are more complex than children and are often needier and more demanding of their parents' time and patience. At the same time, they are pushing for more independence and autonomy. Parents simply don't know what to expect from their daughters, nor do they understand the critical role that they must play during these often difficult years.

I am writing this book for precisely that reason—to help parents know "what to expect," and to help them become more attuned to their daughters' needs. Knowledgeable, aware parents—parents who really understand their daughter's strengths and weaknesses—will be in a better position to provide her with the tools she needs to become a strong, self-confident adult. Knowledgeable, aware parents —who understand their own strengths and weaknesses—will also be better prepared to cope with their own feelings of anger and frustration, which are a natural part of parenting a teenage daughter. Parents *do* have the power to make a tremendous difference in their daughters' lives. Parents can create a climate in which adolescence is a positive time of growth and development for their daughters as well as their sons.

IS YOUR DAUGHTER AT RISK?

The first step is to make parents aware of various situations—at home, at school, out with friends—that may be hazardous to their daughter's emotional or physical health. For this purpose, I have designed a questionnaire to help parents identify girls who may be especially "at risk" during this difficult time.

Some questions relate to your daughter's stage of development in comparison to her peers, some ask about your particular parenting style, and some are concerned with your daughter's personality and friends.

This questionnaire is not only designed to make you, as parents, aware of the girl who is at true risk, but also to help raise parental awareness about the types of situations and issues that can profoundly affect your daughter's life. Your daughter may not show signs of "at risk" behavior now. If, later, she does, you will be savvy enough to pick up the cues early on.

Even if you answer yes to some of these questions, this does not necessarily mean that your daughter has a problem. What this does mean is that you need to take a closer look at your daughter's life, your relationship with her, and any outside influences that could be undermining her self-confidence or steering her in the wrong direction.

1. Is your daughter more physically developed—or less physically developed—than other girls her age? Does she seem to be self-conscious about it?
2. Does your daughter hang out with an older crowd? Do you sometimes worry that her girlfriends wear clothes that are too sophisticated or "sexy," or that they behave in a manner that is inappropriate for their age?
3. Does your daughter have friends who smoke or drink?
4. Does your daughter seem to imitate her friends to excess? Has she adopted the same mannerisms or style of clothing? Are you worried that she is turning into a "follower"?
5. Has your daughter recently made the transition from sixth grade to a middle school or junior high school? If so, have you noticed a drop in her grades, an unwillingness to participate in extracurricular activities, or a lack of enthusiasm about school?
6. Do you feel that your daughter avoids doing anything that is too challenging, mentally or physically?
7. Is your daughter no longer doing well in subjects in which she excelled during elementary school?
8. Is your daughter constantly trying to please her friends? Does she always seem to be the one to give in when they have a disagreement?
9. Does your daughter seem to care more about her boyfriends than they do about her? Is she routinely "dumped"?
10. Is your daughter a chronic dieter? Does she routinely refuse to eat dinner with the family? Do you wonder if she is getting adequate nutrition?
11. If you are a working mother, do you sometimes feel guilty that you are asking your daughter to do too much around the house? If you also have a son, do you divide the chores up fairly between son and daughter?
12. Are you a mother who describes your daughter as "my best friend"?
13. Do you frequently find that after you ask your daughter to perform a household task, you have to finish the job for her because you don't think that she's done it well enough?

14. Do you frequently end arguments with your daughter by saying, "Do what you want. I can't stop you anyway"?
15. Are you disappointed in your daughter's looks?
16. Do you find yourself discussing your son's future more frequently than your daughter's? Do they have equal access to higher education?
17. Are you a father who is spending less time with your daughter than you used to?
18. Does your daughter have a sibling who is so demanding of your time that you are unable to give your adolescent daughter adequate attention? Do you sometimes say to yourself, "She seems to be doing so well that it doesn't matter"?
19. When your daughter entered puberty, did you become more restrictive of her activities? Are you afraid to let her do the same things that you formerly allowed her to do?
20. Is your daughter responsible for caring for a younger sibling, sick parent, or grandparent? Does this responsibility hamper her ability to do her schoolwork or participate in extracurricular activities?
21. Is your daughter the only girl in her crowd who isn't dating? Does she feel bad about this?
22. Do you feel uncomfortable talking to your daughter in clear and frank terms about the perils of unprotected sex (AIDS, other sexually transmitted diseases, pregnancy)?
23. Do you feel uncomfortable talking to your daughter about date rape?

Most parents of adolescent girls will find themselves saying yes to at least one or two of these questions, and many will find themselves saying yes more often than they say no. If you happen to fall into the latter group, take comfort in knowing that even though you may be confronted with more challenges in terms of dealing with your daughter, they are not insurmountable ones. Learning about your daughter and her needs is the first step in helping her surmount the challenges of adolescence.

Although every adolescent girl is a unique individual, different types of girls will exhibit specific patterns of problems. In my experience, adolescent girls tend to fall into three categories based on their particular stage of development: the Fast-Track Girl, the On-Time

Girl, and the Late Bloomer. About 15 percent of all girls are Fast Trackers, that is, they begin to menstruate earlier than the average age of 12.8—some may start as early as 10. Most—70 percent—of all girls are On Time, that is, they begin to menstruate around the time of their 13th birthdays. Another 15 percent are Late Bloomers who begin menstruation later than their peers—sometimes as late as 15 or 16.

FAST, ON TIME, OR SLOW

The Fast-Track Girl

Being the first girl in her group to grow breasts, body hair, and to menstruate can make a girl feel extremely lonely and isolated. As a result of their physical maturity, these Fast Trackers must confront unique problems and are prone to particular kinds of risks.

The On-Time Girl

The On-Time girl is lucky in that she conforms to standard growth charts and matures with her peers. Because she is moving along with the crowd, however, she tends to be constantly comparing herself to her friends, which can make her feel very insecure. Although she is spared many of the problems suffered by Fast Trackers and Late Bloomers, she still experiences a great deal of discomfort and self-consciousness about her body.

The Late Bloomer

As this girl watches her friends develop and mature, she may become very anxious about her own lack of development and needs special reassurance from her parents. In addition, the physical Late Bloomer may lag behind in other important ways. I will discuss her special problems throughout this book.

Whether your daughter is a Fast Tracker, On Time, or a Late Bloomer, there are many issues which all parents have to face. Learning to break down your daughter's "wall of silence" is one of them.

THE WALL OF SILENCE

If you find that you have difficulty reading your daughter's cues, you're not alone. Despite the fact that girls are perceived as being more emotional than boys, girls are actually more adept at concealing their feelings. When a boy is upset, very often he lets his parents or his teachers know by "acting out," for example, by being disruptive at school or at home. Girls are typically not permitted by their parents or their teachers to vent anger or aggression. Therefore, when a girl is upset, she often "acts in," that is, she directs her feelings of anger and aggression toward herself. She feels inadequate and responsible for causing her own problems. When something goes wrong, she is quick to blame herself. When she does badly at school, it is because she is not bright enough. When a boyfriend breaks up with her, it is because she is not pretty enough, or her breasts are too small, or she wasn't giving enough sexually. When she is not accepted by the right clique, it is because she is unattractive or socially inept. This often leads to feelings of depression. Not surprisingly, at least one third of all adolescent girls—twice the number of adolescent boys—experience feelings of depression. Adult women suffer from depression at twice the rate of men. These feelings of depression are inextricably linked to low self-esteem.

HER BATTERED SELF-IMAGE

Girls enter adolescence with an edge over boys. As a rule, they have done better in elementary school, have better social skills, and are generally bursting with confidence about the future. But despite this, by the time a girl starts junior high school, the good feelings that she had about herself vanish. There are numerous studies—some dating back to the 1960s—that document this loss of self-esteem among girls. Many feminists hoped that the women's movement, by expanding the roles and aspirations of women, would give adolescent girls a sense of empowerment that would enhance their self-esteem. But that has not happened. Despite the many social changes brought about by the women's movement over the past two decades, there has been little change in how adolescent girls view themselves. In fact, if anything, perhaps because of the confusion that inevitably arises out of shifting roles, the problem may even have gotten worse.

A 1990 study by the American Association of University Women (AAUW) surveyed boys and girls between the ages of 9 and 15. This study revealed that 8- and 9-year-old girls are "confident, assertive and feel authoritative about themselves." In fact, 60 percent said they were "happy the way I am," as compared to 67 percent of boys the same age. By age 16, however, only 29 percent of girls surveyed said they were "happy the way I am," as compared to nearly 50 percent of the boys. The researchers concluded that as boys and girls grow older, both experienced a loss of self-esteem in a variety of areas, but that "the loss is most dramatic and has the most long-lasting effect for girls."

The negative feelings are manifested in how girls think about their future. Boys dream bigger dreams; they aspire to prestigious occupations and aggressively seek out new challenges. Girls, on the other hand, typically have less-challenging and lofty goals. They are more timid about facing new experiences; they are more fearful and uncertain about what the future may hold. Some girls—through luck or extraordinary personal strength—may be able to "outgrow" these problems on their own, but many will not. Without the proper intervention, many girls will spend much of their adolescence and adulthood trying to cope with these negative feelings about themselves.

There is one notable exception: According to the AAUW study, African-American girls do not experience as significant a decline in self-esteem as do white and Hispanic girls, and I think that there are several explanations for this difference. The primary reason is that the African-American girl often has a powerful role model in her mother, who is often a single mother. Through the years, the African-American community has been portrayed as a matriarchal society in which women are the glue that holds the family together. From early childhood, girls raised in this environment know that they will have to make it on their own—they are not taught to look for a man to "rescue" them, or that they are in any way weaker than or inferior to men. This contributes to the fact that African-American girls may be stronger or more self-reliant.

This is not to suggest, however, that African-American girls have problem-free lives or are any more optimistic about their future than are white girls. Quite the contrary. Despite their high scores on self-esteem tests, African-American girls share many of the same problems as other teenagers, but often in a more virulent form. Where I work, I see many African-American girls follow the same dead-end path: They get pregnant, drop out of school, and end up having to support their children on their own. Many end up on drugs.

Regardless of race, the rules of good parenting remain the same for everyone.

SEPARATION ANXIETY

Why is adolescence such a troubling time for girls? The basic task of adolescent boys or girls is to become adults who are capable of taking care of themselves. Although virtually all children will remain emotionally attached in some way to their parents, parental ties that are typical of childhood must gradually give way to some form of autonomy. Boys have an easier time severing these ties than do girls. Girls generally are more concerned about relationships than boys, and they place great stock in sustaining and nurturing relationships with their parents and friends. Because of these feelings, however, they may have greater difficulty becoming independent from their parents.

It's not just the girls who have trouble letting go—it's also their parents, who tend to cling to their daughters longer and harder than they cling to their sons. The struggle between their need to assert themselves as individuals and their need to remain connected often creates many conflicts within teenage girls.

BODY IMAGE

Adolescent girls are also extremely conflicted about their changing bodies. During adolescence there are of course enormous physical changes in both boys and girls. However, the biology of girls and women is far more complicated than that of boys and men. As a result, "becoming a woman" is much more of a physical ordeal than "becoming a man."

For one thing, even the timing is different. Girls enter puberty about two years earlier than boys and thus must cope with these monumental changes at a younger age. Fast Trackers must deal with these changes even earlier. For another, these changes are far more dramatic for girls than for boys. Between ages 8 and 10, the bodies of boys and girls, with the exception of the genitals, are almost identical—one long, straight line leading from shoulder to torso to legs. As boys develop, they may get heavier, longer, and stronger, but the basic body shape remains the same. No so for girls. The straight lines give way to curves. The breasts begin to grow, the waist goes in, the hips expand. Moreover, girls menstruate, and there is nothing in a pubertal boy's experience that even comes close to the embarrassment and discomfort caused by monthly bleeding.

I have seen girls with string-bean-shaped bodies blossom into voluptuous women practically overnight. A girl as young as 11 or 12 may suddenly find that she has to adjust to a strange new body, and for many, it is a difficult adjustment. Many girls have confided in me, "I don't want to change. I want to go back to the way I was."

As a rule, girls do not feel very good about their new and different bodies. I have never met an adolescent girl between the ages of 11 and 14 who said without reservation, "Gee, I love my body. Growing up is fantastic." I have yet to meet a girl who stepped on the scale and exclaimed proudly, "I've just gained five pounds. Isn't that great?" More likely, a girl will be fretting about how she is too big in some places and too small in others, and almost inevitably, before too long, she'll be on a diet.

Although some boys may be temporarily upset about a changing voice, or the growth of body hair, on the whole, they like what they see. I have heard boys marvel at their new manly physiques and developing muscles. A case in point is a study in which boys and girls were asked what they liked best or least about their bodies. Boys generally answered positively, citing their growing strength and athletic prowess as things that they liked. Girls, on the other hand, had more negative things to say and usually focused on specific areas of the body, such as legs, hips, or facial features. Unlike boys, girls did not view physical development as a source of empowerment that enabled them to do more things; rather, they were most concerned with how they looked. This different mind-set is particularly obvious at the extremes. Adolescent girls will risk their health by dieting to lose weight. Adolescent boys will risk their health—for example, by taking steroids—to bulk up.

THE FAT FACTOR

The obsession with looks goes hand in hand with the obsession with weight. For many teenage girls, weight is a major source of unhappiness. According to a recent study by the Centers for Disease Control in Atlanta, high school girls are much more likely to consider themselves overweight than are high school boys—and they are also much more likely to do something about it. According to the study, dangerous practices such as popping diet pills, frequently skipping meals, and inducing vomiting to maintain a low weight are common among girls. About 5 percent of all 12- to 18-year-old girls in the United States suffer from anorexia nervosa, an eating disorder characterized by such symptoms as excessive weight loss due to an unwillingness to maintain a normal body weight, an obsession with food, cessation of the menstrual cycle, and, often, excessive exercise. Some anorectics are also victims of bulimia, a condition characterized by the consumption of large quantities of food, which are then purged from the body by vomiting or taking laxatives. Anorexia rarely strikes boys and men—90 percent of all anorectics are females, typically from middle- or upper-class homes. About 10 percent of all anorectics eventually die as a result of the disorder, usually from the severe damage inflicted on their organs and body chemistry due to malnutrition or the abuse of laxatives and other "purging drugs."

AT HOME: PUTTING HER IN "HER PLACE"

The different ways in which boys and girls are treated in their own homes is yet further evidence that growing up is harder on girls.

For boys, adolescence ushers in a new period of self-discovery and increasing independence. In most cases, when a boy reaches puberty, his parents loosen their grip, giving their son the freedom to explore his expanding world. It is not unusual for parents to allow a 13- or 14-year-old boy to go out with a friend without adult supervision. Nor is it unusual for parents to allow a boy to ride his bike home after dark, especially if he is tall and physically developed. An adolescent boy's new freedom also means that he is becoming a more equal partner with his parents. Studies show that although a boy and his mother may have more arguments immediately following puberty, after a while the mother backs off, allowing him to win more disputes. In short, the boy usurps some of the mother's power in the household as she accepts his need to be given more authority. (Interestingly enough, this does not happen between boys and their fathers.)

When an adolescent boy challenges authority, it is often viewed as masculine and positive. When an adolescent girl tries to do the same thing, she is quickly put down. Parents are far less tolerant of verbal outbursts from a daughter, which they often view as unlady-like behavior. When a girl attempts to assert herself, she is often accused of "being selfish" or "disrupting the household."

There are other, more insidious ways that girls learn "their place" in the household. At home, the adolescent girl is often treated as her mother's helper. In fact, the legacy of the "overloaded woman" may begin in adolescence. In many two-income or single-parent house-holds, the teenage daughter has become the surrogate mother, baby-sitter and cook. One recent study reported in the *Wall Street Journal* showed that in homes where the mother holds an outside job, a teenage daughter performs an average of ten hours of housework per week, while a teenage son gets away with a mere three hours. This is not only unfair, it sends the wrong message to both boys and girls.

THE SEXUAL DOUBLE STANDARD

As parents "track" girls into traditional female roles, they also im-pose more restrictions on their freedom. After girls reach puberty—particularly after they begin to menstruate—life becomes more con-fining. I know girls who once had the run of their neighborhoods—who were able to visit friends or go shopping by themselves—who now find that their parents are reluctant to let them go anywhere unescorted, especially at night. If they do go out, girls are subjected to earlier curfews, are instructed to call in more often, and are more frequently admonished to "Stay out of trouble," "Avoid strangers," "Stay out of cars," etc.

It's only natural for parents to be concerned about the safety of their daughters, especially since girls and women are more vulnera-ble to such crimes as rape and assault. However, it is counterpro-ductive to make girls feel that they are weak and helpless at the hands of men. Rather, they should be taught the necessary skills to lessen the risks of assault and unwanted sexual advances. Teaching a girl to be "street savvy," or showing her how to avoid dangerous situations is far more constructive than teaching her to live in fear and far better for her self-esteem.

The truth is, boys are also victims of crimes such as mugging—and yes, even rape—yet parents are not as protective of their sons as they are of their daughters. The difference in attitude has a lot to do with the sexual double standard. I rarely hear parents express concern about their sons getting a girl pregnant, but they often express concern about their daughters getting pregnant. Parents are willing to look the other way when it comes to their sons' sexuality, but feel compelled to keep a close eye on their daughters'.

An adolescent girl tends to interpret her parents' view of the world as meaning that "if anything goes wrong, I am to blame." For the first time in her life, she's beginning to feel sexy, attracted to boys, and is probably spending a good deal of time wondering and fantasizing about sex. Although her feelings are natural and normal, she might interpret her parents' concern to mean that there must be something wrong with her sexual feelings. All too often girls associate their "bad feelings" with their changing bodies and thus begin to feel self-conscious and awkward.

DATING AND SEXUALITY

I believe that talking to a girl frankly and honestly about sex is the best way to make sure that she will stay out of "real trouble," that is, that she won't get pregnant or engage in unsafe sex. There is even strong evidence that girls who are close to their parents and can talk to their parents about these issues may be more likely to postpone embarking on a sexual relationship than those who are not.

Parents like to think their daughters are not sexually active, but in many cases, they are. About one third of all girls between the ages of 15 and 17 are sexually active. Unwanted pregnancy is a major problem among adolescent girls. A million teenagers get pregnant every year—half of them become mothers. The high rate of pregnancy is not surprising, considering the fact that one third of all teenage girls do not use contraception the first time they have intercourse.

One out of five sexually active teenage girls does not use contraception at all.

Not only is the girl who does not use contraception at risk of becoming pregnant, she is also increasing the odds that she will contract a sexually transmitted disease such as chlamydia or even AIDS. Although pregnancy may be more common among girls from troubled homes, with the growing number of sexually active girls, it can and does happen to "nice girls" from "good homes."

SCHOOL: POOR PREPARATION FOR LIFE

School is another arena in which girls start first, but, ironically, finish last. As a rule, girls in elementary school get better grades than boys, especially in subjects, such as English, that require greater verbal skill. They also do at least as well as boys in math and science. However, come junior high school, girls—especially bright girls—begin to lose their competitive edge.

Girls' lack of self-esteem is reflected in their attitude about academic performance. When I encounter a girl who isn't doing well in a subject at school, she usually blames herself for being "too dumb" to understand what the teacher is saying. In fact, many girls go out of their way to avoid difficult subjects. When boys don't do well, they blame it on poor teaching or on unusually difficult subject matter, but they rarely blame themselves.

Adolescent girls participate less in class discussions and get called on less often. When they do speak, they are more likely to be interrupted by their teachers than are boys.

From elementary school on up, certain subjects are deemed to be appropriate for girls, while others are not, and this prejudice follows a girl throughout her academic career. For example, studies show that teachers spend significantly more time with boys on math than they do with girls. This lack of attention to math may result in lower grades on college entrance exams. On the SAT exams, 23 percent of boys score over 600 in math, while only 11 percent of girls hit the 600 mark.

Science is another subject that is deemed "male territory." Studies show that teachers are quicker to "rescue" girls from difficult science projects, thus denying them the satisfaction and skill derived from completing a complex task.

While there's nothing wrong with encouraging girls to read, there is something wrong with discouraging girls from studying subjects such as math or science that are essential for their future options: In today's world, math proficiency is particularly important because it is a skill that is required in most of the higher paying occupations. In fact, even though women on average earn about 70 cents to every $1 earned by men, the wage discrepancy is virtually nonexistent for female college graduates with strong math backgrounds.

The workplace has changed enormously over the past two decades.

It is difficult for parents raised in a "low-tech" world to understand the complexity of this new high-tech world, and yet that is exactly what we must do if we want to ensure our daughters a rich and full life. In the workplace of tomorrow, only the most menial jobs will be open to those who are technologically illiterate. Even the "traditionally female" professions—teaching, nursing, and secretarial work—will be closed to anyone who is not comfortable with the new technology. Classrooms are becoming computerized; many hospitals and offices are already technological wonderlands. Whatever career your daughter may choose to pursue, she will need a firm foundation in science and math, and it is up to you to make sure that she gets it.

FOR GIRLS: THE FUTURE IS FUZZY

By late adolescence, both boys and girls are expected to have some idea of their future lifestyle and occupation. Once again, this is a more difficult task for girls than for boys.

For boys, the men's movement notwithstanding, there's no question that they're going to be breadwinners no matter what else they decide to do. For girls, the future is fuzzier. Despite recent and profound changes in family life and the work force, many girls are still being raised to be part of a nuclear family in which they will not be expected to be a serious wage earner. It is the rare parent who sits down with his or her daughter and asks, "Do you expect to have children? Have you thought about how you're going to support them?" The underlying assumption is that a male will be there to provide support. Yet the typical nuclear family in which the husband is the primary breadwinner is fast becoming a thing of the past. By the time your daughter is married, it may be nonexistent: Today, the overwhelming majority of women, married or not, mothers or not, work outside the home. In fact, the average woman will spend about thirty years of her life working outside the home.

In most cases, she is working because she has to. In white families, women account for more than one third of the family income. In African-American families, they provide about half. (That's assuming that, white or African-American, they are married.) If current trends continue, your daughter stands an even chance of getting divorced, and in most cases, that means she will end up as a single mother raising children on her own for a good part of her life.

Today, the poorest person in America is the child of a single mother who needs to rely on welfare or the generosity of relatives to scrape by. Many of these single mothers did not start out poor. Many started out from nice middle-class homes: It can happen to your daughter, too. This cycle of poverty will continue unless the girls of today are taught to dream bigger dreams and to acquire the necessary skills and drive to fulfill them.

SMOKING AND SUBSTANCE ABUSE

Many girls engage in behavior that seriously threatens their health. Alcohol is the number one drug of choice among teenagers, girls included. A recent study reveals that 92 percent of all high school seniors have used alcohol and 20 percent of all 14- to 17-year-olds are considered "problem drinkers." About 5 percent of all women are problem drinkers, and many began during adolescence.

Cocaine and crack—a highly addictive form of cocaine—are also gaining in popularity. Due to females' unique physiology, these drugs are particularly lethal for girls and women. Girls need to know that using these drugs is not chic, it's suicidal.

Although they are legal, cigarettes are also extremely dangerous for girls. Every year, one million teenagers take up smoking. More than half of these new smokers are girls. Experience has taught me that girls smoke not only because they want to look mature and sophisticated, but because they regard smoking as a tool to stay thin. In not-so-subtle ways—such as by marketing brands with names like Virginia Slims—the cigarette companies are targeting and preying upon these young consumers. There is also compelling evidence that girls who are depressed are more likely to smoke. Since for these girls smoking becomes a method of coping with depression as well as a way of satisfying their nicotine craving, it is doubly addictive. Parents should be extremely concerned about teenage smoking, because the earlier in life a girl begins smoking, the more likely it is that she will suffer from a smoking-related disorder down the road. You only need to look at the growing numbers of women suffering from stroke and heart disease to recognize that smoking should not be dismissed as harmless youthful experimentation. The fact is, it can seriously imperil the health of a young woman.

IMPROVING THE ODDS

Clearly, for many girls, adolescence is the defining period in their lives, for it is during this tumultuous period that girls develop their view of the world and their place in it. Whether it marks the beginning of a girl's ascendancy or decline will, of course, depend upon her own unique strengths and weaknesses. But it also depends on you. Appropriate intervention at the right time can make an enormous difference in your daughter's life. Most of the problems of adolescence can be overcome if parent and daughter tackle them together.

Sensitive and creative parenting can help a girl avoid or overcome eating disorders and can help her avoid the anguish of AIDS and teenage pregnancy. A parent who knows the appropriate way and time to intercede can help an insecure, unhappy child regain her self-confidence—before she gets locked into a cycle of disappointment and failure.

In the rest of this book, I will show you what you can do to help your daughter surmount problems and challenges and enjoy the bright future she deserves. *All That She Can Be*

- Will show you how to become a powerful advocate on your daughter's behalf
- Will teach you how to accurately read the problems that your daughter is encountering so that you can help her cope with them
- Will show you how to communicate with your daughter so that you do not operate in separate, hostile worlds
- Will help you to become a more creative, sensitive parent.

Three decades of treating adolescent girls and their parents has taught me this: If we become and stay attuned to our daughters' needs and concerns, and if we deal honestly and directly with their problems, we will send confident, self-assured, and—perhaps most importantly—happy adult women out into the world. Moreover, we will also be establishing wonderful and enduring relationships with our daughters and building stronger and healthier families.

TWO: STILL ANGRY
AFTER ALL THESE YEARS?

I wrote this book to help you to better understand your daughter's adolescence so you can be a more compassionate and effective parent. Before you can do this, however, you need to better understand yourself. The way to do this is to spend some time thinking about your own adolescence and how it may affect the kind of parent you are today.

Our own experiences during adolescence can have a profound impact on the way that we parent our adolescent children. Hopefully, those experiences exert a positive influence over our parenting.

Sometimes, however, painful memories from childhood can interfere with our ability to be good parents. If we are angry about the way our parents treated us, it can sabotage our efforts to parent effectively. If we are angry about other things that happened to us during adolescence—if we remember feeling unpopular, lonely, or isolated—and we try to deny those feelings, that too, can adversely affect the way we parent.

Many parents have a "blind spot" when it comes to seeing the link between their own adolescence and how they react to their children's. They may choose to bury the memories of adolescence simply because they *are* so hurtful. This is understandable. For many of us, adolescence evokes memories of awkwardness and discomfort—not exactly the kind of memories we want to relive.

Adolescence also frequently evokes confusing memories about our own parents. It can be especially painful to confront feelings of anger and rage toward our parents. Yet, if we don't deal with our parents' shortcomings in an honest way, we can end up making even more serious mistakes with our own children.

People who were the victims of bad parenting are often so afraid of inflicting similar pain on their own children that they inadvertently withdraw from their parenting responsibilities. Thus they fail to offer any discipline or guidance at a time when their children need it the most.

Others may react in an opposite, but equally destructive way. They deny their feelings of anger. They convince themselves that the bad things that were visited upon them by their parents really weren't so bad. In fact, they rationalize their treatment by claiming that it made them into the men or women that they are today. Tragically, they often go on to act out their rage on their own children.

As hard as we may try to bury painful memories, we can never truly forget them. Anger and pain have a way of staying locked inside of us, festering and growing for generations to come, coloring and distorting our relationship with our daughters and our feelings about ourselves. Therefore, we owe it to our children and to ourselves to reexamine the past with an open mind.

Looking back on our own adolescence can help build a bridge of empathy between ourselves and our children. It not only helps us to understand our children better, but enables us to gain insight into ourselves and why we may react to our children in the particular way that we do.

In order to help bridge the gap between the present and the past, I have compiled a brief questionnaire to help you reflect on your own adolescence. These questions will stir some memories that will help you identify the types of issues that may be affecting your relationship with your daughter.

Some questions will concern the type of household in which you were raised. Others will ask you to recall your perceptions of yourself during adolescence and how you felt you were treated by your family and friends. Still others will evoke memories of your parents' relationship, how you felt about it, and how it may be affecting your relationship with your family today.

LOOKING BACK

1. Do you feel that an important dream or goal went unfulfilled because your parents did not offer the proper guidance or direction during adolescence, or seemed not to care? Do you feel that you would be doing something very different today if they had acted differently?

2. Were you the type of adolescent whose parents could say, "(S)he never gave me any trouble"? Do you feel that you were so "good" that you missed out on normal adolescent experiences?

3. Do you feel that you "wasted" adolescence by spending too much time "sowing your wild oats"? Do you feel that you were sexually promiscuous during adolescence? Do you wish that your parents had been stricter or watched over you more closely?

4. Was power evenly divided between your parents, or was your father "the ruler of the roost"? How did you feel about the division of power in your household?

5. What were the main issues that you and your parents fought over? Were you ever physically punished? Did either one of your parents have such a bad temper that you were actually frightened of what they would do?

6. Did your family label you in any way (for example, "The Smart One," "The Slow One," "The Selfish One," "The Good One," "The Pretty One")? Do you feel that the label was valid or fair?

7. Do you feel that your parents gave you a voice in matters that concerned you, for instance, did they listen to your views on what camp you'd like to attend, or how to spend money that was given to you as a gift?

8. If you came from a family with siblings, were the males favored over the females? Were you raised to believe that girls were less capable or deserving than boys?

9. Were you popular in high school, or did you often feel left out of the social mainstream?

10. During adolescence, were you On Time, a Late Bloomer, or a Fast Tracker? In what areas? Try to be precise.

11. What were the main points of contention between your siblings and your parents? Between you and your siblings?

12. Did you feel bad about the way the women in your family were treated?
13. Did your father hold the purse strings? Do you (or your husband) do the same thing?
14. If you could do it all over again, what would you change about your adolescence?

From your answers you can recreate your past to determine what issues may be affecting your behavior toward your daughter. Look for any patterns that may emerge from your responses. Do your memories suggest that you may have felt powerless at the hands of your parents? How do you deal with issues of power regarding your own daughter? Do you feel that your parents favored your sibling? How do you deal with sibling rivalry in your home?

Many of these questions are quite specific and, hopefully, may have started you thinking about your own adolescence in a new way. As adults, we tend to look back on adolescence in very broad terms. But our reactions to our children's behavior are often in reaction to the specifics of our past. The more aware we are of the particular issues that we may feel pained or confused by, the more sensitive and flexible we will be in dealing with our own children.

THE TELLTALE SIGNS

Parents allow what happened in their past to negatively affect their parenting in different ways. In the end, how the feelings emerge in parenting depends on how well we have or have not faced our past.

How can you tell if "ghosts" from the past are intruding in an unhealthy way on your relationship with your daughter? Here are some warning signs that could alert you to the fact that you are reacting to a past experience:

Automatic pilot. Certain situations may trigger an extreme response. You react without thinking, as if some outside force is propelling you forward—I call that response "going on automatic pilot." For example, you may find something that your daughter does or says to be so infuriating that you're in a rage for days, but you may not be able to articulate why. Or, in some cases, you become so confused, hurt, or angry over something that she does that you feel completely helpless and pull away from her, leaving your daughter to her own devices at a time when she may need you the most. When your response to your daughter is very exaggerated—when you can't really justify your emotional response—chances are the automatic pilot is kicking in, and something from your own past is triggering this reaction.

Relentless rage. If you're constantly angry at your teenager and often respond in an extreme way to everything that she does, it could be a sign that something else is triggering this continuous flood of emotions.

Apathy. If you find yourself saying "I can't handle this" or "I don't care what she does," it could be a signal that she has touched a nerve, and you find the situation too painful to deal with.

You're obsessed. If you can't sleep at night because you're particularly concerned about some aspect of your daughter's life that you know deep down inside does not warrant that kind of concern (one bad grade, she wasn't asked to the prom, or another "typical teenage" problem), it could mean that some experience from your past is causing your reaction.

Locking horns. If you're locked in a power struggle with your daughter over a particular issue—for instance, if you're furious that she insists on wearing the same pair of faded, torn jeans when she has a closet full of new clothes—ask yourself why. What is so important about this one thing? Obviously, if it's an issue pertaining to her health and safety, your feelings are justified. But if you are constantly battling over something that is not a critical issue, you need to step back and assess your own motives: What in your past could be causing you to act this way? Were your parents overly critical of your appearance? Would it really matter if you relented?

This is the way we've always done it. Are you very rigid about a particular issue? Do you expect your daughter to do something "your" way simply because it's how it was done when you were growing up?

If any of these examples hit home, you need to ask yourself, "Why am I doing this? What in my past is causing me to feel this way?" The answer may be very obvious, or it may take weeks or months of sifting through emotional debris. Some people may do this exercise very successfully on their own, others may require help. Obviously, if the past has intruded on the present to the point that your relationship with your daughter has badly deteriorated, I recommend that you seek outside counseling.

PAST EXPERIENCES: PRESENT MISTAKES

Coming to terms with the past and being able to differentiate between the past and the present is critical for good parenting. If you are aware of your reactions to the past, you will be less likely to be swept away by powerful emotions that can confuse and hurt your ability to deal appropriately with your teenager.

Here are some examples of common mistakes made by parents who have not come to terms with their own past experiences.

Pulling Away: In Memory of Rejection

Before he confronted his past, my patient Jim was totally unaware of how the past can intrude upon the present in an especially harmful way.

Jim had two daughters: The oldest daughter, Karen, was very pretty, but Sarah, who was two years younger, was a gangly Late Bloomer. When his daughters were young children, Jim was close to both of them. However, once Karen reached adolescence, he showered attention on the younger, less-attractive girl. Jim went out of his way to spend time with Sarah and to help her with her homework. In contrast, he was distant and somewhat cool to Karen, who, sensing his disapproval, was very jealous of the close relationship he had with Sarah.

Jim was aware that he favored one daughter over the other, but attributed it to the fact that he was "disappointed" in how Karen had turned out. When I asked him specifically what was wrong with her, he said, "All she wants to do is date and have a good time. My other girl has a much better head on her shoulders."

I later learned that Jim, who had also been a Late Bloomer, was an especially awkward adolescent who was very envious of the popular crowd at his high school. It was easy for him to empathize with his younger daughter and to feel her pain. On the other hand, not only couldn't he identify with his older daughter, but he was somewhat awed by her beauty and popularity. Rather than risk rejection, he simply pulled away from her. The automatic pilot was moving him on a course that was set two decades earlier.

Once Jim recognized what he was doing, he made an effort to reach out to Karen and try to get to know her better. Their relationship began to improve, and Karen no longer felt as if she were being rejected.

Jim's negative feelings about himself during adolescence nearly destroyed his relationship with his elder daughter. Jim's is not an isolated case. Parents very often confuse their past with their daughter's present and, by doing so, completely miss important signs of need on their daughter's part.

Ignoring Her Needs: In Memory of Loneliness

Debby Miller recently sought therapy to help her deal with her 14-year-old daughter, who seemed to be getting into deeper and deeper trouble. Every week, Debby would come in with another story. "Susan came home at one o'clock again last night, with a different boy, and I think that she had been drinking."

"I'm afraid that Susan may be experimenting with drugs."

"I hope Susan doesn't get pregnant."

No matter what Susan did, however, Debby didn't try to stop her. I was completely baffled by Debby's lack of action with respect to her daughter's problems, and I was also growing increasingly concerned about what would happen to Susan. As I learned more about Debby's adolescence, I began to better understand her reaction to her daughter. Debby had been just the opposite of Susan: She had been a "good girl" whose parents kept her on a tight rein until she was well into adulthood. A studious, serious teenager, Debby had not even gone on a date until she was in college. As an adolescent, she felt very lonely and isolated.

It became obvious why Debby was so lax with her daughter—she was reacting to her own rigid upbringing by allowing her daughter to do all the things that she wished that she had done. I finally said, "It must be very difficult for you to know the limits and restrictions that you should be setting for your daughter, because I bet you dreamed of having that kind of life when you were an adolescent." In a flash of recognition, Debby said, "My God, I never thought of that."

Once Debby acknowledged that her past was interfering with her ability to be an effective parent, we were able to discuss the ways in which she could steer her daughter in a less destructive direction.

Getting It Right: In Memory of What Went Wrong

Although many parents attempt to block out the memories of adolescence, for others, the memories are still fresh and all too vivid. They view their daughter's adolescence as an opportunity to revise their own personal histories, to right the wrongs of the past, as a second chance to do it right.

For example, Linda, a 15-year-old girl attending a private school, was recently referred to me because her mother, Kate, was concerned about her acting-out behavior. Within the past year, Linda had begun to smoke and to hang out with a crowd that her mother did not approve of. Much to her mother's chagrin, Linda's grades had fallen off, and she seemed uninterested in school.

As I got to know more about Kate, I began to understand a great deal more about why Linda was doing what she was doing. Kate, who was raised in the 1960's, had an older brother who consumed most of her parents' attention and resources. Although Kate had gotten better grades than her brother, he was sent to an Ivy League school, while Kate attended a mediocre state university. Feeling she had few options, Kate became a teacher and always regretted that she had not gone to law school.

When Linda was born, Kate vowed that her daughter would have the chances that she had never had.

As soon as Linda began school, Kate made it clear that she expected her to be the best. Every afternoon, they would do Linda's homework together, and Kate always pushed Linda to do extra work. Initially, she did extremely well in school, bringing home "A" papers and perfect report cards. Once she reached adolescence, however, Linda began to cut classes and complain about being bored in school.

Kate was furious at Linda for "wasting away" the very opportunities that Kate had so desperately wanted for herself. Linda, on the other hand, was also furious at Kate, and although she couldn't articulate it, sensed that her mother was using her as a surrogate to fulfill her own dreams.

Kate unfairly expected Linda to make up for all Kate's past hurts and disappointments, and by doing so, was seriously damaging her relationship with her daughter.

Once Kate realized what she was doing, she stopped pushing Linda so hard, and Linda stopped rebelling.

Through this experience, Kate learned an important lesson: Part of the task of confronting the past is recognizing that we can't change it, we simply have to learn to live with it. Nor can we expect our current relationships to make up for past losses. It is unfair to pin our hopes and dreams on our children, we have to let them find their own.

"It Did Me Good": In Memory of Otherwise Unacknowledged Pain

Unacknowledged pain is perhaps the most dangerous kind of all, because it can make us hurt the ones we love.

June referred her daughter, Lynn, to treatment because she said that the 16-year-old was "wild and out of control." But after a few sessions with the two of them, I realized that June was the one with the problem.

June had had a very strict, rigid upbringing in which she was severely punished for even the most minor of infractions. June should have been furious at her parents, but instead seemed to go out of her way to justify their harsh treatment of her. Outwardly, her attitude was "I was such a wild kid, if they hadn't stopped me I don't know what would have happened." But inside, she was raging, and she took it out on Lynn, who was also being subjected to severe punishment and an equally mindless brand of authoritarianism.

June was trying desperately hard to legitimize her parents' actions by adopting them herself. Her response is not uncommon. It is very hard for people to come to terms with the fact that they may have been treated badly by their parents and that their parents may not have been as caring and considerate as they should have been. For some, this is tantamount to admitting that their parents didn't love them, and that is something that they do not want to believe. Therefore, like June, they distort reality by claiming that they had the best parents in the world and set out to imitate their destructive and painful style of parenting.

Keep Her Safe: In Memory of My Mistakes

Some parents may blindly repeat the mistakes of the past, but others may try so hard to avoid them that they make even bigger mistakes.

I recently treated a 15-year-old girl whose life was being made miserable by her mother's desire to protect her from the mother's own past mistakes.

Nancy was twenty pounds overweight, very passive, and very unhappy. Her clothes were drab, her hair was pulled back in an unflattering ponytail. In contrast, her mother, Terry, was a strikingly attractive woman who dressed impeccably. Nancy's parents were concerned that their daughter was deeply depressed, and they couldn't figure out why.

After talking to Nancy, I realized that what Nancy wanted was to be like other girls. She wanted to look pretty, dress nicely, and go on dates, but that was not what her mother wanted for her. Her mother, Terry, had been a classic Fast Tracker, a beautiful girl who looked older than her years. She dated early, experimented with sex long before her girlfriends, and as a result, took on more than she was emotionally capable of handling. Her grades suffered, and she decided not to bother with college, which she always regretted. Terry was determined that her daughter would not repeat her mistakes and encouraged her to focus solely on academics.

Nancy didn't mind concentrating on school during childhood, but once she hit puberty, she began to feel very isolated and alone. It hurt when the boys that she was interested in didn't give her a second look, or when the girls she wanted to befriend considered her to be a "nerd." Frustrated, and unable to find any other pleasure in her life, Nancy turned to eating. She put on a few extra pounds at first, but then her petite body practically doubled in size. Terry, however, did not consider this to be a serious problem. "Look, so what if she's a bit overweight, she could be getting herself into a lot more trouble than that. Believe me, I know."

In an attempt to "protect" her daughter from the painful experiences that she had had as an adolescent, Terry had pushed Nancy into an equally painful situation. In reality, her attempt to control her daughter was actually stifling her and creating a very unnatural environment. Through family therapy, Terry eventually began to see how her actions were hurting her daughter, and she eventually loosened her grip. Once Nancy was permitted to be a normal adolescent, she rapidly lost weight and began to enjoy what was left of her adolescence.

The important lesson Terry learned: You can't shield a child from all of life's mistakes, nor should you try to. Adolescents need to find their own way. Only through experience will teenagers grow and learn.

Parents do, however, need to offer a reasonable amount of protection and guidance. They do need to give their daughters the tools to make good decisions about their lives. However, overprotection to the point of suffocation denies a teenager the opportunity to learn on her own. Even more important, it prevents a girl from developing the self-assurance she needs to feel that she is capable of taking care of herself.

PUTTING THE PAST TO GOOD USE

Parents who understand the past and how they may have been affected by it can use that knowledge to create a better environment for their daughters.

The past can enhance your understanding of the present. By looking backward, you may be able to anticipate problems in your daughter's life before they happen, or at least spot little problems before they career out of control.

The past can also be a powerful tool in increasing empathy and understanding between the generations. If you remind your teenager that you were once young too, with similar feelings, she may be willing to listen longer and harder.

Here are some ways in which your understanding of your own past can help:

You can convey your love and concern naturally and calmly.

Daughters and parents often drift apart during the more difficult stages of adolescence—but some drift farther apart than others.

I knew one mother who became distraught when her 14-year-old daughter began to shut her out of her life, as adolescent girls often do. When the mother tried to ask any questions, she would receive one-syllable answers, or a sullen nod of the head. The mother found her daughter's actions to be particularly upsetting because it reminded her so much of her strained relationship with her own mother, who, unlike her, had been distant and unloving.

One afternoon, when her daughter had been especially uncommunicative, the mother felt herself becoming furious. She wanted to grab her daughter and scream, "You never tell me anything, I'm always here for you, but you shut me out," but she knew instinctively that anger would only drive a bigger wedge between them. Nor did she want to do something that her mother had done to her, blame her daughter for the sorry state of their relationship. Instead, she said calmly, "You know, I keep asking questions about what you're doing or what you're thinking or what you're interested in, and you just give me a cold shoulder. The reason I'm so interested in us talking about these things is that I always dreamed that when I was a mother, I would be able to have these kinds of conversations with my daughter, because I wasn't able to have them with my mother."

The mother then dropped the subject. But the next time she tried to talk to her daughter, she found her somewhat more receptive, and, eventually, her daughter began to fill her in on what was going on in her life.

This mother was able to share her past with her daughter without imposing it on her. More importantly, she was able to present herself as a caring human being with feelings and dreams. By doing so, she was able to bridge the growing gap between herself and her daughter.

You can help your spouse better understand his or her behavior.

Another mother was able to draw upon the experiences of the past to stop a potentially dangerous dynamic that was developing in her household between her daughter and her husband. Anne, who had been the classic "good girl" most of her childhood, had a great deal of difficulty asserting her independence from her parents. Anne was kept in line by her father, who had an unpredictable temper, and her mother, who cautioned Anne not to get Daddy angry.

When Anne finally graduated from college, she was a confused, unfocused young woman who had no sense of what she wanted to do with her life. With the help of therapy, Anne spent her twenties sorting out her relationship with her parents. Today, she is a self-aware, self-directed person.

Anne is now the mother of an 11-year-old girl who is just beginning to show signs of adolescent rebellion. But her husband, Dan, doesn't like it. "She made a comment that was designed to provoke him, and he really flew off the handle. I've never seen him so angry. I looked at Julie's face, and she was terrified, and it reminded me of me. All I could think was, Oh no, not again."

Following that incident, Anne had a long talk with her husband. "I told him that he had a right to get angry, but that there was a difference between saying, 'Please don't talk to me in that manner' and strutting around screaming and appearing to be out of control.

He knew how I felt about my father, and he felt terrible. He was unaware of how his anger had affected Julie. He apologized to her."

In many households, this story would have had a dramatically different ending. If Anne had been less enlightened, she might have passed down the commandment: "Don't ruffle Dad's feathers," sending a message that men are to be feared and obeyed. But Anne taught her daughter a different lesson—that she did not have to accept abuse. She also taught her husband an invaluable lesson in parenting. By remembering the pain of her youth, Anne was able to calmly get her spouse to see what he was doing and the destructive effect it was having on their daughter.

You can better understand the pressures of adolescence and help your daughter to better cope with them.

Sometimes a parent can tap his or her own experiences to see a potential problem budding in his or her child.

Jenny, the mother of a 12-year-old girl, remembers that during her adolescence, popularity was all that mattered to her. "I went out of my way to do things so that the 'right' kids would like me, even if I didn't want to do them," she recalls. "I was really interested in politics, but only nerds joined the debating team, so I didn't do it. I would have loved to go folk dancing, but the folk dancers were a different crowd that my crowd didn't like, so I didn't go. There were so many really interesting, worthwhile people that I avoided because I didn't want to be associated with them."

Now that Jenny's daughter is entering adolescence, Jenny is beginning to see signs of the same behavior. Recently, her daughter came home from school in tears because her best friend didn't like her haircut. "We had a long talk about why her friend didn't like the haircut, I told her I liked it, I pointed out that the hairdresser thought that she looked great, and I also reminded her that she had liked it very much before she went to school. I stressed that she and her best friend don't have to agree about everything. You know, it's perfectly okay to say, 'Thanks for your opinion, but I still like it.' I wasn't sure that any of this conversation had sunk in, but a few days later I overheard her on the phone saying, 'Well, I like it anyway.' I don't know what it was about, but I was really proud of her."

Jenny's ability to connect to the past helped her daughter to better cope with the intense peer pressure typical of adolescence. Jenny's past experience made her a more aware, better equipped parent, and it will also make her daughter stronger and more self-confident.

You can tap the past to enhance your relationship with your adolescent daughter. Looking back can increase your compassion and understanding; it can prevent you from repeating the mistakes of the past and from inflicting past pains on your children.

Understanding the link between the past and the present will not only make you a more effective parent, but will provide your daughter with a good parenting model. She will pass on a tradition of compassion and understanding rather than one of pent-up anger and rage. She will feel closer to you and closer to her own children, and you will be leaving behind a legacy of good parenting for future generations.

THREE: HER CHANGING BODY

> Dear, dear! How queer everything is today! And yesterday things went on just as usual. I wonder if I've been changed in the night? Let me think: was I the same when I got up this morning? I almost think I can remember feeling a little different. But if I'm not the same, the next question is, "Who in the world am I?" Ah, that's the great puzzle.
> —Lewis Carroll, *Alice's Adventures in Wonderland*

"I feel just like Alice in Wonderland," confessed my patient Stacey, a bright, articulate 12½-year-old who was trying to describe the physical and emotional sensations that have been making her life miserable. "Alice didn't know what was happening to her, and sometimes I feel the same way."

To an adolescent, puberty is a lot like falling down a rabbit hole and landing in a world where everything is topsy-turvy. Like Alice, who could grow or shrink several feet in the course of a day, an adolescent girl's body undergoes a radical transformation in a relatively short period of time. As a result, she often feels confused and uncertain about who she really is and who she is becoming—and so do her parents.

Although I wrote this chapter for parents, it is also written with your daughter in mind. I urge you to share this information with her. Much of the anxiety that girls experience about puberty stems from their not knowing what to expect—of feeling that they are being "ambushed" by a barrage of strange physical changes. Parents need to do a better job of communicating what is going on and explaining what these strange sensations are all about. Girls who fare the best during puberty are those who are best informed; the girls who will be the most overwhelmed will be those who are least prepared.

PREPARING YOUR DAUGHTER FOR PUBERTY

When I ask parents if they've explained puberty to their daughters, they usually reply:

"We've had 'that talk' and she knows all about it," or "She's read this terrific book . . ."

Their daughters tell another story: "Mom showed me this book and it was kind of boring and I didn't understand too much," or "Yeah, I know how babies are made. But I'm curious about something. I have this friend and she got her period once and it went away for six months and then it came back and then it went away . . ."

These girls are filled with questions, and no wonder. Puberty is not something that can be explained in one "mother-daughter talk," or read about in a book. As I frequently remind parents, children are not adults—they do not have adult minds, they cannot grasp difficult concepts in one or two discussions. Parents need to maintain an ongoing dialogue with their daughters, in which they continually review what is happening and why.

By late childhood, most children have a rough idea of where babies come from and even how they are made. They have not yet, however, begun to focus on what will happen to their bodies as their hormones switch into high gear. The ongoing dialogue between parent and daughter should begin before this happens, at around age 9. Her mother (in this case, the child will probably feel more comfortable if this information comes from a woman) should introduce the general concept of puberty and begin to describe in detail how her daughter's body is going to change. This may not make a lot of sense to a 9-year-old, but at least she will have some warning that she is about to enter into a new phase.

Later, when a mother notices the first sign of breast development or pubic hair, she should pick up where they left off by saying, "Remember what I told you six months [or a year, or whatever] ago about how your body will be changing? I notice that you're beginning to look different. Do you know why that's happening?"

Most importantly, a mother should ask her daughter, "How do

you feel about this? Do you have any questions?" If a girl resists talking about these changes, her mother may be able to break down the wall between them by drawing on her own past. "When I was 10, my breasts were starting to get big and I was so embarrassed that I walked around with my arms folded over them, but some of the kids teased me anyway and I felt miserable."

Girls at this age are very egocentric: They think that they are the only ones in the world who have ever had these kinds of feelings. I have found that it can be very helpful to remind a girl that others before her have had similar experiences, as will others who come after her. Not to mention the fact that many of the girls in her class probably feel just as embarrassed or confused as she does right now!

As the physical signs of puberty become very obvious, parents should begin to stress that everybody develops differently—there is no right or wrong way to experience puberty, and girls need to be told this. Some girls will grow at a faster pace than others, some will lag behind. About 15 percent of all girls will menstruate early and another 15 percent will menstruate late. Girls need to understand that regardless of where they fall on the pubertal timetable, they are normal.

DO TELL DAD

Although girls may be more comfortable talking with mothers about the more intimate details of menstruation or other body changes, their fathers should also be involved in some of these discussions. Very often, when a girl starts to menstruate or gets her first bra, her initial response is "Don't tell Dad." Some mothers go along with this because they feel that their daughters would be embarrassed if their fathers knew; others tell the fathers in secret. What these mothers don't understand is that their daughters often don't mean what they are saying. I think most girls desperately want their fathers to know about the major events in their lives, but they have difficulty articulating their feelings. They may be a little self-conscious and embarrassed, but they are also proud that they are growing up and really do want Dad to know. I also think that by not telling Dad, mothers are sending the message that menstruation, or other signs of puberty, are deep, dark secrets that need to be hidden from men. This attitude will only make their daughters feel even more self-conscious. Rather than immediately agreeing with a girl's wish to exclude her father, a mother should say, "Well, I think Dad would be very happy to know that you are growing into a young woman. This is an important moment in your life. Are you sure that you don't want to share it with him?" Many girls will jump at the opportunity to include their fathers.

Some girls have told me that they don't want to tell their fathers because they don't think that their fathers will understand or take the time to listen. "My mom went through the same things, I don't think that my father will know what I'm talking about," explained one 13-year-old. Fathers can counter this attitude by telling their daughters, "I remember what it was like being a boy growing up, but I don't know what it's like to be a girl. But that doesn't mean that I'm not interested in what's happening to you. Tell me about some of the things you're experiencing. I really do want to know what you're going through."

THE GROWTH SPURT

Before puberty officially takes over, a girl's body begins to experience a "growth spurt" that separates the girls from the boys.

Throughout infancy and childhood, at least on a physical level, boys and girls have similar growth patterns. At around the age of 9½ —approximately two years earlier than boys experience their growth spurt—the female biological clock takes over. Hormonal changes trigger the prepubertal growth spurt in which girls begin to grow at a much more rapid pace.

Over the next three to four years, the average girl will become 25 percent taller and will almost double her body weight.

The basic configuration of the female body undergoes a radical transformation. The angular prepubescent body will develop curves. Fat will develop on the stomach, hips, and breasts. If a girl is lucky, her body will fill out as she is growing taller. In some girls, however, the weight gain may precede the height gain, causing what is known as "baby fat," characteristic rolls of fat on her midsection and abdomen. Although this is a source of great anxiety among girls, and in fact has been linked to the later development of anorexia nervosa, in most cases, the fat melts away when the girl grows taller.

During the growth spurt, girls become very self-conscious about their bodies. As one part grows longer and the other grows fatter, the reflection in the mirror never looks quite right. Girls of this age frequently change their clothes two or three times before going outside: They're not just being vain, they are demonstrating their discomfort with their physical selves.

A Fast Tracker may be particularly upset about what she sees in the mirror, especially if it's "baby fat" and she's the first one in her crowd to get it. This girl is going to feel especially unattractive and alienated from her body, and her parents need to be extremely sensitive to her feelings.

Parents should be very careful not to make any girl feel self-conscious or overly concerned about her pubertal weight gain and should take great pains to explain that it is usually temporary. Girls need to be told that over time they will "grow into" their bodies and that what seems strange and awkward now will within a short time seem comfortable and natural.

Once a girl begins menstruating, the growth spurt stops—she will only grow another one to three inches. Increased levels of estrogen prevent the bone cells from dividing as rapidly as before.

During this period of rapid growth, you may notice that your daughter may sleep longer at night or require a nap after school. Some parents attribute this to adolescent laziness, but the hormones associated with growth are secreted during sleep at much higher levels than during periods of wakefulness (which explains why infants require so much sleep). Parents also may notice that their adolescent is developing a voracious appetite. This increased need for food is triggered by the hypothalamus and is meant to ensure that the body has enough energy to fuel these enormous changes. (If your daughter is constantly hungry, and you're worried that she's gaining too much weight, now is not the time to put her on a diet. Rather, stock your house with healthful, nourishing snacks and don't buy junk food that provides "empty" calories.)

BREASTS

At around age 10½, girls begin to develop what are known as secondary sexual characteristics. Breast development is often very gradual and can take an average of four and a half years, although in many cases, it may take even longer. After perhaps some initial self-consciousness, girls tend to regard breast growth in a positive light because full breasts are considered a sign of beauty in our society.

The On-Time Girl, who is developing at the same rate as her peers, will fare the best because she won't attract undue attention. Fast Trackers, who develop breasts earlier, may be the subject of cruel jokes or teasing at school or from siblings. It's important for parents to stress to these early bloomers that the other girls will be catching up with her soon and that early growth does not mean that she is always going to be so noticeable.

The flat-chested Late Bloomer may also be fretting—over her lack of breasts. She may be the butt of cruel jokes, not just from boys, but from other girls. One Late Bloomer told me about a particularly humiliating experience in which a more developed girl at school felt around her shoulders for bra straps. When she didn't find them, she announced loudly to the class that "Lisa still wears undershirts." Adolescents can be very cruel to each other, especially to those whom they consider "slow" or "different."

Even if your daughter is spared this kind of public embarrassment, she may feel that she is far less attractive than her more developed friends. Parents of Late Bloomers need to counter this outside pressure by continually stressing that everybody grows at a different pace and that, in many cases, a flat-chested 14-year-old will fill out nicely by 16 or 17. However, parents should also point out that all bodies are different. Breasts come in different shapes and sizes, and no one "style" is better than any other. Parents need to emphasize that this would be a boring world if everybody looked the same.

At the same time, they should go out of their way to compliment their daughter on her particular strengths: "You've got the most beautiful eyes I've ever seen," or "You're the most wonderful dancer." By doing so, they can help her to feel good about what she does have.

BODY HAIR

The appearance of a small amount of pubic hair usually follows the onset of breast development. Pubic hair begins on the lips of the vagina, and over the course of several years, gradually spreads over the outer labia and in some cases onto the inner thighs. Underarm hair also appears after the first signs of breast development, and the hair on the arms and legs may also become thicker and darker.

Although most girls are fairly nonchalant about pubic hair, they become very upset over the hair that grows on the more noticeable body parts. This is especially true if the hair is especially dark. In some cases, a Fast-Track girl who grows hair before her friends do may also be very embarrassed.

Parents often make light of their daughters' negative feelings about body hair, but they wouldn't if they understood the depth of their daughters' unhappiness over this issue. Very often, parents refuse to allow a girl to shave her legs before a designated age— usually around 13 or 14—regardless of her hair growth. I have talked with young adolescent girls who are terribly self-conscious about their body hair. These girls literally dread putting on a bathing suit or wearing a pair of shorts.

My own feeling is that girls have enough to go through during this period without having to feel unhappy about something that is so easy to fix. That is why I applauded the mother of a 10½-year-old with unusually heavy hair growth who bought her daughter an electric razor. This sensitive mother realized that her daughter was far better off shaving her legs than limiting her activities because of body hair.

THE MENSTRUAL CYCLE

Of all the physical changes that occur during puberty, menarche, the first period, which typically happens a few months before the 13th birthday, creates the most anxiety among girls. The other physical changes of puberty are far less dramatic. Breast buds, pubic hair, and even body hair develop very gradually. Menarche typically begins without any warning: One day, a girl discovers that she is bleeding, and it can come as quite a shock. Although preparing a girl for menarche can make her feel more positive—and less frightened —when it actually happens, even the best prepared girl is going to have mixed emotions, often ranging from excitement to dread. Girls who are totally unprepared are going to have the roughest time.

Numerous studies show that girls are very ambivalent about menstruation. In her diary, Anne Frank summed up these mixed emotions with great eloquence. "Each time I have a period . . . I have the feelings that in spite of all the pain, unpleasantness, nastiness, I have a sweet secret and that is why, although it is nothing but a nuisance to me in a way, I always long for the time that I shall feel that secret within me again." Like Anne Frank, many girls recognize that even if it is not apparent to others, menstruation is a significant turning point in their own lives. It is concrete evidence that they are growing up.

On the other hand, they are filled with negative emotions. Blood is a powerful symbol associated with injury and trauma, and it can conjure up some very primitive feelings.

Even for a girl who feels reasonably positive about menstruation, monthly periods can complicate life: Girls worry about everything from getting bad cramps on a day they have gym, to whether or not they will leak through their sanitary napkins. Many girls are convinced that no matter how hard they try to hide it, everybody knows when they have their periods. "I feel really weird on those days, like everybody's staring at me," is how one 12-year-old sums it up.

Although girls may tell a few close friends that they have gotten their period, it is not usually something that they want publicized. They almost never talk about getting their periods with boys, and in fact would be embarrassed if a boy knew that they were menstruating. "Most girls keep it a secret. They don't want too many people to know. They don't want people to make fun of them or to say bad things," explains another 12-year-old girl.

It's not surprising that so many girls are uncomfortable about menstruation—so are many grown women. In our so-called enlightened society, menstruation is still pretty much a taboo subject. It is not a topic that is routinely discussed at the dinner table, and in many families, it is not discussed at all (except during the "mother-daughter talk"). Many mothers are secretive about their own menstruation; they do not let other family members know when they have their periods. As a result, girls are getting a very negative message about menstruation, which not only affects how they feel about menstruation, but how they feel about their bodies.

The Fast Tracker, who menstruates earlier than her peers, will have to cope with these emotions without support from her friends. She is bound to feel very lonely and isolated and in need of extra support from her parents. The Late Bloomer, who sees all of her friends start to menstruate, may also feel lonely and isolated. As she waits for her periods to begin, she wonders, "Is it ever going to happen? What's wrong with me?" The Fast Tracker needs to be assured that the other girls will be catching up to her shortly; the Late Bloomer needs to know that her time will come.

WHAT SHE NEEDS TO KNOW

Girls who make the best adjustment to their changing bodies in general and menstruation in particular are those who come from homes where these issues can be discussed in an open, free manner. In fact, girls who do the very best come from homes where their fathers know that they have begun to menstruate and where they can talk to both parents about these sensitive issues.

First, parents should offer an easy and concise explanation of the biology (I think parents can do this better than any book), and not just once, but several times before and after their daughter begins menstruating, certainly by age 11. If your daughter appears to be a Fast Tracker who is developing faster than average, I would start talking to her about this at age 10. Very likely a girl of this age will have some general knowledge about monthly periods from previous discussions with her parents, friends, older sisters, or from television commercials for "female protection." But now it's time to get specific.

A mother could begin the discussion by saying, "It's getting to be about the time when you're going to begin menstruating. I can't tell if it's going to be next month or in six months, but I think we should talk about it."

Some daughters will be happy that their mothers have brought up this subject that undoubtedly they have been thinking about, but others may be embarrassed or may try to appear very sophisticated by dismissing the suggestion with a "Oh, I know all about that, Mother." Follow up with, "Well, I'm sure that you know a lot, but let's talk about ovulation for a minute. Do you know about ovulation?" or "Do you know about estrogen?" Chances are she won't and she'll say, "What's that?" and you can begin your discussion.

The discussion should be a true dialogue—not just a lecture—in which your daughter feels free to ask questions. Try to make your explanation as simple and warm as possible—avoid using technical terms.

The best way to begin is to try to engage your daughter with some interesting fact:

MOTHER: Did you know that the menstrual cycle starts in the brain? Isn't that a silly idea?

DAUGHTER: Uh? What do you mean by that?

MOTHER: What I mean is that it starts in the brain because it is triggered by a hormone that is controlled by the brain. The menstrual cycle is actually activated by key hormones that are "switched on" as the body approaches puberty. Have you heard about the body's master gland—the pituitary gland that controls growth?

The discussion should continue along those lines. Keep in mind that you will not be able to cover everything in one discussion. Take any opportunity that comes your way to continue your talk. For instance, if your daughter announces that a friend has begun to menstruate, you should ask how her friend feels, and how your daughter feels about the prospect of getting her period. If you're watching television together and see a commercial for sanitary pads, you can comment on whether you think that that particular pad is a good product or not, and this may trigger a discussion of menstruation.

Once your daughter has a basic understanding of menstruation, you can then give her some books (which you should read also) to further enhance her education.

HER CONCERNS

Adolescent girls are often unnecessarily frightened by their first period because the blood doesn't look like blood; it tends to be a very dark or brownish color. Girls need to be reassured that this doesn't mean that there is anything wrong, merely that the blood has been collecting on the uterine wall for quite some time. If girls were told this ahead of time, they could be spared unnecessary anxiety.

In addition, many adolescent girls are under the mistaken impression that the menstrual cycle always takes twenty-eight days. They get very concerned if theirs doesn't. They need to be told that the menstrual cycle can vary from woman to woman. Adolescent girls in particular tend to have irregular cycles: Some months they may not ovulate at all, and some months they may have very heavy flow. Instead of having the typical twenty-eight-day cycle, they may have a twenty-one- or thirty-four-day cycle. Usually, within two or three years, however, a regular pattern is established.

Many adolescent girls have told me that they are very worried that the loss of menstrual blood will lead to anemia. Parents should reassure their daughters that no more than a few tablespoons of blood are lost in any one cycle, and the blood is meant to be lost. Girls should also be told that if they eat a well-balanced diet, they will not become anemic.

Menstrual cramps is another big area of concern for adolescent girls, and one that often goes unnoticed by parents. About 60 percent of all adolescent girls suffer from mild to severe menstrual cramps, and in fact, a good number of them miss school because of it. I think that it's important to discuss this with your daughter. Although I wouldn't present menstruation as a debilitating illness, I would tell the truth: Some women experience some discomfort. This way, if your daughter feels changes in her body, she will know that it is normal. I would alert her to the fact that some women—not all women—may experience premenstrual syndrome (PMS), in which they may feel a little depressed or irritable right before their periods; their breasts may feel tender, their stomachs may feel bloated. I would talk about menstrual cramps. In some cases understanding what they are will help your daughter learn to cope with them. Even though menstruation shouldn't interfere with daily activities, if the cramps are severe there are many over-the-counter painkillers that can help. After she begins menstruating, I would ask her, "How do you feel? Do you get cramps? Do you have any questions?" If you provide your daughter with honest explanations and clear answers, she will turn to you as her main source of information about menstruation and other sensitive issues.

COMMUNICATING THE RIGHT MESSAGE

Many girls are confused about what menstruation really means in their lives, and adults add to this confusion. When a 12-year-old girl begins to menstruate, we congratulate her and say things like "Now you are a woman." When we describe menstruation we tend to focus solely on its reproductive role. Neither approach makes much sense. First of all, we don't want to even suggest to a 12-year-old girl that she is ready, either physically or emotionally, to have babies. Nor do we want her to equate menstruation with adulthood. She may be menstruating, but she is still very much a child. I also don't think that we should communicate that the sole purpose of becoming a sexual being is to bear children. Not only are women having fewer children these days, but some are opting not to have any. Therefore, it is important to put these changes in the context of your daughter's life. The message that we should be giving her is: "Menstruation is one of many important physical changes that occur as a girl grows into a young adolescent, an adolescent grows into a teenager, and a teenager becomes a young adult. There are many tasks to accomplish before adulthood. You will go on dates, finish high school, go to college, and choose a career. You will move out of our home into a home of your own. And at some point, way down the road, you may meet someone that you want to marry and think about having children. But right now, you are a 12-year-old girl whose body is working right on schedule."

BODY ODOR

Next to menstruation, young adolescent girls are most concerned about body odor. For the first time in their lives, their perspiration smells like sweat. As their vaginal lining thickens, it begins to produce secretions that have a distinct odor. Menstrual blood also has a mild odor.

Parents tell me that their daughters spend hours in the bathroom each day, bathing and showering, and I don't doubt it. Countless girls have told me that they really think that they "stink" and are dreadfully concerned that other people think so, too. Part of this preoccupation with odor is inflicted upon them by the media, which targets young girls for products such as underarm and vaginal deodorants. Girls are also responding to the fact that they are detecting new smells on their bodies, and this combined with all the other changes that are going on, can be quite overwhelming. Once again, the Fast Tracker who is detecting these new odors earlier than her friends is going to feel even more self-conscious about them.

Although you may think that a fixation on body odor is quite silly.

you should not trivialize your daughter's concerns. Let her talk about it. If she wants to use an underarm deodorant, there's no reason not to let her. I would, however, discourage the use of vaginal deodorants; they can cause yeast infections, not to mention the fact that they are unnecessary. Try to reassure your daughter that adult women have these same odors and, in most cases, they're not noticeable. Take heart in knowing that by midadolescence she should overcome this obsession.

ACNE

Acne is another problem of adolescence that is particularly painful for girls, who are self-conscious about their looks under the best of circumstances. Acne is a skin disorder that is caused by the increased secretion of male sex hormones by girls during puberty. These hormones stimulate the oil glands of the hair follicles to produce sebum, a fatty substance that is normally discharged by the pores to lubricate the skin. Excess amounts of sebum makes the skin oily, which clogs the pores and results in the pimples, pustules, or blackheads typical of acne. Although acne often clears up by itself, in many cases, it doesn't.

Depending on their personalities, girls respond in different ways to acne. Some girls will spot one pimple and yell, "Mom, do something! Call the doctor!" Others will suffer in silence. The "silent" type may feel acne is a punishment for all the sexy or hostile thoughts she is having lately—she may live in fear of her mother saying, "I see that you have acne, have you been masturbating?" or "Have you been thinking about that boy in school again?" It's important for parents to respond appropriately and say, "Gee, your skin needs help. I'll call the dermatologist. There's a lot that they can do about acne now." It's important for your daughter to understand that acne is nothing more than a common medical problem—it is no cause for shame or embarrassment—and in most cases, it can be treated quite successfully.

WHAT SHE NEEDS FROM YOU

During this period of rapid growth, your daughter needs to sense your approval and acceptance of her developing body and her "new self." The ongoing dialogue between you and your daughter will help her to understand that these changes are a normal, natural part of a bigger process of becoming an adult woman. Appropriate and encouraging comments, such as "You seem to be growing up in such a lovely way" or "You certainly are looking good," will help her view these changes in a positive light.

Most of all, by offering your support and sympathy when she needs it, you assure your daughter that although she is undergoing a major change, your love for her and your relationship will always be a constant in her life.

FOUR: HER INTELLECTUAL AND EMOTIONAL GROWTH

The physical changes that occur during adolescence are very dramatic and obvious. The emotional and intellectual changes, however, are less tangible and far more difficult for parents to comprehend. Yet they are very real. If parents better understood their daughter's state of mind, it would reduce their sense of powerlessness and frustration and would make them more empathetic and effective parents.

Although every adolescent develops differently, and some may be strong in certain areas and weak in others, most girls experience similar patterns of growth at roughly the same time. Therefore, adolescence is usually divided into three groupings based on chronological age: early (11–13), middle (14–16) and late (17+).

I am defining adolescence here as ending after college, but many psychologists believe that the issues of adolescence are not fully resolved until the early 30s. I personally believe that adolescence doesn't really end until a child has completed her education and is ready and willing to function as a self-supporting, independent adult.

"I'M NOT YOU"—EARLY ADOLESCENCE, 11 THROUGH 13

At this stage your daughter usually

- Feels self-conscious and unsure of herself
- Begins to establish her own identity as a separate and unique individual

- Has a poor sense of her strengths and abilities
- Strives to assert her independence from her parents, notably from her mother.

Early adolescence is known for its wild mood swings; one minute a girl can be perfectly calm and the next minute she can explode in anger. Typically, this anger is directed at her parents, often at her mother.

Why does this happen? Overwhelmed by the changes in her body, the adolescent begins to focus on herself in relation to the world. As she adjusts to her new physical self, she needs to create a new concept of who she is—a new persona to fit the new body. Before she can identify who she is, she needs to rule out who she is not: She needs to differentiate herself from others. I call this the "I'm not you" phase because adolescent girls use their parents as negative models—as examples of everything that they think they don't want to become. This is why these girls tend to become hypercritical of their parents during this period. The criticism is not particularly rational. "She really gets on my nerves," observed one 13-year-old about her mother. "She does a lot of things that annoy me. Like, she chews funny, I hate the way she chews. We fight a lot about that."

An adolescent daughter will attack her mother for just about anything: If her mother asks a reasonable question, the girl is likely to respond in a very unreasonable, surly fashion, and her mother will typically wonder what in the world she said or did to deserve this treatment.

The young adolescent tends to be melodramatic and will hurl insults, such as "I hate you. You're the worst mother [or father] in the world." Keep in mind that when an adolescent uses words like "hate" it is not the same as when it is used by a more mature adult. One of the hardest parts of parenting an adolescent is learning to cope with your own hurt feelings that can result from these undeserved and unfair attacks.

Sometimes adolescents use even more offensive language. To show how independent or different they are from their parents, young adolescent girls often go out of their way to try out new curse words at home. Tell your daughter directly, "You don't talk that way to me. If you feel that it's necessary to use those kinds of words, you can use them, but I don't want to hear it. I find it very demeaning, disrespectful, and very uncommunicative."

How She Feels

In two words, she feels conflicted and confused.

At the same time that your daughter is pushing you away, she is holding on to you for dear life. Adolescent girls are very emotionally needy; for all their bravado, deep down inside they are very frightened of being left on their own. No matter how much they strut or scream, they are still very dependent on their parents, for emotional and financial support. On one level, the fact that they are so dependent and needy makes them even angrier. They deflect this anger by blaming their parents for holding them back, for treating them "like a baby." But on another, deeper level, they are very grateful that their parents are there for them. This is especially true of daughters and mothers.

"I fight with my mother a lot, but I also feel closer to her now because she went through what I'm going through," explains one 12-year-old. "I feel more comfortable with my mother. I say, 'Mom, guess what happened?' and she really listens."

Unlike boys, adolescent girls have to deal with yet another conflict. Up until puberty, the rules for boys and girls are pretty much the same. Academic achievement, doing well in sports, a special talent in art or music, are all measures of success. But now the girl who used to get a pat on the head for bringing home an "A" paper will discover that good grades are not enough to win praise. An adolescent girl begins to hear other voices that are judging her by a different standard. Looks, popularity, and attractiveness to boys become of paramount importance. Instead of striving to improve their intellectual skills and increase their level of competency—as they have been doing all along—girls are pulled in a different direction, thus throwing them off balance and, I believe, off course. As a result, they feel confused and unsure of themselves.

How to Deal with Her Anger

Parents are typically startled and hurt by the amount of hostility and anger in their daughter; they simply don't know how to respond. It's very difficult for parents to accept that this unbridled anger is directed toward them, so they often attempt to deflect or minimize it by saying things like:

"Oh, you must be suffering from PMS."

"Something must have happened at school today."

"Are you in a bad mood again?"

Some respond by putting their daughter back "in her place" by saying:

"I raised you. How dare you talk to me that way?"

"Don't stamp your feet like that at me . . ." A pause and a sarcastic, "young lady," with a strong emphasis on the *lady,* hit home the unspoken message: "This is not appropriate behavior for a girl."

Parents may indeed succeed in subduing their daughter, or even humiliating her, but the anger doesn't go away. The girl bottles it up and directs it toward herself. Many of the grown women that I treat in my practice have difficulty expressing anger and are unable to clearly articulate their needs. Typically, these women had been "trained" from childhood never to show anger and are paying dearly for it today.

As difficult as it may be, the parent under attack has to try to remember that the child is out of control and it will only make matters worse if the parent loses control too. As an adult, a parent should be able to detach herself or himself from the situation and respond in a calm manner, particularly if she or he is aware that this is perfectly normal adolescent behavior. If the girl is in a rage, the parent should simply say, "Look I see that you're very angry and I can't seem to do anything right. When you're able to talk about it, we will."

If the girl is saying something very hurtful, the parent should acknowledge this—a girl needs to be taught that other people's feelings are important too. "You're really hurting my feelings, and I feel very bad about what you're saying. I don't want to talk to you when you're like this. When you calm down, we'll talk about it."

Your ability to stay calm may defuse the situation—your daughter may actually start talking—or she may stalk off in anger, depending on her mood. In either case, you've let her know that although you don't enjoy being the recipient of her hostility, you're not going to reject her because of it. At the same time that you're telling her that it's okay to feel anger, you're also communicating that fighting is not the only way to resolve conflicts. Most importantly, you're letting her know that you're willing to listen to her concerns, and she will learn to expect this from other relationships.

How She Thinks

At the same time that the adolescent's body is budding into womanhood, she is making a monumental leap in her cognitive development—she is beginning to think in new and more sophisticated ways. Unlike a child, she is now able to understand abstract concepts and can reason in a more adult fashion. The early adolescent is somewhat more adept at comparing and discriminating, at making more logical and informed decisions than the child. Her way of thinking, however, still tends to be "black or white." She often misses the subtler gray areas, which she will see by middle or late adolescence.

The young, egocentric adolescent spends much of her time thinking about herself. However, she doesn't yet have the insight or self-awareness to see her strengths and weaknesses clearly. Therefore, she needs to continually compare herself to her peers to get a sense of who she is.

For example, a 12-year-old might look around her classroom and ponder, "My friend Janet may be smart, and she always seems to have the answer, but I raise my hand a lot too, and my grades are pretty good. Is she really smarter than me? Is my friend Emily smarter than Janet? Is Emily smarter than me?"

The early adolescent sizes herself up against her friends to see where she fits in. However, she is still locked into the black or white "who is smarter?" way of thinking. Either you're the "smartest," or you're not; the subtle range in between is lost on her.

Your daughter's "black or white" view of the world often distorts her vision, especially when it comes to evaluating her parents' relationship. For example, if her father asks her mother for another cup of coffee during dinner, and her mother serves it to him, the daughter accuses her of being "his slave" and is quick to add that she would never do that for any man. If her mother asks her father not to do something that he may have wanted to do, the daughter accuses her mother of being a "tyrant" and adds that she isn't going to be like that with her husband.

Obviously, the young adolescent girl is missing the subtle nuances in the relationship and can only see it at its most extreme. Since your daughter's view of the world is obscured by her "partial vision," it's important for you to correct what she thinks she is seeing. In reality, some of her challenging questions may be her way of asking for clarification. For instance, if she accuses her mother of being a "slave" to her father, she may really be asking, "Are you Dad's slave?" The mother can respond by explaining that she and her husband have divided up chores in a way that makes them feel comfortable and that there are plenty of times when Dad does special things for Mom. Your daughter will begin to see things more clearly if you take the time to explain them to her.

Peers and Friendship

As the adolescent girl uses her parents as negative role models to define who she isn't, she turns to her peers to help her establish who she is. At around 11 to 13, many girls become part of a clique—a group of friends that seem to do everything together. One of the clique's primary features is that it has to exclude others to know that it is special, and this is sometimes done in a cruel and thoughtless way. Cliques are not known for their encouragement of individuality: Members typically dress the same way, adopt the same hair styles, and generally tend to copy each other. At this vulnerable point in their lives, many girls lack a strong enough ego to establish an individual identity and require the support of other adolescent egos to define them.

Dating and Sexuality

As girls begin to experience new and exciting sexual feelings, they become very preoccupied with sex: They talk about it, they think about it, they worry about it, but they rarely do anything else about it. As a rule, young adolescent girls tend to socialize with boys as part of a group. Boys of the same age are usually a year or two behind in terms of physical development and may not be interested in dating. There is a lot of teasing, roughhousing and flirting between boys and girls, and there is a great deal of curiosity about each other. In most cases, however, girls will stay with girls and boys will stay with boys as they explore their feelings about these new budding relationships.

The more developed girls, the Fast Trackers, are extremely vulnerable and require special handling. These girls may feel pressured to start dating and to behave as if they are teenagers, and it is important for their parents to remind them that they are not. A 12-year-old should not wear clothes that are appropriate for a 16-year-old, she should not walk out of the house laden with makeup. Young adolescents are not emotionally ready to date, nor to tackle the other tasks of middle and late adolescence.

The Fast-Track girl needs her parents to continually emphasize the fact that they like her the way she is. For example, if someone says to your daughter, "Oh, you're so mature, I thought you were 18," you should tell your daughter, "That's nice that they thought that you were so mature, but that's not important. We respect you as the 12-year-old you are. We know that you're not 18 and we're happy that you're not."

The Fast-Track girl who is heading for trouble—the girl who dates too early, hangs out with an older crowd, and acts as if she is much older—is often a girl who is being "pushed" into growing up by her parents. Her parents may be confused by her "maturity" or she may be acting out her parents' subconscious wish to be free of their responsibility of raising a child. Very often, these parents have withdrawn from their daughter, leaving her to her own devices. This girl is at great risk of unwanted pregnancy, substance abuse, or dropping out of school.

What She Needs from You

Give her concrete evidence of her growing maturity. Your daughter needs concrete signs that you recognize that she is entering a new stage of life. Often, parents expect a lot of help with household chores from their adolescent girl, whom they now view as mature enough to handle the responsibility, however, they fail to extend her any real privileges.

By early adolescence, a girl should be given a weekly allowance to cover her daily living expenses (transportation to and from school, lunches, recreation), which she should be expected to manage on her own. This responsibility will not only make her feel more mature, but will teach her an important lesson about how to handle money.

The 11- to 13-year-old girl should also have the right to pick out at least some, if not all, of her clothes. Young adolescents should be permitted to baby-sit for money and to use that money as they want. If it is financially feasible, by the age of 12, a girl should be given a modest budget to decorate her bedroom—or her own designated area in a shared bedroom. Letting her pick out some posters and a new bedspread can go a long way in letting her know that you are aware that she is growing up. It may also give her greater incentive to keep her room neat, eliminating a major bone of contention between adolescents and their parents. Giving your daughter an increased level of autonomy over various aspects of her life will make her feel better about herself and will help boost her confidence.

Practice setting limits while letting go. As your daughter fluctuates between dependency and independence, you must learn how to start letting go. You need to help your daughter develop a sense of competence and confidence in her own strengths and abilities. This doesn't mean that you don't set boundaries and guidelines, but it does mean that you look for ways to make her feel capable and independent.

Follow your daughter's cues. In an attempt to flaunt her new independence, a 12- or 13-year-old girl will make many new demands on her parents. Typically, she may insist that she be allowed to go to the mall by herself on public transportation, or demand to go to a party without adult chaperons. It's your job to determine which demands are reasonable and which are not and to modify her demands so that her safety is not compromised. For example, if you feel uncomfortable letting your daughter go to the mall by herself, don't veto the idea entirely. You might suggest that she travel with a friend and agree to let her go as long as she's home by a designated time. On the one hand, you're encouraging her to be independent, but on the other, you're teaching her how to do it in a safe, sensible manner.

There are times when you will have to say no, as in the case of her wanting to go to a party without adult chaperons. When you refuse, she probably will reply, "Well, everyone else is doing it, why can't I?" You will reply that you don't feel that teenagers of her age should be at parties without adult supervision, and she will repeat that everyone else is going. At this age, she is not going to understand that "everyone else is going" or "everyone else is doing it," is not a good reason. No matter how much you explain your feelings, she lacks the reasoning skills and the ego strength to make a conscious decision not to follow the pack. So you're going to have to make it for her.

In all likelihood, these kinds of discussions are going to end with her running to her room in tears and slamming the door behind her. This may be upsetting, but it is perfectly normal. You're doing what you have to do, and she's doing what she has to do. In situations such as these, parents have to remember that they are adults, their daughter is an adolescent, and this, too, will pass.

Emphasize the "two A's"—academics and athletics. Society is pulling your daughter in a direction that will lead to a loss of self-confidence and will limit her options—you need to help her counteract these forces. Your daughter needs to know that your values haven't changed: You still consider school to be of paramount importance, and your expectations for her haven't changed either. Continue to talk to her about what's going on in school, express interest in her homework. Let her know that you are there for her if she needs help.

Athletics is another area that can help your daughter develop body confidence and increase her flagging self-esteem. During puberty, girls often stop participating in sports, and many become totally sedentary. I think that's a shame. Team sports are not only a way for girls to learn how to be competitive in a healthy way, but can give them a sense of accomplishment and self-worth. If possible, parents should encourage participation in sports, or at least some form of physical activity such as an exercise or dance class.

Give her lots of praise and love. Because there is frequent tension between parents and their adolescent daughter, communication is often hostile. Both sides forget how to relate to each other in a loving manner. For instance, one mother recently described an incident in which she was shocked by her own behavior. Her 13-year-old daughter came home from school very excited because she got an A on a math test, but instead of congratulating her, this mother said, "That's nice. Why did you leave your room in such a mess this morning?" After she said the words and saw her daughter's crushed expression, she knew that she had made a terrible gaffe. "I should have made more of a fuss over the test, but I was still annoyed with her about something she had said to me that morning. It seems we're always angry with each other these days."

Parenting an adolescent can be very frustrating, and it does require enormous amounts of patience. As exasperated as we get with our adolescent girls, we need to remember that they are still developing children. More than anything else, they still need our love and approval.

"TODAY, I AM..."—14 THROUGH 16

At this stage your daughter

- Enters a highly experimental period in which she "tries on" many different roles
- Begins to see the "gray areas" of life, though she is still not thinking like an adult.

The negativity that marked the "I'm not you" phase of the past two years is beginning to wane. A 14- or 15-year-old girl is not constantly baiting her mother as she did when she was 12 or 13.

As she enters the more positive and highly experimental "Today, I am . . ." phase, the middle adolescent girl is beginning to focus on who she is—or more specifically, on who she'd like to be.

The middle adolescent girl is opening herself up to a world of possibilities. She daydreams a lot about the kind of woman she wants to become. As she looks for a positive identity, the teenage girl flirts with many different potential careers and lifestyles.

An after-school job in a hospital may trigger an interest in medicine or nursing; a sales job in a dress shop may steer her toward retailing; a successful experience as a counselor in a summer camp may lead her to consider teaching. A normal girl of this age is going to fantasize about many different options, and although some parents may view this as being "flighty," it is an important step in her quest for identity. Only by being allowed to try on different roles will she eventually find the ones with which she is comfortable.

Although middle adolescence is a time of increased emotional maturity, most girls still don't have a realistic view of what their future lives will be like.

How She Feels

The middle adolescent girl is more at peace with herself than the young adolescent girl. She no longer longs to be a child, and in fact can see some real benefits to being a teenager. The 14- to 16-year-old is much more sure of herself in social situations than the young adolescent; she has lost much of her awkwardness.

Unfortunately, in many cases, she has not regained her childhood confidence in other important areas, notably at school. In many cases, not raising her hand in class, tuning out of math and science classes, and accepting lower grades has become a way of life: She has lowered her sights and in some cases scaled down her dreams and future goals. Her resignation in the academic arena reflects her lack of confidence in her ability to think and take on new challenges. It also reflects her fear that being smart will make her unattractive to boys and earn her the label of "nerd," which will make her unattractive to everyone.

Expressing Herself

Your middle adolescent daughter has an enormous need to express her uniqueness. She may take a stand on a particular issue and go to the mat for that cause if need be. She may become a vegetarian to prove how "caring" she is, or she will adopt a political point of view different from yours to prove what an independent thinker she is. She has reached a point in her life when she feels capable of standing up and making a statement, and it is a very important milestone. Even if you disagree with her, you should respect her right to her own opinion, but make clear that that doesn't mean that you shouldn't be given the opportunity to express yours.

Sometimes her statement is a fashion statement. As they look for ways to define their individuality, girls of this age are highly experimental when it comes to fashion. It is perfectly normal for a 14- or 15-year-old girl to, for example, streak her hair three different shades of orange, pierce three holes in each ear, and wear a different earring in each one of them. Although parents may find these "fashion statements" to be very disconcerting, it is certainly not new. When I was 14, I remember painting my fingernails "Sable Black" because I believed that it would make me look very sophisticated. I probably looked ridiculous, but I felt very grown up. Although you may find your child's style of dress to be personally embarrassing—and you may wonder about the reactions of your friends and neighbors—as much as possible, try to ignore it. Unless your daughter's health or safety is at risk (for example, I would not let a girl hobble around at school in shoes with four-inch-high heels) this is not an issue worthy of a confrontation, and the stage passes rather quickly.

How She Thinks

The middle adolescent girl is beginning to show greater maturity in her ability to think and reason. There is a refinement in the thought processes that allows her to sometimes differentiate beyond black or white. It is no longer a matter of who is smarter than whom, or who won or who lost—she is beginning to see the middle ground.

The 15-year-old, with her growing maturity and stronger sense of self, should be able to say with some degree of confidence, "Janet is really smart, and her hand always goes up in class, but I write terrific stories, and I'm really talented in math—I'm pretty smart too."

She has made great strides, but she is still not thinking like an adult. On certain issues, many middle adolescents still see things in a black-or-white, all-or-nothing perspective. For example, girls of this age are especially anxious about the prospect of juggling multiple roles in the future. Perhaps by watching their own mothers struggle with family and career they have become wary of trying to "do it all." Perhaps they are still limited by their own inability to focus on several goals at once. Whatever the reason, they often feel as if they have to choose between family and career. Typically, they will say, "Mom works but she doesn't give her job 100 percent because she's too busy worrying about what's happening at home. Boy, when I grow up I'm just going to devote myself to my career and forget about this family stuff," or "Mom's never around, she's so torn between her job and taking care of us. I'm never going to do that, I'm just going to stay home with my babies."

Setting Limits and Making Deals

By 14, a girl is capable of independent thought. She does not need to slavishly follow the crowd. You can begin to reason with your daughter in a new, more sophisticated way.

For example, if your daughter wants to do something that "everyone else is doing," but you don't approve, you can now try to engage her in dialogue:

"Just because everyone is doing something, does it mean that it's good or right?"

"Are there things that everyone does that you don't want to do?"

"I think that this particular idea is not a good one for you because . . ."

"Isn't there something else that you can do instead?"

Parents will find that the right words can be very effective tools in dealing with their daughter. Unlike the stormy days of early adolescence, she may actually understand and accept your position, or she may remain calm and levelheaded enough to present a strong case in her favor.

Although there are times when no will have to be no, give and take on these issues is important. From these discussions, girls learn the art of negotiation—how to ask for something, how to fight for it, and, if necessary, how to compromise. A sophisticated 15- or 16-year-old usually knows better than to try to get her way through direct confrontation; rather, she will bargain and haggle. "If I can't have the $200 dress, can I have the $100 jumpsuit?"

"If I don't go to the party where there are no chaperons, can I stay out an extra hour later on my next date?"

Once you reach an agreement, however, it is your job to make your daughter adhere to it. If you and she agree that she can spend $200 on her spring wardrobe and she blows the whole wad on a "gorgeous sweater," she should not be allowed to come back to you a week later for another $22 for a pair of jeans, even if it's "just $22."

At this age, teenagers are very proficient in testing limits and seeing how far they can push. A teenager will typically come home after curfew or "forget" to do chores around the house. It's critical for their own sense of security to see that their parents have set secure boundaries and care enough to enforce them.

Peers and Friendship

As your daughter develops a stronger sense of herself, she will gradually move away from the clique and establish friendships on her own—she no longer needs to go everywhere surrounded by her "gang."

At this age, boys typically have many friends that they do things with, girls often have fewer but closer friends in whom they confide.

Dating

Middle adolescence is a time when girls leave the safety of their groups to explore boys on their own. Most girls begin dating at around 14, and many are simply terrified about what that entails. Their greatest fear is appearing awkward and inexperienced. Girls are very concerned about whether or not they should open their mouths when they kiss, or they're worried that they're not going to know what to do if a boy wants to hold their hands in the movies or tries to touch their breasts. If a girl has a close relationship with her mother, she may try to talk to her about some of these issues.

Some girls, however, may want to keep this aspect of their lives "secret" from their parents and may rely on their friends for this kind of information. This is perfectly normal. Even a girl who talks to her parents about sex and dating may look to friends for more specific advice.

Dating is one area in which input from Dad can be very beneficial. He can offer his daughter some insight about how boys think and help her understand that they are every bit as insecure and uncomfortable as she is.

What She Needs from You

Broaden her view of herself and the world. During middle adolescence, parents need to expand their daughter's contracting world by opening her up to a wide range of possibilities. During the experimental "Today, I am . . ." phase, girls are very receptive to exploring different options, and parents should take advantage of this. Encourage your daughter to try new things—whether it's joining a new club at school or attending a camp with a particular theme, such as one specializing in tennis instruction or dramatics. Encourage her to get involved in a political campaign or a worthwhile community project. These activities are not only educational, but will also help her to develop a sense of competence.

Encourage her to speak her mind. The girl whose voice is routinely silenced at home will not be able to speak up in school. Your daughter should be encouraged to express her opinion, unfettered by frequent interruptions or ridicule by other family members. (Males in particular tend to be big offenders in terms of jumping into conversations, interrupting girls and women.) Make sure that your daughter has the same opportunity to speak as other members of the family and that her views are treated with respect.

Help her to develop good values. Encouraging your daughter to speak up doesn't mean that you have to agree with everything she says. If your daughter makes a statement that you disagree with, don't get angry. Use it as an opportunity to let her know your values and your feelings on the subject.

For example, during dinner, your daughter announces that her best friend's parents have just bought her a sweater for $300, and you won't even let her spend $100 for a sweater. She's telling you this for two reasons: First, as an indirect dig at you for not being as "generous" as her friend's parents, but second, because she's trying to get a sense of whether or not this is the right thing to do. Is it okay to spend $300 on a sweater? This is a perfect opportunity for you to discuss your values and the economics of your family. Without lecturing your daughter, you can point out that $300 would cover the family's food bill for a couple of weeks, or a month's car payment. You can let her know that you think that there are better ways to spend $300 than on one sweater.

Your daughter will probably find reasons to disagree with you, but later, when she is talking with her friends and someone says, "Marsha is so lucky, her parents spent $300 on a sweater for her," your daughter may interject, "Well, I think that there are many better ways to spend $300." Although you'll never know it, your daughter has thought about what you said and recognized that your values were better than those of her friend's parents. I have seen this happen numerous times in my practice—I know that when a girl is espousing an opinion that is much more mature and adult than her peers', very likely she is imitating her parents, although she would never admit it and may not even know that she is doing so.

Continue to give her more autonomy. At this age, many girls want to take on an after-school job for one or two afternoons a week, and as long as it's not interfering with their schoolwork, I think that it's a good idea. Work will help a girl feel confident about her ability to function in the "real world" and will give her a taste of what it's like to earn money.

Parents should look for ways to help their daughters feel autonomous. For example, a teenage girl should be consulted about important family decisions, such as where the family will go on vacations, or how she would like to spend her summer. Whenever possible, she should be allowed to make choices. Keep in mind that within a few years she will be in college, perhaps even living on her own. This is the time to help her develop the decision-making skills that will enable her to make the right decisions at the right time.

TOWARD A NEW RELATIONSHIP— 17 AND BEYOND

At this stage, your daughter

- Has a better sense of who she is and who she wants to be
- Thinks in a more long-term, realistic fashion
- Begins to see the shades of meaning.

The older adolescent is heading for a more equal relationship with her parents. She is now better able to understand their point of view, and this relationship has vastly improved over the stormy days of early adolescence.

The 17-year-old no longer feels the need to constantly assert her "differentness" by disagreeing with her parents. She now feels comfortable enough with herself to know that if she agrees with her parents, she is not sacrificing her independence, and that if she disagrees with her parents, she is not threatening the relationship.

Because she no longer feels threatened by her parents, she is now able to view them as a potential source of information and advice. More and more, the 17 + teenager consults her parents before making decisions and seeks out their opinions.

However, don't be deceived by your daughter's growing maturity; a 17-year-old is still capable of reverting back to very childish behavior. Even the most mature-sounding or -looking 17-year-old is still an adolescent at heart and may at times be very unreasonable. There will still be fights, and there will still be tears, but not as often as before.

How She Thinks

As she matures, the older teenager begins to see the world in a new light: the one-dimensional, "either/or" world of middle adolescence disappears as she is able to distinguish the subtler tones. She can make more thoughtful judgments, and is capable of more sophisticated comparative thinking. Life is no longer a matter of "good" or "bad," of "winning" or "losing." Whereas the younger adolescent would feel she was a failure if she tried and lost, the older adolescent can now understand how it is possible not to win at something yet, nevertheless, to have gained and benefited from the experience.

The older teenager is no longer thrown by seemingly insignificant occurrences as she would have been when she was younger. For example, a pimple is no longer a major disaster: A 14-year-old might dissolve in tears if she got a pimple on the day of an important date, but the average 17-year-old would be able to look in the mirror, spot a pimple and say matter-of-factly, "I better do something about this." This is not only a sign of maturity, but of her developing sense of having greater control over her life and surroundings.

How She Feels About Herself

The late adolescent is beginning to establish a firmer sense of who she is and has a more realistic sense of her abilities. She takes responsibility for her actions: She no longer believes that if she doesn't do well at something, it is simply because she isn't good at it. She now understands that in many cases she can improve her performance by working harder.

She also knows, however, that there are dreams that she may never be capable of achieving. For instance, if she had always wanted to be a professional ballet dancer but really wasn't that good, she may now realize that she isn't as talented as others in her class and may look for another career. She has also reached the point where she may decide that some dreams are not worth the pursuit.

It's Harder to Set Limits

Although the relationship has improved, late adolescence is hardly a honeymoon period between parent and child: There are still many conflicts. The three C's—curfews, car, and chaperons—are a constant source of tension. Since the older adolescent feels so grown up, she believes that her parents should recognize her maturity by permitting her to stay out as late as she likes, letting her drive the family car all hours of the day and night, and allowing her to attend parties where there is no adult supervision. If you attempt to set limits, she will accuse you of not trusting her. It is very important that you let her know that these are not issues of trust, but of safety, and as a parent, you can foresee potential problems that she as a teenager cannot.

Dating

By late adolescence, many girls have begun to date in a more discriminating fashion; they now have a sense of what kind of boy they like and choose their dates based on friendship and companion-ability. By age 18, around half of all girls will be sexually active, and many will have had a serious, relatively long-time relationship with one boy.

A Late Bloomer, however, who may not have started dating until 16 or 17, will be less experienced and therefore more like a middle adolescent when it comes to establishing relationships with boys. This girl needs time to catch up with her more mature friends and should be encouraged to take her time before embarking on a more serious relationship.

What She Needs from You

Get specific. By 17, you and your daughter should be having fairly specific discussions on her school and career plans. Talk about different careers with your daughter—be sure to discuss work in the context of earning a living so that your daughter is aware of potential salaries. If you have a friend or relative with a particularly interesting job, try to arrange for your daughter to spend a day or an afternoon observing him or her at work. Some local colleges offer career days or even special summer programs for high school students interested in specific professions such as law or journalism. This is an excellent way for your daughter to see if she is interested in pursuing a particular field in college.

Help your daughter devise a plan to achieve her goals. For instance, if she expresses an interest in becoming a teacher, you and she need to work out how she can best achieve that goal. What college should she attend? What kind of courses should she take? Does she want to teach grade school or high school or college? Is she interested in teaching a particular subject? Will she need to go to graduate school? These types of discussions will help her to face the future in a fairly realistic way.

Let her know that her new freedom allows for mistakes. As your daughter begins to make plans for her future, she needs to understand that things may not always go according to plan.

The older adolescent is entering a very exciting time in her life when she will be confronted by many new experiences. She needs to feel free to try her hand at many different things, and she also needs to understand that she can and will make mistakes. Few people get everything right the first time—trial and error is an important part of the learning process.

Many girls may begin at one college, and a year or two later, find that it doesn't meet their needs and they want to transfer to another. The 18-year-old prelaw student may at 20 decide that she's unhappy with her choice and want to switch majors. The girl who's engaged at 19 may have second thoughts at 20.

As your daughter makes more and more decisions for herself, you need to prepare her for the fact that she may at times make wrong decisions. She needs to be assured that few decisions made at 18 or 20 are irrevocable, and that the only real mistake is recognizing that you've made a wrong choice and not doing anything to correct it.

Let her know you know she can do it. As your daughter prepares to enter college and perhaps even to leave home, it's important for her to have a sense that you feel that she can handle what lies ahead. You need to communicate that she was raised to be a strong, confident young woman who is capable of making intelligent decisions. She needs to feel that she has been adequately prepared to tackle the challenges of school and eventually the world of work. Your vote of confidence is important to her, and you need to go out of your way to show her that you believe in her.

Your daughter also needs to know that even though she is well prepared, it is not going to be an easy ride. Tell her, "I know that you're going to do extremely well in whatever you decide to pursue. However, some things are going to come to you fairly easily, and some things aren't. You've still got a lot to learn, and you're going to have to take some blows along the way. But I know that whatever happens, you can handle it."

II

YOUR DAUGHTER'S WORLD

FIVE: THE FAMILY DYNAMIC

Of all the factors that influence and shape a girl's life, her family is by far the most important. Parents and to some extent even siblings can provide role models that profoundly affect future relationships. How she is regarded by her family affects her view of herself and her future dreams and aspirations. Within the context of her family, a girl develops a sense of who she is and who she will become.

How well—or how poorly—a girl adjusts to adolescence is often a reflection of how well her family understands and accepts her new stage of development. If her family is pleased to have a maturing girl, takes pride in her growth, and encourages her to express her new ideas, she will grow into a self-confident woman who has a strong sense of who she is. If her family finds her growth to be more of a nuisance than a joy, or overprotects her to the point of suffocation, or routinely puts her down with "What do you know, you're only 13," the girl is going to grow into a woman with a poor sense of herself. She will be hampered by nagging self-doubt, and she will feel too insecure to express her opinions or assert herself in the workplace or in her personal relationships. She will not be able to live a full and satisfying life.

The family unit consists of several different relationships all operating under the same roof. Each child in a family has a distinctly different relationship with each of his or her family members. The adolescent girl relates to her individual parents one way and differently when they are a "unit." She has separate relationships with her siblings, and her parents treat her in certain ways in relation to her siblings.

BETWEEN MOTHERS AND DAUGHTERS

> What makes the mother-daughter relationship so poignant is its bewildering reciprocity. What one person does, feels, inevitably affects the other.
>
> —Nancy Friday, *My Mother/Myself*

Mothers and daughters share a unique bond. Although this bond can be tested and strained during adolescence, it has proven to be a powerful and enduring one. During the first days of life, when all infants—boys and girls alike—experience their mothers as extensions of themselves, much of the world is experienced through her feelings. If Mother is relaxed and happy, it feels good to the infant. If Mother is nervous and upset, the infant shares in her distress. Eventually, sons and daughters begin to connect to their mothers in distinctly different ways. At the time when boys begin to differentiate from their mothers in recognition of their own "maleness," the boundaries between mother and daughter remain blurred.

When the mother looks at the infant daughter, she invariably sees a part of herself, and when the infant gazes at her mother, she sees a glimpse of the woman she will become. This identification creates a connection between mother and daughter that is very special but can also be very threatening to an adolescent girl who is trying to establish a separate identity.

From this bond, a girl learns what it's like to be a female. She learns how to nurture, how to be loving, and how to develop and sustain close, meaningful relationships. Throughout her childhood, her mother is a girl's primary role model. Girls imitate their mothers —they play dress-up in her clothes and parent their dolls in much the same way that their mothers parent them.

A girl begins to focus on her outside world as she enters kindergarten and comes under the influence of her teachers and her peers. During this period, the mother-daughter bond is somewhat loosened as the daughter's world expands. Yet the mother-daughter relationship remains close, and for the girl, the mother is still the positive mirror of impending womanhood, that is, until puberty.

Because of the intense bond between mothers and daughters, mothers bear the brunt of the storms of puberty. As the girl attempts to find her own identity, she uses her mother as a negative role model, often cruelly rejecting her mother in many ways. At the same time, the girl is very insecure in her new role and desperately needs her mother's support to sustain her. The typical adolescent will one minute lash out at her mother, then the next cling to her for comfort and assurance.

MOTHERS AT MIDLIFE

There are issues in the mother's life that can also exacerbate the tension between mother and daughter. Mothers of adolescents tend to be in their late 30s or 40s, which are extremely vulnerable years for women. As a woman approaches midlife, she becomes increasingly aware of the physical aspects of aging: Her daughter's budding womanhood may be a grim reminder that the mother is growing older. Women of this "certain age" often begin to compare themselves to younger women. If a woman has put a lot of stock in her appearance (which is hard not to do in our beauty-oriented culture), she will begin to feel threatened. At work, she may feel that she is being passed over in favor of younger employees.

If she's invested a lot of time in raising children, she may feel that she deserves some time to pursue her own dreams, but at the same time, the demands of parenting are actually increasing. As her daughter begins to date, the mother may remember her own dating experiences, which may appear to be a good deal more romantic than her current situation. As her daughter dreams of her future life, the mother may realize that many of her dreams may never be realized. Even the most devoted of mothers will feel an occasional twinge as she watches her daughter begin her journey toward adulthood.

WORKING VS. NONWORKING MOTHERS

Because girls identify so closely with their mothers, parents frequently ask whether the daughters of mothers who work outside the home have different feelings about the role of women than the daughters of stay-at-home mothers. The answer is no. If a full-time homemaker is excited and enthusiastic about her work, she will communicate those feelings to her daughter. Her daughter will in turn believe that whatever you choose to do in life, it should be interesting and fulfilling. On the other hand, if a mother who works outside the home is constantly overwhelmed and exhausted, she will communicate those negative feelings. In turn, her daughter may take a dismal view of work in particular and women's lot in life in general. The issue is not whether a woman has a job outside her home—it's how good she feels about whatever career she chooses.

RELATIONSHIP STYLES

During adolescence, there are different styles of relationships that typically emerge between mothers and daughters. I write here about five particular mother-daughter dynamics that I have observed in my own practice. As you read about these different types of relationships, some of you may be struck by one style in particular that "hits home," but most likely most of you will find that you relate to elements of each one.

The Overprotective Mother
Your daughter is at risk of

- Not learning to be street smart
- Lacking the confidence and skill to handle herself in difficult situations.

"I used to baby-sit for my brother, and now my mother sends him to the mall to walk me home," complained a 13-year-old girl who was humiliated that her mother thought that she needed the protection of her 11½-year-old brother. "She has to know where I am every second. She was never like this before." This story is not unusual; mothers typically become more restrictive of their daughters' activities after their daughters reach puberty.

First, mothers are reacting out of a genuine concern that their daughters are unable to protect themselves in a "dangerous" world. Second, a mother may see her daughter's bid for independence—a perfectly normal part of adolescence—as an attempt to sever the maternal bond, and the perceived loss can be emotionally wrenching.

Over time, the mother-daughter relationship has to be renegotiated. The mother must give her daughter more responsibility and freedom, at the same time teaching her the necessary survival skills to fend for herself. If she doesn't, the daughter will leave home a vulnerable and fearful young woman who is totally unprepared to function in the outside world.

The Competitor

Your daughter is at risk of

- Never feeling that she is quite "good enough"
- Engaging in destructive behavior to prove she is as good as her mother.

Some degree of rivalry is inevitable between mothers and their adolescent daughters, but in its extreme form, it can be very destructive to the girl's growth and development.

During the awkward pubertal years, the competitive mother is often very supportive and encouraging of her daughter. During the middle adolescent years, however, when her daughter begins to look and act like a young woman, and when other people begin to react to her as such in a positive way, the mother becomes threatened, fearing that the girl will surpass her. Jealousy and competition begin to surface and are manifested in any number of ways. One of the most obvious ways is through appearance: The mother may adopt a more youthful or flashy style of dress in an unconscious effort to upstage her daughter.

At the same time, she may become overly critical of her daughter's behavior or competence. This mother attacks the girl any chance she gets, mocking her ideas and putting her down in a very demeaning fashion. This kind of woman often deludes herself into believing that she is "educating" her daughter and therefore her criticism is justified. No matter how hard her daughter may try, she can never please this kind of mother.

The girl who is locked in a competitive struggle with her mother usually feels dominated by her mother and may lash out in dangerous ways. In extreme cases, the daughter may try to prove she is really "better" than her mother by getting a man (to prove she is attractive) and getting pregnant (to prove that she can do everything her mother can do).

The girl who grows up in this situation is never going to feel confident about herself. She will always feel that she somehow doesn't "measure up," she will always feel insecure and will hold herself back from taking on new challenges.

The Best Friend
Your daughter is at risk of

- Emerging from adolescence without a sense of who she really is and what she really wants
- Never learning how to speak her mind or to expect reciprocity in a relationship.

"We have a wonderful relationship. We're each other's best friend."

When a mother uses these terms to describe her "perfect" relationship with her teenage daughter, my heart sinks—this is not a healthy relationship for either one of them, but it exacts an especially steep toll on the girl.

First, this is not a friendship of equals: It is friendship in which the daughter must take on a subservient role in order to bolster her mother's ego. In the process, the daughter surrenders much of her own. "Mom's best friend" is usually a passive girl who rarely expresses an opinion without first checking with her mother. In fact, her mother is always raving about what a "good" girl she is as compared to other girls her age (who are acting like normal adolescents).

The "best friend" mother often rules her daughter's life, making most of her decisions for her, right down to the most trivial: Her mother picks out her clothes, plans her summers, and often chooses her friends. This mother is desperate for love and companionship, but due to her own insecurities, she is unable to get it from more equal relationships.

The "good girl" never gets to differentiate herself from her mother. These girls are being cheated out of their adolescence; they never get to rebel or to assert their independence. They grow up to be confused, unhappy women who are poorly prepared to make their own decisions. They are out of touch with who they are and what they really want.

The Hands-Off Mother
Your daughter is at risk of

- Feeling that she is a "bad" person who is not worthy of love and attention
- Experimenting with sex, drugs—getting into serious trouble.

There are times when every parent, out of sheer frustration, throws up her hands and says to her daughter, "Do what you want, just leave me alone," but this is the modus operandi of the hands-off mother. The hands-off mother rationalizes her inaction by saying, "Well, she's going to do what she wants anyway, so why should I fight?"

There are two reasons why a mother chooses this style of parenting. First, the mother may be acting on a subconscious wish to absolve herself from the responsibility of raising her daughter. She rationalizes her behavior by contending that her child is old enough to make up her own mind and doesn't listen to her anyway, so why should she waste her breath?

Second, a hands-off mother may be protecting herself from having to confront her own weaknesses. For example, if she smokes and her daughter takes up the habit, she is not in any position to lecture her 12-year-old about the dangers of smoking. In order to be an effective role model, she would have to quit, which she may be unwilling or unable to do. Rather, this mother holds her tongue, but absolves herself of guilt by blaming her daughter for her own inability to be an effective parent.

The daughter of a hands-off mother feels terrible about herself and truly believes that if only she were a better child, worthy of parental attention, her mother would be more interested in her. Often she will fill this "vacuum" in her life by engaging in sexual relationships long before she is emotionally ready, or by attaching herself to a "bad crowd," which if nothing else, provides the emotional support that she is not getting from her mother. This girl will grow up to be a woman who feels unloved and undeserving.

The Stage Mother

Your daughter is at risk of

* "Sharing" her life with Mother and failing to create a life of her own
* Never becoming her own person.

In *Gypsy,* the musical about Gypsy Rose Lee's life, we saw the classic stage mother-daughter duo in action. Like Gypsy Rose Lee's mother, the stage mother works herself to the bone so that her daughter can achieve where the mother has failed. Unlike the competitive mother, the stage mother is content to bask in her daughter's glory. She doesn't need to be in the limelight herself—as long as her daughter is center stage, she's content to live vicariously through her. In turn, the daughter's sense of self is derived from her mother —her mother defines who she is and what she wants.

In *Gypsy,* Gypsy Rose Lee finally freed herself from her mother's grip, but in real life, that rarely happens. In reality, these daughters typically never learn to say no; their lives become so intertwined with Mother's, that they never achieve a sense of independence or autonomy.

Although the true stage mother is an extreme case, there are subtler versions of this dynamic that are quite common. For instance, I had one patient who was quite unhappy because her mother forced her to take ballet lessons at a very exclusive studio in New York frequented by professional dancers. Although her mother was thrilled that her daughter was talented enough to "keep up with the professionals," the daughter felt that she could barely hold her own in class, and she would have preferred to take lessons at a less competitive studio in her suburban neighborhood. This daughter was afraid to tell her mother the truth because she didn't want to disappoint her, but at the same time, she felt that she was being used by her mother "so that she'd have something to brag about to her friends." In this case, the mother derived so much pleasure from her daughter's special ability that she lost sight of her daughter's needs. When her daughter finally confessed her feelings, the mother felt terrible about the way that she had been pressuring her and allowed her to go to her local studio. This mother stopped looking to her daughter to bolster her own sense of self-worth, which is a lot healthier for both of them.

The "Good Enough" Mother

There is no such thing as a "perfect" mother. At times, even the best of mothers can find themselves locked in a less than ideal dynamic with their adolescent daughters. A well-meaning mother may be a bit of a "stage mother" about certain aspects of her daughter's life; a loving mother may be an overprotective mother at times when she should be encouraging her daughter to strike out on her own.

The "good enough" mother is the mother who, despite occasional lapses, is able to provide her daughter with the love and guidance she needs to become a self-assured, competent adult. The good enough mother accepts the dual challenge of adolescence: She understands that at the same time that she is letting go and allowing her daughter to become more independent, she must also continue providing her with love and emotional support. The good enough mother does not turn her daughter out into the world to fend for herself before she is ready—she is there to steer her through the difficult times. And when it is time for her daughter to enter the adult world, the good enough mother feels confident that she has given her daughter the basic skills on which she can build a successful life.

DAD: "THE OTHER PARENT"

Until very recently, the father of a daughter was viewed as "the other parent," with a rather nebulous role in that relationship. Contrasted to the all-important mother, the father has been regarded as a minor character, definitely not as a leading man.

We now recognize that a father plays a more important role in the father-daughter relationship, and the degree to which he is involved or detached can have a profound effect on a girl's development.

Her father is the first man a girl will ever love, and from this relationship she will learn about other heterosexual relationships. On a deeper, more primitive level, a loving father can make a girl feel well cared for and protected. He above all others can endow her with a strong sense of her worth as a person and her worth as a sexual being.

THROUGH HIS EYES

From her early infancy, the father's expectation of what his daughter should be shapes the girl she will become. For example, in one fascinating study, fathers and mothers were asked to describe their newborn sons and daughters. Both mothers and fathers used adjectives such as "strong" and "hardy" to describe their sons and were more likely to view their daughters as "beautiful," "fine featured," and "delicate." The fathers of daughters, however, carried the sex-role stereotyping to the extreme and were much more focused on appearance than were the fathers of sons. Ironically, the researchers noted that the girl infants were actually more robust and stronger than the boy infants, a fact that eluded their parents. Parents see what they want to see, and in my experience, I have found that fathers can be especially blinded by sex-role stereotypes.

Once a girl becomes an adolescent, her father often takes on the role of "taming" her masculine impulses by reinforcing feminine behavior. In other words, helping her mother cook dinner will win her praise, playing touch football with the guys next door will elicit a scowl or a comment such as, "Do you really have to get that dirty when you play?" Overt displays of anger are usually poorly tolerated by fathers, who make it clear that such behavior is simply not permissible. Fathers, more so than mothers, are likely to react negatively to the "clumsiness" and "awkwardness" that is typical of early adolescence.

DADDY'S GIRL

Throughout a girl's lifetime, her father assumes many different roles. During the baby and toddler years, he is the "fun" parent, who by virtue of his frequent absences, is viewed as special. At around age 4 or 5—in what is called the "Oedipal phase"—a girl begins to feel a strong heterosexual pull to her father, and for many fathers and daughters this marks the beginning of a "honeymoon" period, during which she becomes "Daddy's little girl": She loves her father in a naïve, uncritical way, and this "blind" love may last until early adolescence.

Through her relationship with her father—and her father's relationship to her mother—a girl learns how to relate to men and sustain a heterosexual relationship. Future relationships are often modeled on this special one—this is what love should feel like.

If a girl finds her father to be a dynamic, exciting man, she often seeks the same feelings from her relationships with other men. If a girl finds that she is forever trying to woo a cool and distant father, she may repeat the pattern in her future relationships. In some cases, however, a father becomes a negative model, that is, because her relationship with her father was so painful, a woman may seek a man who is his complete opposite. Or, in some cases, a girl who found her relationship with her father to be very painful may feel ambivalent about pursuing any relationships with men at all. Whatever the end result, the relationship with her father is a criterion by which other relationships with males are measured.

LOOKING FOR APPROVAL

Father is also the man with whom a girl "tests" out her femininity. Girls usually love to go shopping with their mothers, but they also make it a point to model their new purchases for their fathers. They are not only seeking his approval, they are using him to gauge the reaction of other men.

How and when a father gives or withholds his approval sends a powerful message to his daughter, whose vision of herself is often reflected through his eyes. If a father praises her for being pretty, but for nothing else, she is bound to place undue importance on her looks. Although she will be proud that he thinks she is pretty, on a deeper level she will feel rejected because he has failed to notice the person within the body. If a father praises a girl for her achievements, it will give her permission to continue to succeed. However, if the father fails to admire any of her feminine virtues, a girl will also feel rejected because she will reason, "If your own father doesn't think you're pretty, then chances are, nobody else does either." If a father is evenhanded in his approach and is careful to praise both beauty and accomplishment, a girl will feel empowered to succeed in all aspects of life.

"DEMYSTIFYING" THE OTHER SEX

Father can also play a valuable role in a girl's life by making the other sex more comprehensible. A father who is willing to talk about how males think and behave will be helping his daughter learn how to relate to men—not only with boyfriends, but with teachers at school and with the men she will encounter in the workplace. By "demystifying" the male sex, the father will be giving his daughter the confidence to develop friendships with men and to compete with men as an equal.

THE PUBERTAL TRIANGLE

During the key pubertal years, a girl may turn to her father as she distances herself from her mother, seeking an ally within the family. Sometimes the father becomes a buffer between mother and daughter. This scenario was vividly portrayed in *Anne Frank: The Diary of a Young Girl.* Thirteen-year-old Anne and her mother, who showed little patience for Anne's adolescent angst, were frequently at odds with each other. The normal mother-daughter tension was undoubtedly exacerbated by the fact that the Frank family was hiding from the Nazis and living in very close quarters. Yet, despite the tumultuous world events, Anne sounded like any other normal teenager when she wrote, "Mummy kicked up a frightful row and told Daddy just what she thought of me. Then she had an awful fit of tears so, of course, off I went too; and I got such an awful headache anyway. Finally I told Daddy that I'm much more fond of him than Mummy, to which he replied that I'd get over that." Although Anne's father offered Anne a sympathetic ear, he wisely avoided becoming enmeshed in the conflict between Anne and her mother.

In some cases, however, a father and a daughter may ally against the mother. This often happens in homes where the marital relationship has splintered or hardened to the extent where the partners are on different "sides." The father who allows this to happen may outwardly appear to be very sympathetic and loving to his daughter, but he is actually using her as a pawn in his struggle with his wife. The adolescent girl caught up in this situation is at serious risk of getting "stuck" in this tender stage of development. Instead of turning away from her father to pursue other romantic interests, which is what she should be doing, she be will be investing much of her adolescent passion in him. Her alliance with her father will prevent her from forming healthy relationships with boys and later with men.

SEXUAL TENSION

As adolescent girls develop, the sexual tension between the pubertal daughter and her father is another force in this dynamic that many fathers find greatly disturbing. When a five-year-old jumps into Daddy's lap and showers him with kisses, his usual reaction is, "Oh, isn't she cute," and he hugs her back without giving it another thought. When a 12- or 13-year-old with full breasts and curvy hips jumps into his lap and gives him a hug, a father is bound to feel some sexual response. Uncomfortable with his feelings, he will probably yank her off his lap and reprimand her for "acting like a baby" or for "bothering him." Hurt and rejected, she will either lash out that he doesn't love her, or that she hates him, and will start to cry.

It is far better to acknowledge that human beings are sexual creatures. It is normal to feel sexual impulses, even toward our children when they grow into attractive and desirable young men and women. What is not normal is to act on these impulses. There is a big difference between a fleeting sexual response and committing an act of incest. Fathers would do themselves and their daughters a favor if they anticipated these "taboo" feelings and understood how to respond to them as a natural part of raising an adolescent girl.

A sensitive and aware father can find better ways to handle these kinds of situations. For instance, I was at a wedding recently where I observed an absolutely striking fourteen-year-old girl climb into her father's lap and give him a kiss. The father very calmly picked her up by her elbows and stood her on her feet. He then smiled and said, "When you were little, we had a lot of fun when you used to sit on my lap. But now, you can't fit on my lap anymore and we have fun in different ways." I admired this father for how he got his point across without humiliating his daughter or harming their relationship.

WALKING ON EGGSHELLS

Even the most attuned fathers can become exasperated with their adolescent daughters. Adolescent girls can be argumentative—they'll readily provoke a fight, but they are also moody and overly sensitive. During this often tumultuous period, even when a father thinks he is trying to be sympathetic and understanding, he may find that his daughter takes offense. Rather than risk rebuff and rejection, many fathers simply pull away from what appears to them to be a no-win situation.

HIS OWN ANGST

Surrounded by turmoil in his household, the father, like the mother, may be experiencing some turmoil of his own. The father of an adolescent may be grappling with his own midlife conflicts, which can be pretty intense. For men in particular, the 40s are the "make you or break you" years—many men believe that if they don't achieve their dreams in their 40s, they never will. During this time of self-reassessment, family demands may seem like more of a burden than a joy, and an adolescent daughter can be very demanding.

RELATIONSHIP STYLES

As with daughters and mothers, there are several styles of relationships that emerge during adolescence between fathers and daughters. The typical father will identify with one or more of these styles, but many will find that their father-daughter relationship is actually a mixture of several or even all of them.

The Withdrawing Father

Your daughter is at risk of

- Feeling she is "at fault" or unworthy of love
- Feeling insecure in her future relationships with men.

By far the most typical response among fathers of pubertal girls is withdrawal, emotionally if not physically. A "withdrawing father" may spend less time alone with his daughter, engage her in conversation less often, and he may become overly critical of her, almost as if he needs a reason to justify his actions.

We know from several important studies that girls often feel less accepted by their fathers during this critical time. In my own practice, girls who once felt that they had close relationships with their fathers now admit, "Dad and I don't get along very well these days." More often than not, their fathers agree but are quick to blame the situation on the fact that their daughters are "going through a bad patch" or "a phase."

A daughter responds to her father's withdrawal in one of two ways: A very insecure girl, or one who is extremely egocentric, will view her father's desertion as validation of her own unworthiness. "I am a fat, boring, acne-ridden mess, and nobody, not even my father, wants to deal with me."

The girl who doesn't blame herself will wonder if there is something wrong in her father's life that is forcing him to behave so strangely: She will speculate that he is in serious financial trouble, or that he has met another woman and is planning on leaving the family. Whatever her interpretation of the events, a girl is bound to be puzzled and hurt by her father's mysterious behavior.

Girls who lose this precious relationship with their fathers may grow up to be women who have difficulty learning to trust other men with their love; some may react by placing themselves in subservient positions with men out of fear of losing them, too.

The Overprotective Father

Your daughter is at risk of

- Having her emotional growth thwarted
- Developing a poor sense of who she is
- Looking to a man to solve all of her problems.

There are two kinds of overprotective fathers: The "too empathetic" father wants to protect his daughter from emotional pain. The "control freak" wants to protect his daughter from any "harm."

Although they mean well, these fathers are both inflicting harm by refusing to let their daughters live and feel their own lives.

The too empathetic father is unable to maintain the appropriate emotional boundaries between him and his daughter. He is killing her with kindness. The too empathetic father typically gets very upset when his daughter gets upset—he feels what she feels. For instance, if she has a fight with her mother and runs to her room in tears, he will run after her and stand outside the door saying, "I'm here, darling, I want to talk to you, don't be so upset." He will not allow her to work through her feelings on her own, he wants to do it with her or even for her.

Very often, these fathers may have felt misunderstood or neglected by their own parents during adolescence and are trying to overcompensate with their own children. Unfortunately, their good intentions often backfire. Adolescents need to have an opportunity to assert their independence. It is critically important for an adolescent girl to be allowed to take a stand, to defend her position, and if necessary, to stalk off into her room (by herself) to prove that she is right. By trying to "make things nice," the too empathetic father is denying his daughter this essential form of self-assertion. The daughter of this kind of parent will have a poor sense of herself because she will have difficulty distinguishing her own feelings from those of her father.

Although he behaves differently from the too empathetic father, the control freak wreaks the same kind of psychic destruction. The control-freak father tolerates no dissent in his household; if his daughter misbehaves in any way, if she speaks harshly to her mother, or if she brings home a bad report card, she is banished to her room. This father's message is simple: "Everyone in my household lives by my rules, and if they don't like it, they can leave."

In his own warped way, the control freak is trying to protect his daughter from his perception of danger. By stripping her of her independence, however, he is not preparing his daughter for the real world outside her home, where she will have to make decisions on her own. Often women raised in these kinds of households are attracted to men who, like the womens' fathers, bully them under the guise of protecting them. Very often, these women end up in therapy, because these relationships are very unsatisfying.

The "Ruler of the Roost"

Your daughter is at risk of

- Developing a distorted view of "male" and "female" roles
- Feeling that she should be subservient to men
- Feeling that what she has to say is unimportant.

The "ruler of the roost" is the king of his castle. In his best form, he is the benign dictator, in his worst, he is the tyrant. The ruler of the roost comes home from work after a long day and expects everyone to tiptoe around him so that he is not disturbed. Even if his wife works, she is expected to attend to his needs, and in many cases, so is his adolescent daughter. The ruler of the roost is a rather detached father; he leaves the care of the children to his wife.

Adolescent girls often resent "rulers" because they feel that they cast their mothers in a weak, submissive role. In reality, rulers and their wives may have a far more equitable relationship than meets the eye (she may cook the meals and he may make most of the money, but she is the one who actually pays the bills and decides how the money is spent); however, such subtleties are often lost on adolescent girls.

Although rulers are not hands-on parents, they can still have a good relationship with their daughters if they make an effort to maintain contact. Rulers in particular use work or outside commitments as an excuse for removing themselves from the responsibility of parenthood. During adolescence, daughters need recognition and approval from both parents, and no matter how busy a father is, he must reserve some time to spend with his daughter.

The "tyrant" is a ruler gone out of control. Although it is hardly typical, there are men who run their households with iron fists, and wives who go along with them, no matter what. Unlike a control freak, a tyrant's primary motivation is not protecting his family, rather he is concerned with meeting his own needs to the exclusion of the needs of others. A daughter raised in a home with a tyrant is not only getting a very distorted view of marriage, but she herself is being "programmed" to obey men, which will hamper her ability to form a normal, loving relationship.

The Most Wonderful Dad in the World

Your daughter is at risk of

- Never finding a man who can compete with Dad
- Believing that blind devotion and subservience is what love is all about.

The "most wonderful dad in the world" wants his daughter to believe that he is the most wonderful man in the world and no other man will ever love her as much as he does, and he tells her just that. When they are together, he is very complimentary but always manages to turn the conversation around to himself. As long as she thinks he's terrific, he thinks she's terrific. In reality, the "most wonderful dad" is using his daughter as an appreciative audience to prove his own self-worth. The most wonderful dad uses his relationship with his daughter to enhance his own ego, perhaps because his relationship with his wife or his other children is not meeting his emotional needs.

Although these fathers may talk a good line, very often, they have been fairly uninvolved in their daughters' upbringing. I have treated many grown women who are still locked into the idea of most wonderful dad and are unable to find a man who can compete with their fathers. I had one patient who used to talk for hours about how her father was the only man who was ever attuned to her feelings and appreciated what she had to say. When we finally got to talking about how much time she actually spent with her father, I learned that this man who was supposedly so interested in her, and so giving of himself, would spend about half an hour with her a couple of nights a week. Gradually, she came to understand that the ideal relationship she believed she had shared with her father was actually an illusion.

The "Good Enough" Father

Similar to the "good enough" mother, the "good enough" Father enjoys watching his daughter grow up and takes joy in her newfound maturity. He is able to adapt his style of parenting to her new stage of development; he neither clings to the "child" nor pushes her prematurely toward adulthood. This father recognizes that he has an important role to play in his daughter's upbringing—he does not rationalize his absence by saying, "This is a time when a girl needs her mother the most." The good enough father sets aside special time for his daughter and lets her know that he feels she is an important and worthy person.

BETWEEN PARENTS AND SIBLINGS

Siblings are the wild card of the family dynamic: Their impact on an adolescent girl is unpredictable. In some families, siblings are loving and close, in others they are constantly hostile. In still others ambivalence is the key emotion. Whether or not siblings get along often depends on their age difference, their personalities, and how their parents treat them separately and collectively.

SIBLING COEXISTENCE—
NOT ALWAYS PEACEFUL

When a daughter enters adolescence her relationship with her siblings inevitably undergoes a change, sometimes for the better, sometimes for the worse. I have seen situations in which a "pesky" younger sister reaches puberty and suddenly becomes a friend and confidant to her older sister. I have also seen situations in which an older girl who had previously been close to her siblings reaches puberty and suddenly wants to disassociate herself from them. This can cause a good deal of hurt feelings among the younger children in the family. What very often happens is that the younger children retaliate by teasing their adolescent sister, and often their jokes can be quite cruel. I recently spoke with one mother who was beside herself because her 8-year-old son was reducing her 12-year-old daughter to tears with his persistent teasing. "I've threatened him every way I know how, but he still does it. How can I get him to stop?" she asked. She was surprised when I told her that I doubted she would be able to, nor did I think that the brother was the real problem.

Teasing is a fact of life for adolescents. If they're not teased at home, very likely someone is teasing them at school. Teasing per se is not a problem: It only becomes a problem when the girl actually believes what is being said about her. There is no way to stop an 8-year-old boy from pointing at his sister's breasts and telling her that she looks fat or that she's ugly. As many times as you reprimand him, he will "forget" and do it again. But it is important to take that girl aside and to assure her that she looks fine and that she is growing normally. It is also okay to teach her a few "showstopper" lines to use if the teasing is really bothering her, such as "Oh, you're just jealous." (That usually shuts boys up very quickly!) This will give her the strength to deal with teasers at school too.

There are some situations when parents should intercede. If one sibling is constantly pushing another to tears—if his or her teasing is particularly relentless or cruel—parents need to make it clear that no member of the family should be subjected to verbal abuse. The sibling who is guilty of chronic emotional battering, who is compelled to use others as an emotional punching bag, is very often frustrated and unhappy and, in my opinion, is in need of help.

Passions run high during puberty, and clashes between siblings can often turn into hand-to-hand combat. It's important for parents to separate the children before anyone gets injured—the rule of any sane home should be "nobody gets hurt." At this point, children should have the verbal skills to work out their problems without resorting to hitting.

If brothers and sisters resort to physical fighting, parents should be careful about the approach they use to intervene. They should not rush in to "protect" the "helpless" sister; this will make her feel as if she is fragile and defenseless in the hands of men. In reality, many teenage girls are quite capable of holding their own in these situations. Simply break up the fight in a matter-of-fact fashion. "We don't do this kind of thing in this house" is the only message they need to hear.

Sibling Styles

In homes where there are two or more children, parents have a way of labeling and defining each child and then treating each accordingly. Here are some typical labels that parents unconsciously place on their daughters and the inherent problems in each of these situations.

The Fine on Her Own Girl vs. The Attention Grabber

The "fine on her own" girl is at risk of

- Being forced into a role she is not emotionally ready to play
- Learning to submerge her true feelings.

In this home, the adolescent girl is cast as the "good" sibling, and her brother or sister is the "bad" or needy sibling. The parents' gaze is often firmly fixed on the "bad" or needy child, who requires a great deal more time and attention than the "good" girl. The parents tend to exaggerate the good girl's maturity and frequently praise her for being able to do things for herself. Thus the good girl's needs are often neglected or ignored. The good girl doesn't want to "burden" Mom and Dad with her problems, so she internalizes her feelings. By middle adolescence, the good girl has a poor sense of herself and is at serious risk of depression.

The Problem Girl vs. The Perfect Sibling

The "problem girl" is at risk of

- Believing that she is "bad" or inadequate
- Believing she can "never do anything right."

In this scenario, the adolescent girl is cast as the "bad" child who is constantly being compared to her "good" sibling, who more often than not, is a "perfect" girl.

A case in point is my patient Jennifer, 13, who used to throw violent temper tantrums in which she would fall to the floor and literally kick her feet and scream, much like a 2-year-old. Jennifer was also doing poorly at school both academically and socially. During our meetings, Jennifer would complain that her parents didn't love her. Although they spent countless hours reprimanding her and discussing her "problem," they saved their affection for their 6-year-old daughter, Wendy, whom Jennifer had grown to hate. One week I asked the parents to bring Wendy along so I could see how the family members related to each other. Much to my amazement, during the entire one-hour session, Wendy sat quietly on her mother's lap, never trying to get up or to contribute to the conversation—highly unusual behavior for a 6-year-old. Wendy was the prototype "good" girl, the passive, no-maintenance child who made few demands on her parents. Jennifer, however, was a more emotional, complicated personality who required more work on the part of her parents. It was easier to cast Jennifer as a problem—and to withdraw from her emotionally—than to understand that her childish tantrums were an attempt to get the attention that Wendy was getting. Jennifer's parents eventually began to pay more positive attention to Jennifer—they went out of their way to find reason to praise her and to bolster her place in the family—and her behavior rapidly changed.

Although Jennifer's case is an extreme example, modified versions of the problem girl/perfect sibling scenario are quite common in homes with adolescent girls. Pubertal girls are at special risk of being cast as the "problem" child for the simple reason that they are often demanding and difficult to handle.

Girls raised in this atmosphere are made to feel that they are behaving in a bizarre or deviant fashion, whereas they are merely behaving as normal adolescents. Unfortunately, it is often a self-fulfilling prophesy. These girls often grow into women with very low self-esteem who feel that they are incapable of doing anything right.

The Daughter Among Sons

The "daughter among sons" is at risk of

- Believing that her needs are unimportant
- Growing up to be subordinate to men.

There are special risks facing a "daughter among sons," who in many households, becomes the forgotten sibling who is overwhelmed by the boys. In many families, the needs of males are deemed more important than the needs of females—few parents will come right out and admit this, but this attitude manifests itself in more subtle ways.

First, resources are often unevenly divided, with "male" interests being deemed more worthy of funding. Parents "find" money to buy football uniforms or to send a son to a private college, whereas they might be reluctant to go into debt to pay for a daughter to go to an expensive school. Second, the daughter is often expected to help her mother out around the house, but not the sons. If the boys are asked to help, it is rarely to the same degree as the daughter. I have seen parents rationalize this by saying, "Well, Jim and Charlie have football practice after school and really can't be home in time to baby-sit for Mark, so that's why Sharon has to do it," or they will say, "But Sharon is so good at these things, and whenever I ask one of the boys to do anything around the house, I end up having to do it over again." But nobody ever bothered to ask Sharon if there was something else that she would rather be doing.

Even in homes where parents try to be equitable, boys are often more aggressive at asking for what they want and in making sure they get it.

When a girl is being raised with brothers, her parents need to go out of their way to make sure that she is given the opportunity to express herself without being ridiculed or put down. Her parents must make sure that she is given an opportunity to be in a supportive environment with other girls, such as the Girl Scouts, Girls Incorporated, or a sports team at school, which can help foster a strong sense of self and her own competence. In addition, parents might even consider sending the daughter among sons to an all-girls school, where she will see girls and women in strong, leadership positions.

Although there are many potential pitfalls, there are also some positive aspects about being raised among boys. A girl who lives with brothers—and is taught how to hold her own—will be less awed by other males and will probably feel less self-conscious when she is around boys.

THE "GOOD ENOUGH" HOME

Just as there are no perfect parents, and no perfect children, there are no perfect homes. But there are some homes that work better than others, that produce daughters who are strong, confident, and ready to face whatever challenges may come their way. These are homes that subscribe to the "separate but equal" philosophy in which parents maintain an evenhanded approach between siblings.

In the separate-but-equal home, family resources are divided equally, parents try to spend equal amounts of time with each one of their children, and each child is expected to do his or her share around the house. Although equal treatment doesn't eliminate sibling rivalry, it does instill in each child a sense of her or his own importance, individuality, and ability to work with others.

Separate but equal also means that parents don't pit one sibling against another; each child is valued and recognized for her or his own individuality. In this house, parents don't say, "If only you were more like your brother [sister]." The unspoken message is "We're glad that you are you."

Under the best of circumstances, there are times when one child's needs will supersede another's, such as in the case of illness or if a child is going through a rough time at school. In these cases, parents in the good enough home are careful to explain why they need to spend extra time with that particular child and to make it up to the other children at a different time.

The creed of this home is that no child should feel neglected or left out, and it usually works fairly well.

Here are some other suggestions for maintaining a healthy home environment:

A room of her own. Ideally, siblings should have separate rooms. However, if this is not possible, an adolescent girl should absolutely not share a room with an adolescent brother. Aggressive and sexual impulses are simply too strong during this period. Two adolescent girls sharing a room is also a poor idea. Girls of this age are very territorial about their "things" and are likely to fight bitterly. A better match would be an adolescent girl with a younger sibling—boy or girl. In order to avoid jealousy, partition the room equally with a divider, such as a bookcase or a screen, and let each sibling decorate his or her own portion.

Privacy: hers and yours. It's reasonable for an adolescent to ask her parents and siblings to knock on her door before entering her room. Such common courtesy is showing her that you respect her and her "private" space. Don't be stunned or shocked, however, if she sometimes forgets to respect the private space of others. During adolescence, doors fly open when you least expect it; your daughter "accidentally" enters your room when you're undressing or barges into the bathroom while you're showering. During these "brief encounters" she may be satisfying her curiosity, and I wouldn't get too disturbed over it. Simply remind her to knock first before entering.

Family dress code. Although nobody should have to walk around fully dressed in the privacy of their own home, all sexual parts should be well covered up. Depending on the style of your home, darting around the house in a bra and a half-slip may be permissible if you're racing to work or if your daughter is hurrying off to school, but a sexy, sheer nightgown is not. If you feel that your daughter's attire has exceeded the bounds of good taste for your household, simply tell her to put on a robe. Don't rant or yell or make her feel that there is something wrong with her body.

BETWEEN PARENT AND PARENT

By observing her parents, a girl learns what goes on between men and women—this is the model that she will emulate in her future relationships with the boys and men she dates and the man she finally marries. She doesn't need to see perfection. In fact it can be very healthy for an adolescent girl to see that people who love each other can fight and later make up. Adolescent girls often have very romantic and unrealistic notions of love. They believe that when you fall in love, you will feel the same feelings and think the same thoughts as your boyfriend or husband. If they take this fantasy into adulthood, they will be in for terrible disappointment.

It is also important for a girl to see that differences of opinions can be aired without fighting—that adults can talk, listen to, and reason with each other, and at times, even politely disagree. Each parent should be able to express different points of view without being subjected to bullying or ridicule by the other.

There are times when even without being told, a girl is going to know that her parents' marriage is in trouble. She will pick up on anger and hostility, even if parents try very hard to hide it. Or, if a parent is absent a good deal from the home, she may suspect that he or she is having an affair.

A girl who detects a marital problem may ask you directly, "Are you happy with Mom [Dad]?" She may want to know if you are planning to get divorced. I believe that parents should respond honestly—up to a point. A simple and direct response is warranted. "You're right, Dad [Mom] and I are not happy, but we're seeing a marriage counselor, and we're trying to make things better" or "We're getting counseling from our minister" is quite enough to say. You need not burden your daughter with exactly what you don't like about Dad or Mom, or the problems in your relationship. If she asks specific questions, you can answer as many as you are comfortable about answering. I would keep in mind that a young adolescent is not going to understand the complexities of male-female relationships, so I would keep my explanation simple.

On the other hand, a mother may be able to sit down with her more mature 16-year-old daughter and have a true heart-to-heart talk. However, the mother should be careful not to pressure her daughter into choosing sides; the daughter presumably loves her father, and this is an unfair request.

Parents who lie and say that everything is fine when it is not are performing a terrible disservice to their daughter. By not validating what their daughter actually sees and hears, they are making her feel as if there is something wrong with her for "imagining" things that are not there. Even if the truth is painful, it is far better than having her live with a lie.

Keep in mind that no matter what you do, as a parent of an adolescent girl, you have an audience, like it or not. No matter how secretive or "clever" you think you are being, or how "naïve" you think the rest of your family is, the truth always comes out, and it is far better that you deal with your marital problems honestly and openly than let your daughter speculate.

FAMILY VALUES THAT WORK

Parents need to set a tone that fosters a loving, close bond among family members. They need to create an environment that downplays sibling rivalry and makes each member of the household feel respected and valued.

The household that truly values each member—that makes each person feel important—will produce children of both sexes who are happy, strong, and confident.

SIX: "WHO AM I NOW?"

What are girls concerned about? The first thing that pops in my head is looks. Many girls are very upset by the way that they look. They're always saying things like, "I hate this about myself," or "I'm so fat!" or "I wish I had her hair," or "Why wasn't I born with her legs?"

—Leslie, age 16

On the surface, Emily appeared to be a perfectly normal 16-year-old: She was attractive, bright and popular. However, her parents sent her to me for treatment because they noticed that their once-ebullient daughter seemed to be depressed.

During our third session, Emily's secret came out.

"I have a little problem," she confessed. "Most of the time, I can stick to my diet. I mean, I'm really good. But when I go off, I can't eat like a normal person. Once I get started, I just can't stop. I can't eat five potato chips—I have to eat the whole bag. I can't eat one scoop of ice cream—I have to eat the whole quart, and then I'll go after a bag of Oreos. I must eat a million calories at a time!"

Emily, who was a svelte size 5, had devised an interesting way of keeping slim. After each bout of uncontrolled eating, Emily would sneak into the bathroom, stick her fingers down her throat, and force herself to vomit. If she still thought that she "looked heavy," she would pop a few laxatives to induce diarrhea.

When Emily began dieting three years ago to rid herself of "baby fat," she resorted to vomiting only once or twice a month. But lately she'd been doing it three or four times a week, and she was becoming concerned that she couldn't stop.

"You don't understand, I don't *want* to do it, I *have* to do it," she explained in tears.

Emily has an eating disorder known as bulimia, which is characterized by frequent bingeing and purging. Bulimia is more than a "little problem": It can seriously disrupt normal body chemistry and in severe cases can be fatal.

As bizarre as Emily's eating habits may sound, they are not uncommon. Studies show that

- Up to 20 percent of all adolescent girls engage in highly abnormal behavior regarding food, usually to control their weight.
- About 5 percent of all women ages 15–22 develop anorexia nervosa, an eating disorder characterized by self-imposed starvation.
- Approximately 9 percent of all young women in the same age group are "hard-core" bulimics, that is, they binge and purge at least twice a week.

At least half of all anorectics are also bulimic. Both of these eating disorders are extremely difficult to treat and are also difficult to detect. In many cases, parents may not even suspect that their daughter has a problem until she is in serious trouble.

Unfortunately, for many girls, adolescence is the beginning of what becomes a lifelong obsession with physical appearance and weight. This obsession can have serious long-term consequences, severely damaging their health and emotional well-being.

HER LOOKS: A LIFELONG OBSESSION

I believe that there are several reasons why girls—and women—become fixated on their "physical selves." During puberty, boys gain muscle, girls gain fat, and some girls gain more fat than others. Many girls begin puberty with the telltale rolls of midriff fat commonly called "baby fat." Although this condition is usually temporary, these girls feel simply terrible about their bodies, and in some cases, carry these scars throughout their adolescence and adulthood.

Many women who aren't the least bit overweight still think of themselves as pudgy, awkward adolescents. These women can identify with the 30-year-old svelte fashion designer who recently told me, "I was a chunky kid. I couldn't wear the normal preteen sizes,

I had to wear the 'Chubbies,' because they were cut a bit bigger. I hated shopping for clothes, it was very embarrassing. I still feel uncomfortable about my body. No matter how thin I get, I still see myself as a 'big' person."

The fact that girls feel shame and embarrassment about their bodies is understandable given the fact that in our culture the tight and trim, prepubescent "malelike" body is the one that is admired— even on women.

Body preference is not just a matter of aesthetics; it is a reflection of our values, notably the way men and women are viewed in society. The hard masculine body is associated with power and strength— attributes that are held in high esteem. The soft, round lines of the feminine body are associated with nurturing and emotion—attributes that are deemed relatively unimportant.

As her body changes its shape and form, as it is transformed from the "androgynous" child's body into a woman's body, the 11- or 12-year-old girl becomes particularly self-conscious and uncomfortable with herself. Although many girls establish an uneasy "peace" with their bodies by midadolescence, few girls—or women—ever feel that their bodies are "good enough."

The girl who feels bad about her body does not feel good about herself. Self-esteem—especially during adolescence—is inextricably linked to a teenage girl's perception of her own attractiveness. The girl who is overly critical or negative about her body—as many girls are—is going to have a poor sense of self. The girl with a poor body image and thus low self-esteem is at much greater risk of developing a life-threatening eating disorder or other potentially debilitating emotional problem.

The girls at greatest risk of running into trouble are the Fast Trackers, those who reach puberty earlier than their peers. Because they tend to be somewhat heavier than other girls, Fast Trackers typically develop more baby fat. These girls seem to suffer the worst loss of self-esteem and have the most negative feelings about their bodies and thus are at particular risk of developing an eating disorder.

On the other hand, Late Bloomers, girls who develop later than average, fare the best, probably because they get to keep their prepubertal bodies the longest and have a longer time to "grow up."

Parents can play a major role in preventing this obsession with looks from destroying their daughters' lives. Astute, understanding parents *can* make a difference. In order to be effective, however, parents need to be aware of the seriousness of this problem and its potential lethal consequences. Parents also need to recognize the insidious role society plays in perpetuating this obsession—the role that they themselves may inadvertently be playing—and how they can best counteract these forces.

LOOKS ARE WHAT COUNT

Societal pressure to be pretty starts very early. From infancy on, girls quickly learn that looks are what will get them the most attention. As babies, girls are admired by their parents more than boys and are more likely to be complimented on their appearance.

Even in school, where academics should be the primary concern, girls are taught that looks count more than substance. When a teacher makes a comment to a girl, more often than not it is not to praise her for her good grades or astute contributions to classroom discussion, rather, it is to compliment her physical appearance, her clothes, or her hairstyle.

By adolescence, girls begin to view themselves as part of the scenery; the message has finally sunk in that appearance is what really counts. In contrast, boys view themselves as a part of the action, focusing on their growing level of competence.

This is not to say that boys are not also concerned about their looks, or that they don't spend time experimenting with hairstyles or agonizing over acne or oily hair. In reality, boys *do* care, but not nearly to the same extent as girls. Boys care about other things a lot more.

A case in point is a study in which boys and girls were asked what they liked best or least about their bodies. Boys generally answered positively, citing their growing athletic strengths and abilities as things that they liked about themselves. Girls, on the other hand, had more negative things to say and usually focused on specific areas of the body such as legs, hips, or facial features. Unlike boys, girls did not view physical development as a source of empowerment that enabled them to do more things, rather they were fixated on how they looked. This obsession with the physical self becomes apparent if you listen to adolescent girls talk among themselves. I have heard girls in my adolescent group devote hours of conversation to who has the thinnest body, the longest neck, the "best" legs, the flattest stomach, the trimmest waist, the shiniest hair, etc. When adolescent boys get together, they are no less competitive, but their focus is usually on sports or other accomplishments.

FAT PHOBIA

The female adolescent's focus on her body often leads to a full-blown case of "fat phobia," which continues throughout adulthood. According to a recent study by the National Centers for Disease Control in Atlanta, female high school students were three times more likely to be on a diet than their male counterparts. Moreover, 27 percent of all female students who considered themselves to be of normal weight were still trying to lose weight. In other words, girls really do believe that "you can't be too thin."

The report concluded that "female students were significantly more likely than male students to report having exercised, skipped meals, or resorted to dangerous practices such as taking diet pills or inducing vomiting for weight management during the seven days preceding the survey . . ."

Several recent studies have noted other alarming trends among high school and college females. One Massachusetts study found that up to 20 percent of all high school girls interviewed admitted to having induced vomiting or resorted to laxative abuse to reduce.

Girls are so phobic about fat that they seek continual reassurance that they're not overweight. "The girls in my school are constantly complaining that they're fat. They're so thin, but they think they're enormous. I think they say they're fat so that they'll be told that they aren't. Saying to someone that they're thin is like the best compliment you can give," notes one 12-year-old.

Another study of college women revealed that up to 40 percent follow diets of 800 calories a day or less, about half of what they actually need to function normally. Not only are untold thousands of girls walking around hungry (and probably tired) as a result of this dieting, but they may be causing long-term damage to their bodies by not providing them with enough essential vitamins and minerals.

THE LONG-TERM CONSEQUENCES

Many girls are not getting adequate nutrition, and your daughter may be one of them. Adolescent girls are not particularly careful about their diets. As one 14-year-old said with a laugh, "What kind of diet are most of my friends on? Basically, the kind where you don't eat."

Girls on severely restricted diets are at risk of developing serious medical problems during adulthood. Half of all adolescent girls do not get the 1200 mg recommended dietary allowance (RDA) of calcium, a mineral that is often sacrificed in the name of dieting. *The Surgeon General's Report on Nutrition* noted that "chronically low calcium intake, especially during adolescence and early adulthood, may compromise development of peak bone mass," which, as it goes on to explain, may cause osteoporosis later in life. Osteoporosis, a debilitating bone disorder, is a leading cause of death among older women.

Iron is another vital mineral that many girls lack. Adolescent girls —especially those who don't eat red meat—are prone to iron-deficiency anemia, which causes fatigue and reduces the body's ability to fight infection.

Low-calorie diets have also been implicated in menstrual disorders and may even cause fertility problems down the road.

Despite the very real risks associated with chronic dieting, teenage girls are too focused on achieving the "impossible body" to consider what they are doing to their health.

THE IMPOSSIBLE BODY

Most of the teenage girls whom I encounter want to look like someone else, usually someone they've seen in a magazine or on a movie screen. They want to be taller, leggier, and skinny—the skinnier the better. Just thumb through any issue of *Seventeen, Sassy,* or any other magazine that your daughter may read, or go to any movie, and you will see women who are a lot thinner and taller than normal. In fact, the typical model is far from typical—she is 9 percent taller and weighs 16 percent less than the average woman.

Height, body build, and to some extent even weight are largely determined by genetics. For most girls and women, tall and thin is only a dream, and an impossible one at that.

WATCHING FOR SIGNS OF TROUBLE

Given our cultural preoccupation with beauty and thinness, it is perfectly normal for an adolescent girl to be concerned about her weight and appearance. In fact, it is the rare adolescent girl who is not on a "diet" of one kind or another. If a girl is not on a weight-loss diet per se, she may adopt an alternative or "trendy" style of eating, such as vegetarianism or macrobiotics, in part because she may believe it is healthier or more humane, and in part to flaunt her individuality. Even girls who are of normal weight will talk about losing weight and will carefully watch what they eat. Some girls may even look enviously at a picture of an especially thin model and say wistfully, "I wish I was as thin as she is." In most cases, parents need not worry—the normal girl may talk in extremes, but she will not act in an extreme way.

Your support can be critical in counteracting the many negative messages your daughter is hearing about her body. Tell her, "You have only one body to last you for your whole life. Now, it's a strong, beautiful body, and you should be very proud of it. If you want to keep it strong and beautiful, you need to take care of it. And that means giving it the proper nutrition so that it stays strong and beautiful."

Tell her that you understand her desire to stay slim—pretending that the social pressure isn't there won't make it go away—but you can also point out that dieting is actually the worst way to keep off weight. The statistics are on your side. More than 90 percent of all dieters eventually regain the weight that they had lost. You can probably cite countless examples of people whom you both know who have lost weight only to regain it after they went off their diets. Your daughter needs to know the truth about dieting—that the only way to maintain weight loss is by making permanent changes in her eating habits, that is, by learning how to eat a well-balanced diet with the right amount of calories for her body, and by getting enough exercise.

There are some girls, however, who cross the line of normalcy. For these girls, dieting becomes a dangerous obsession.

ANOREXIA NERVOSA

Anorexia nervosa is a baffling, bizarre disorder about which little is really known. Around 95 percent of all anorectics are female, typically from middle- or upper-class homes. No one is exactly sure what causes anorexia, although there is compelling evidence that it may be a combination of psychological and biological factors, which may vary from girl to girl. Experts even disagree over how to establish a positive diagnosis. (Some experts will not diagnose anorexia until someone has dropped 10–15 percent below their normal body weight. Others, however, feel that if a girl has lost a significant amount of weight and is behaving as if she is anorectic, then she is.) Generally, anorexia is diagnosed on the basis of

- An unwillingness to maintain a normal body weight
- Amenorrhea, the loss of the menstrual cycle, for at least three cycles due to excessive weight loss.

Although many anorectics take an incomprehensible pride in controlling their appetites on their own, some resort to diet pills to quell the hunger pains. This practice can have serious side effects, including irregular heartbeat and stroke, and diet pills can be addicting.

The Risks

Starvation wreaks havoc on the body in many ways:

- The delicate balance of body hormones is disrupted, causing the cessation of the menstrual cycle and infertility. In 75 percent of all cases, menstruation will resume once the girl reaches normal weight, although periods may remain irregular and infertility is a common residual problem.
- As the body systems switch into "starvation mode" to conserve energy, the blood pressure drops to dangerously low levels and the heart rate slows, which is why the anorectic often complains of feeling cold or light-headed.
- The immune system is weakened, leaving the anorectic girl vulnerable to infection.
- Major body organs, such as the brain, heart and kidneys, may suffer irreparable damage.
- The bones begin to weaken and are vulnerable to fractures. Anorectics may suffer from premature osteoporosis.

The Prognosis

About 12 percent of all anorectics die due to complications caused by starvation. About one third will regain normal weight, another third will gain weight but still remain underweight, and the remainder will probably not gain weight. Generally, an anorectic is not considered "cured" until she has maintained a normal weight for five years.

Warning Signs

Parents often miss the telltale signs of anorexia, which include a specific pattern of behavior that has become associated with this disorder. In addition, anorectics develop specific symptoms that should not be ignored.

Anorectics often have a distorted body image. Anorectics typically develop a distorted body image, that is, no matter how much weight they lose, they still consider themselves too fat. I have seen girls hospitalized at seventy-five pounds. They look emaciated and starved. Their faces are hollow and gray. Bones jut out everywhere. They are covered in a fine, dark hair called lanugo, which is believed to be the body's way of making up for lost heat. Yet, when they look at themselves in the mirror, they don't see the ravages of starvation; instead, they claim to see a girl who could still stand to lose a few more pounds! Their distorted view of themselves makes it extremely difficult to try to reason with anorectics when they are in this starvation state.

Anorectics are often obsessed with food. Although these girls are literally starving themselves, they are often obsessed with food. When they're not talking about food, they're thinking about food. When they're not thinking about food, they're in the kitchen handling food. Many of the anorectics I've worked with were gourmet cooks—they loved to prepare food for others, but never partook of the feasts themselves.

Anorectics develop bizarre eating habits. When they actually do eat, anorectics eat very little. Their eating habits are very infantile: These girls typically take minuscule portions, cut them up into tiny pieces, and push them around their plates. Eventually, their range of foods becomes evermore restrictive. Very often, they will eat only certain types of food, such as a particular type of vegetable, or only grains, or only foods of a certain color or texture.

Anorectics are very secretive. Anorectics try very hard to hide their problem and very often succeed. In most cases, they will refuse to join the family for meals, often finding excuses to eat by themselves in their rooms, or not at all. ("I can't stand the smell of what you're eating," "How can you expect me to watch you eat meat?" and "I already ate" are standard excuses.)

Anorectics rarely let other people look at their bodies. Typically, anorectics wear baggy, loose-fitting clothes to camouflage their weight loss. Often they refuse to go to the doctor for fear of being "discovered."

Anorectics often go on "exercise binges." Paradoxically, although she should be weak from hunger, the anorectic often engages in frequent and excessive exercise. There are several reasons for this. First, the anorectic knows that activity burns calories, therefore, she tries to use as many calories as possible by exercising. Second, there is evidence that vigorous exercise may depress the appetite. During strenuous exercise, the body produces morphine-type chemicals called endorphins that not only numb pain (including hunger pain) but produce a feeling of well-being—the so-called runner's high described by marathon competitors. These chemicals are also believed to affect the appetite center of the brain, reducing the urge to eat. By exercising, the anorectic is killing two birds with one stone: She's shedding calories as well as killing her appetite.

Anorectics may become depressed and isolated. The anorectic may appear to be uninterested in what's going on around her and may have difficulty concentrating at school. She may say things like "Nothing matters to me anymore" or "I don't want to go on."

Anorectics do not look like girls in the "bloom of youth." Anorectics look sickly. Their hair becomes dull and lifeless, their nails may turn yellow, their skin often looks gray. Any girl who looks like she is constantly ill should be taken to a doctor.

BULIMIA

Although half of all anorectics are also bulimic, bulimia is far more widespread and, in many ways, a far more insidious problem. *Bulimia,* which literally means "great hunger" or "ox hunger," was first mentioned by Galen, a famous physician who lived in the second century. Galen, as did many doctors after him, believed that bulimia was caused by a stomach problem that forced the person to vomit immediately after eating. Not until several centuries later did the real truth emerge and did we fully understand the true nature of this disorder. Today, *bulimia* is defined as the ingestion of an enor-

mous quantity of food (some bulimics consume more than 8000 calories at a time—about three to four times the amount the average
adult eats in a day), followed shortly by self-induced vomiting or
diarrhea.

In order to promote "purging," bulimics often resort to

- Ingestion of drugs such as ipecac that induce vomiting
- The abuse of over-the-counter laxatives
- The abuse of diuretics, or "water pills."

At least 20 percent of all college women engage in some form of
bulimic behavior to control their weight, but only those who binge
and purge at least twice a week are considered to have full-blown
eating disorders. Typically, a bulimic may binge and purge several
times a day. The binge is usually triggered by stress or anxiety. The
girl who binges usually eats "forbidden" foods such as chocolate, ice
cream, or bags of cookies. As she is gobbling up the goodies, she feels
a sense of calm and relief, but when she is done, she often feels
uncomfortably stuffed and disgusted by her actions. Then she
throws up. Very often, the bulimic feels terrible and ashamed about
what she is doing—as with other forms of compulsive behavior,
during these episodes, she is literally out of control—but she doesn't
know how to stop.

The Risks

- Bulimia, like anorexia, wreaks havoc on body chemistry. Ipecac and diuretics in particular dehydrate the body and deplete
  it of important minerals such as potassium, which is essential
  for normal heart and kidney function. If the body's potassium
  balance is sufficiently disrupted, the heart could be thrown
  into a fatal arrhythmia, or the kidneys could fail.
- Excessive and prolonged vomiting can cause the stomach to
  rupture.
- When the bulimic vomits, hydrochloric acid from the stomach
  is pushed into the mouth, which, over time, can destroy tooth
  enamel, causing severe dental and gum problems.
- Vomiting causes a rise in blood pressure in the head. Excessive vomiting can cause broken blood vessels in the eyes,
  which can lead to impaired vision.
- Overdependence on laxatives can cause bowel damage.

Warning Signs

Similar to anorectics, bulimics are very adept at keeping their problem a secret. In fact bulimia is much more difficult to detect than anorexia because the bulimic typically remains within ten pounds of her normal weight. (The anorectic/bulimic, however, may in fact speed her weight loss along by excessive purging.) Bulimics can function for a long time without being discovered.

There are certain patterns of behavior and telltale physical signs common to bulimics that can help alert a watchful parent to the problem.

Bulimics often rush to the bathroom after eating. Bulimics live in fear that their bodies will absorb the food before they can vomit it up. Therefore, they are panicky if they can't get to the bathroom within a half hour after eating. Although bulimics are usually very careful to clean up after themselves, they may leave evidence, which parents should not ignore.

Bulimics may hide food in their rooms, or steal money. Like the alcoholic who stashes a bottle wherever she or he can, the bulimic stashes bits of "forbidden" food in her room. Very often, bulimics binge and purge in private and therefore need to keep their own supply of food. The habit can be very expensive: The bulimic may need to steal money to pay for food.

Bulimics may engage in other forms of compulsive behavior. Bulimics may be out of control in other areas as well. Some may shoplift, go on spending sprees, abuse alcohol, or enter into sexual relationships indiscriminately.

Bulimics develop telltale physical symptoms. Over time, bulimics develop a skin rash or calluses on their knuckles as a result of rubbing them against their teeth when they stick their fingers down their throats to induce vomiting. Many have chronically sore throats and swollen glands as a result of constant vomiting.

The Prognosis

Because bulimia is so widespread and hidden, we simply don't know the mortality rate. The normal-weight bulimic can survive for a much longer period of time than an anorectic (or an anorectic/ bulimic) but there is always a risk that she will go too far. The girl who is constantly pumping her body with diuretics and ipecac or abusing laxatives is causing serious damage to her organs and could even die. As with the anorectic, psychiatric treatment is required to help this girl overcome her problem.

IS YOUR DAUGHTER AT RISK?

Although eating disorders can happen to any girl, in any kind of family, there are some girls who may be more prone to these problems, whose parents, therefore, need to be especially alert. I have listed six different situations in which a girl may be particularly vulnerable to developing an eating disorder.

In some cases, a particular family dynamic may be responsible or at least a contributing factor to the problem. By pointing out the parental or family role, I am not out to pin "blame" on either parent. Rather, I do feel that it's important for parents to know how their words or actions may be affecting their daughter.

The Overzealous Dieter
- Does your daughter go from diet to diet?
- Does your daughter always have "just another five pounds" to lose?

What begins as a harmless diet could become a lethal obsession.

When the human body is denied food over an extended period of time, certain biochemical imbalances occur that could, among other things, affect hunger. Just as endorphins are produced during vigorous exercise, the body may produce chemicals to relieve hunger pains. Although the anorectic may initially feel hunger, after she drops to a certain weight, she may lose the urge to eat and in many cases can't keep food down even if she wants to. Thus her condition is no longer voluntary, she is "trapped" into starvation by her body.

If your daughter is on a diet, be especially careful to watch for signs that she is losing too much weight or getting too thin.

Starving for Love
- Are you spending less time with your daughter than you did before she became an adolescent?
- Does your daughter have a sibling with a problem or special talent that garners him or her tremendous attention?

I had one chronic bulimic patient who felt that her family cared more about her brother than about her. When this girl felt slighted or angry, she would seek her revenge by eating vast quantities of ice cream and then promptly vomiting. I always felt as if she were trying to fill her body with what her soul lacked: a sense of being loved. In this case, food provided the comfort that she felt she couldn't get anywhere else. In other, similar cases, anorectics who feel unloved may starve themselves to a point of physical deterioration that forces their parents to care for them much as they did when they were children. I don't think that it's coincidental that the onset of eating disorders very often coincides with the adolescent years, when parents may withdraw from their daughters. Many girls do begin to feel unloved and uncared for, and they will do what they have to to regain their parents' attention, if not love.

Don't Want to Be a Woman

- Was your daughter particularly upset about the physical changes of puberty?
- Does your daughter say things like "I wish I looked the way I used to"?

There are some girls who may use anorexia as a means of retarding their development into women. I have seen girls who are very upset about the physical changes of puberty actually try to "starve" them away. Or a Fast Tracker who may have experienced an early—and in her eyes frightening—sexual encounter may try to revert back to her childlike body. Good communication between parents and their daughters regarding puberty and sexuality may help prevent this kind of situation.

The Superachiever

- Is your daughter the type of girl of whom you could say "She never gives me a bit of trouble"?
- Does your daughter always have to be the best?

The superachiever comes from a family where achievement and appearance are all that matter. This girl gets praise for her A+ grades or her looks, but for nothing else. She doesn't have a sense that she is loved just for being her. In order to get her parents' attention, she needs to be special and she rises to the occasion.

Superachievers are often excellent students and compliant daughters—they are the "good girls," or "mother's best friend." Very often, they are attuned to the needs of others—especially to their parents'—but are out of touch with their own. Longing to be the best—and for her parents' recognition—this girl approaches dieting in the same competitive, compulsive fashion that she approaches her schoolwork and hobbies.

On the outside, the superachiever and her family may appear to have the "perfect" relationship, but deep down inside, the superachiever is furious at her parents and is turning her body into a weapon to hurt and control them. This type of anorectic is very manipulative: She has an uncanny way of taking control of the household, getting everyone in the family to focus on her and her problem.

The Jock

- Does your daughter deliberately keep her weight down to enhance her athletic performance?
- Does her teacher or coach encourage dieting?

Dancers and athletes are especially susceptible to eating disorders, because they are taught that thinness will give them a competitive edge—the lower body mass supposedly helps the ballet dancer leap to greater heights and the athlete run, jump, or swim faster. In recent years, the standard for body size of both dancers and athletes has become lighter and leaner, and as a result, the number of eating disorders has risen among both groups. In fact the situation had gotten so bad among high school and college athletes that recently the National Collegiate Athletic Association passed guidelines forbidding coaches from weighing in female players for fear of promoting eating disorders. If you have a daughter who participates in a sport or is serious about dancing, it is very important to make sure that her teachers and coaches are not encouraging her to drop a size or two to help her perform better.

The Compulsive Household

- Do you have a family history of alcoholism or drug abuse?
- Do you or your spouse tend to "obsess" over work?

There is a definite connection between eating disorders and other types of compulsive behavior. In fact many bulimics come from families in which a parent or close relative has had an eating disorder or has abused drugs or alcohol.

Substance abuse is not the only manifestation of compulsive behavior. I have seen households in which the pursuit of money and success had become all-encompassing; the parents were obsessed with material acquisitions, and for them, success was an addiction. Their daughters picked up the obsessive style of the family, but instead of focusing on money, focused on the teenage version of success—maximal good looks and minimal weight.

In some cases, food may be the obsession of the household. The parents who for health or weight reasons watch every morsel of food that goes into their mouths, or into their children's mouths, are sending their children a message that food intake must be rigidly controlled.

NO QUICK FIXES

Eating disorders rarely go away by themselves: Professional intervention is essential for the anorectic's or bulimic's survival. There may be a temptation on the part of parents to try to keep their daughter's problem a secret, or to try to deal with it themselves. This can be a terrible and deadly mistake. It is far too complex and dangerous to try to deal with your daughter's problems without professional help. Your daughter will not eat simply because you ask her to and in fact may become even more stubborn if she feels that she is being watched or can gain attention by not eating.

Even with adequate professional support, recovery can be very slow. Patients with eating disorders are notoriously difficult because they are masters in the art of self-deception—they have built up walls of resistance that need to be broken down. In addition, eating disorders are often a symptom of a far deeper problem, and it can be years before the anorectic girl gains the necessary insight to understand and control her behavior.

Treatment for anorexia and bulimia varies depending on the seriousness of the situation, but any of the following may be appropriate.

Hospitalization. In severe, life-threatening situations, when a girl is seriously undernourished, she will be hospitalized. Very often she will be fed intravenously or through a tube to insure adequate nutrition. In many cases, once a "critical weight" is established, she will be able to eat on her own, but only when the girl's health is sufficiently improved is she ready to begin dealing with some of the underlying problems that may have led to the eating disorder. At this point, nutritional counseling may be helpful to "reprogram" her eating habits.

Family therapy. Some practitioners feel that it is imperative to treat the entire family, especially if the anorectic or bulimic girl seems to be "controlling the family," or if a particular family dynamic is exacerbating the problem.

Individual therapy. Most anorectics and bulimics will require some form of psychotherapy to help them deal with their feelings of unhappiness and despair. The initial goal of therapy is to make the patient acknowledge the serious health consequences of her actions. The typical anorectic or bulimic girl often denies she has a problem, and it can take many months or even years before she recognizes what she is doing to herself. Only then will she be able to deal with the root causes of her eating disorder.

Support groups. Support groups such as Overeaters Anonymous are particularly good for these girls because many believe that they are alone—that they are the only ones in the world who engage in such "sick and disgusting" behavior. Seeing that others are in the same boat can be a great source of comfort.

Medication. Drugs are rarely prescribed for eating disorders because they have not proven to be effective. If a girl is diagnosed with clinical depression, however, she may be given an antidepressant such as Prozac.

Eating disorders treatment centers. Throughout the United States there are special medical centers devoted solely to treating patients with eating disorders. These facilities provide intensive medical care, psychotherapy, and outpatient services. An eating disorders treatment center may be preferable to dealing with a hospital or doctor who is inexperienced in working with these types of patients.

THE OVERWEIGHT TEENAGER

About 15 percent of all teenage girls are considered to be obese; that is, they are 20 percent or more above their ideal body weight for their height and body type. Ironically, although we live in an era in which thinness and fitness are exalted, the number of truly overweight teenage girls is on the rise. One reason is that many teenage girls live very sedentary lifestyles. Their main after-school activity is often sitting and talking, watching soap operas, or talking on the phone, none of which is conducive to burning calories. The popularity of snack foods such as soda, pizza, and candy bars is also contributing to the increase in obesity.

Given the pressure to be slim and attractive, the overweight girl is probably very unhappy with herself and sensitive about her size. The wrong comment at the wrong time will bring her to tears. Many parents are well aware of how painful this is for their overweight daughters and how difficult it is for them to talk about it. As a result, many parents may be reluctant to talk about it at all. Even if they want to, they may not know how to broach the subject. In addition, given the tendency of teenage girls to develop eating disorders, many parents may feel that it is better to "let well enough alone" than to push their daughters into an even worse problem.

I think that this conspiracy of silence is a mistake—not dealing with the problem will only make it worse. The obese girl knows she is overweight, and if her parents don't deal with it directly, she may feel that her problem is "so bad" even her own parents won't discuss it. In some cases, parents may displace their concern about their daughter's weight by picking on her for other things, and the girl may rightly pick up that her mother (or father) disapproves of something about her, without knowing exactly what it is.

It is far better to deal with the problem directly, as long as you do it with some thoughtfulness and sensitivity. There are certain ways to approach your daughter that are guaranteed to fail. Girls don't want to hear "You have such a pretty face, you'd be a real knockout if you lost a few pounds." They will find this very demeaning and will respond with an angry "What am I? Just a pretty face? Why can't you accept me for what I am?"

Girls also don't want to hear "Why do you eat so much when you know how heavy you are!" or "Why can't you control yourself?" This is not the time for criticism.

Far better to just say as casually as possible, "Gee, I see that you've put on a little weight lately. Maybe there's something we can do about it." Some girls will be greatly relieved by your offer and in all likelihood will ask for help.

If you are also overweight and would like to lose some pounds, you could enlist your daughter's help. Say to her, "I've put on a lot of weight lately, and I'd like to take it off. Want to go on a diet with me?" If she's not interested, begin the diet alone—she may join you later.

However, even this low-key approach may offend some girls. If your daughter bristles at your comments, you should try to find out why she has taken offense. Say to her, "I'm sorry that I've embarrassed or offended you. I didn't mean to, I wish you'd tell me why you're so angry." If she lashes out, "It's none of your business," you can counter with, "Look, I really didn't want to upset you. Do you think that I'm putting you down, because that's the last thing that I want to do." You may be able to open up the discussion, or she may stalk off in anger. If she cuts you off, you have no choice but to wait for her to bring it up again—she may when she's ready.

If your daughter accepts your offer of help, there's a lot that you can do. One good approach is to take her for counseling by a qualified registered dietitian. The dietitian can help her devise a reasonable eating program that will help take off pounds slowly and steadily. It's very important for the dietitian and the teenager to set a realistic weight goal. Once your daughter reaches the goal, it is critical to make sure that she goes off the diet before she loses too much weight, and that she begins a sensible maintenance program. You don't want to trade one problem for another, potentially more lethal one.

I have also seen girls lose weight during the summer at special weight-loss camps. One of the good things about these camps is that they encourage girls to become more physically active, which not only helps them to shed pounds, but also helps them to develop a healthier lifestyle.

Sometimes it is useful for the whole family to diet together, particularly if everyone can stand to lose a few pounds. Your daughter will feel less self-conscious about her situation if everyone is following the same diet. It's also easier for her to join the family for meals if everyone else is not indulging in high-calorie fare.

If weight has already become an emotionally charged subject in the family, try a more indirect approach. I knew of one mother who, for Christmas, gave her overweight daughter a certificate for a "Day of Beauty" at a popular salon. The girl felt so good about herself after her make-over, that she decided on her own to complete the package by losing some weight.

If your overweight daughter goes on a diet, you can help her by providing healthy, low-calorie food, but it is not your job to police her!

A quiet, understated approach is far healthier than overinvolvement. Don't talk about her diet (unless she wants to), don't allow your household to revolve around her diet, don't offer "rewards" for losing weight. (If she takes off some weight, you can surprise her by buying her a new dress or something special to wear, but I would not use it as a carrot to get her to lose.)

Finally, be prepared for the possibility that she may fail. Recent research shows that many people are, for whatever reason, simply unable to lose weight and keep it off. Although a teenager entering the arena of dating may be more motivated to lose weight than an adult woman, there is a chance that she may not succeed. If she cannot stick to a diet, she should not be made to feel like a failure, or that you love her any less. Your disapproval will not make her feel any better about herself; simply leave open the possibility that she may have better luck at a later date, and let the issue rest.

PLASTIC SURGERY

In recent years there has been a dramatic rise in the number of teenage girls who are turning to plastic surgery to improve on nature's work. In fact, nearly 20 percent of all cosmetic surgery on noses is performed on patients under 18. Other procedures that are now attracting teenagers include breast implants and breast reduction, liposuction and chin implants.

Given the current emphasis on physical appearance, it is not hard to understand why teenagers would opt for surgery, or why so many parents would pay for it. However, there are many parents who are genuinely confused about how to handle a child's request for plastic surgery. In fact I have consulted on a number of cases in which parents wanted to know whether their daughter's desire for plastic surgery was actually a sign of an underlying emotional problem. There's no single answer: It all depends on why the girl is turning to surgery.

There are right reasons and wrong reasons for a girl to want to change her appearance. Let's start with the wrong ones. Some girls believe that if only they looked like a particular actress or model, all their problems would be over. Suddenly, they would be happy and popular and would no longer feel awkward with boys or uncomfortable with their bodies. These girls—who, ironically, are usually pretty enough to begin with—march into the plastic surgeon's office with a picture of the "ideal woman" torn from a magazine and say, "Make me look like her." A reputable surgeon will refer them for counseling.

I have worked with a number of these girls, and it is very difficult to get them to understand that surgery is not a quick fix for all of life's ills. Some ills can't be fixed. What stops them is the fact that their parents won't give their consent for the surgery or pay for it. I have had numerous girls stalk out of my office saying, "Well, when I'm working, I'll get my own nose job [breast implants, etc.]." We can only hope that maturity will change their minds.

There are some girls, however, who recognize a true physical shortcoming and want to remedy it. Sometimes a 14-year-old will be miserable because her nose really doesn't suit her face. I don't think parents should lie and say, "Your nose is terrific," because she knows what she sees. However, parents should point out that her face has not fully developed, and the nose that seems out of place on a 14-year-old can look perfect on a more mature 17-year-old. That's why I feel it's important to wait until a girl is in her late teens before allowing her to have plastic surgery.

The same situation may be true for the flat-chested Late Bloomer. A 15-year-old girl whose breasts have not yet fully developed may be constantly badgering her parents for breast implants. Given the potential health risks involved in this procedure, I would not advise it for women at any age. However, girls can be very persistent, and many parents may be tempted to succumb to the constant nagging. This can be a terrible mistake. The flat-chested 15-year-old is still growing; her breasts can fill out over the next five years and even more after she has children. Her parents should explain to her that her flat chest is probably temporary: If she's really embarrassed, she can enhance her bustline with a padded bra. Chances are, as she matures and starts to date, she's going to see that the lack of full breasts is not going to hinder her relationships with boys or men.

There are situations in which surgery can make a big difference in a girl's life. For instance, I treated one patient who from her midteens on was extremely upset about her huge breasts, which did make her look much older and much heavier. She was frequently teased at school, and needless to say, was terribly self-conscious about her body. Although the girl wanted breast-reduction surgery, her mother was adamantly opposed on the grounds that "You should be happy the way you are."

Although her mother may have meant well, this girl was really unhappy and miserable, and I greatly sympathized with her. If anyone needed breast-reduction surgery, she did. At 23, she paid for the surgery herself, and it has turned her life around. In her case, her mother should have allowed it earlier.

Plastic surgery can be expensive and is not covered by many insurance companies. If you can't afford to pay for a particular procedure that both you and your doctor feel is age appropriate and medically sound, it's reasonable to ask your daughter to chip in by working during the summer or after school.

HELPING HER TO LIKE HER BODY/HELPING HER TO LIKE HERSELF

Parents cannot singlehandedly counteract the social pressure to be thin and beautiful—their daughters are listening to too many other voices. However, they can help bring some perspective and balance to this issue.

First, parents need to de-emphasize the importance of looks. This doesn't mean that they can't tell their daughter that she is pretty or that she looks especially nice on a particular day. All girls need to be reassured that their parents find them attractive, even though they often pretend not to care what their parents think. (Your daughter may retort, "You're my dad, of course you think I'm pretty!" but imagine how bad she'd feel if she couldn't take your admiration for granted.)

Girls also need to be praised for reasons other than their looks. I have treated many extremely pretty girls who had developed a poor sense of themselves because all they ever heard was how pretty they were—and nothing else. They had no sense of being worthwhile, important human beings. Parents need to convey a sense that the whole person is important—body and soul.

A girl should be praised if she brings home a good test paper, if she plays well on her team, if she is helpful around the house, or if she handles herself especially well in a difficult situation. If she tries hard to achieve something, but fails, she should also be praised for trying. If a girl receives positive reinforcement for being a thoughtful, well-rounded person, she may still be concerned about her appearance, but will be less likely to obsess over it.

Moreover, parents need to emphasize the importance of diversity. Unless your daughter is one of the few who fit the "fashion model mold," she is going to be unhappy that she does not measure up to the media ideal of beauty. She needs to be told that that's okay, that there are many different ways to be beautiful. And she also needs to be reminded that very few women actually look anything like the women in magazines or on the movie screens. Comments like, "Gee, she looks more like a Barbie doll than a human being" or "I don't know anyone who looks anything like that" can help bring her back to reality. At the very least, they will help her become more critical and less accepting.

If your daughter is not a "standard beauty," she needs to be taught that every woman is attractive in her own unique way. Find something special about her that is worthy of notice—perhaps she has terrific eyes, an appealing expression, or dresses with a particular flair. Go out of your way to point out unusual-looking women who may not conform to the typical standard of beauty but who are perceived as extremely attractive. Be careful not to dwell on her looks in the mistaken belief that she needs constant reassurance—it is equally important to praise her for her accomplishments and to encourage her to focus on other aspects of life.

SEVEN: PEERS, PRESSURE, AND FRIENDSHIP

What does it take to be popular? You have to be friendly with the right people. You can't be too smart or study too much. You have to wear the right brands. Everything has to have a label. You have to wear Gap clothes or Champion—that's really important. Who's unpopular? The really smart ones—the "nerds." The ones who wear the same clothes every day and don't have a lot of money.

—Alexa, age 12

At any age, friendships are an important factor in helping a girl develop social skills and self-confidence. Up until adolescence, however, a strong and loving connection to her parents is the critical factor for a girl's normal emotional growth and development. Although childhood friendships are important, they are not nearly as important as the bond between a child and her family. During the childhood years, no one can exert more influence over a girl than her parents. They are her role models; their voices are heard above all others. All this changes, for better or for worse, after puberty.

Once a girl begins to experience the physical and emotional changes typical of adolescence, she begins to seek out and listen to other voices. Her parents are no longer the center of her universe because alone they can no longer meet her needs. In order to feel like a valuable, important human being, an adolescent girl needs to feel connected to her peers. In order to grow and develop into a strong, self-assured adult, she needs to develop strong friendships with girls who are undergoing similar experiences. These relationships will not only teach her how to establish and maintain future adult relationships, but they will help her to learn about herself.

When a girl turns away from her parents to her friends, many parents feel as if they are being rejected. In fact, adolescent girls have a real knack for making their parents feel outdated, outmoded, and altogether unnecessary. Parents have to remember, however, that although their daughter may prefer to spend time with her peers, it doesn't mean that she doesn't need parents. In reality, she needs them more than ever. For many girls, the adolescent years are filled with rejection, hurts, and slights that can leave lasting scars. The right guidance from parents at the right time can help girls through this difficult period, providing them with the insight that adolescents, by nature of their immaturity, lack.

Although parents can't protect their daughter from getting hurt, they can help her recognize the different between good relationships that are mutually beneficial and those that are destructive. However, in order to be effective in this role, parents need to understand the social system that their daughter's world revolves around and her place in that world.

WHAT FRIENDSHIPS MEAN TO HER

There are several reasons why peer relationships become so important during puberty. First, a girl needs to feel that she is not alone —that there is someone else who is going through the same turmoil that she is going through. Interestingly enough, adolescent girls tend to choose close friends based on pubertal status, that is, Fast Trackers who menstruate early tend to choose other early developers as friends, and the converse is also true: Late Bloomers tend to stick together. Obviously, the physical changes of adolescence are so overwhelming, and girls are so preoccupied with them, that this experience alone may be the basis of some of these early adolescent friendships.

Second, as the body matures, so does the mind. The young adolescent is on the threshold of developing a "self-observing ego" as she seeks to forge her own unique identity. In order to learn about who she is—and who she isn't—she needs to compare herself to others. But in this case, her parents just won't do. A girl of this age is very rebellious: In order to assert her independence from her parents, she needs to demonstrate her separateness from them. Therefore, she turns to her peers.

Young adolescent girls are constantly comparing themselves to others to see who is prettier, who is smarter, who has the best boyfriend, the best clothes, the best body, etc. They are constantly ranking themselves against their peers to assess their own strengths and weaknesses. Adults find this behavior troublesome, but it is merely a reflection of the girl's inability to stand up and say "I am this kind of person." Rather, she still needs to compare herself to others to determine who she may or may not be. Through these comparisons, she will eventually develop a sense of her own individuality.

These adolescent friendships not only help a girl learn about herself but prepare her for the time when her relationships with others will be of equal or even greater importance than her relationships with her family members. Early adolescent relationships between girls help them learn how to relate to a nonrelative on a more emotional level than they did in the past.

Childhood friendships tend to revolve around specific activities; female adolescent friendships are not based on going somewhere or doing something so much as they are on sharing thoughts and feelings. Through these friendships, girls learn about what goes on between two people in a fairly intimate setting and how to care about someone else. From the inevitable hurts and rejections typical of this period, they also learn how to be more discriminating in their friendships and how to discern true friends from false friends. These lessons will eventually carry over into future relationships with boys and men.

STRENGTH IN NUMBERS

From 11 to 14, most girls will establish some kind of an informal affiliation with a "group" or a "clique." These are the girls that she usually sits with during lunch at school, or meets after school at one another's houses. The group serves several purposes. During early adolescence, most girls feel too vulnerable to face the world alone and need the security of the group to provide strength. In addition, by observing the girls in the group—what they say and how they react to certain situations—a girl learns how to be an adolescent girl. From a safe distance, then, surrounded by her friends, she can also observe and learn about boys.

Within your daughter's social world there are several different groups. Typically, there are one or two "in crowds," consisting of the very popular girls or the trend setters. The popular girls tend to be the Fast Trackers in that they date early, wear sophisticated clothes, and are allowed to do things that the other girls are not. Some may even smoke. These girls have "reputations," and they are often held in awe by the others. Popular girls constitute a small minority, but nevertheless, most of the excluded girls wish they were members of this exclusive club and feel bad that they're not.

The popular girls are not necessarily the nicest or even the most well liked. Although they're looked up to, the girls on the outside know that their values are not necessarily good ones. "There's a lot of the popular kids getting together and ganging up on the not so popular. They pick on them and make them feel bad. Nobody says anything because they're afraid that they're going to be picked on next," observed one 13-year-old.

The majority of girls are in the "other crowds." Although these groups are not the "best" or the most popular, from the girls' point of view, they are still better than no crowd. A sizable minority of girls fall on the fringe; for some reason, they don't connect to any particular crowd, although they may desperately want to.

Girls of this age can be extremely cruel in the way in which they exclude others who they feel are "social liabilities." As they search for their own self-identity, they believe in "guilt by association," that is, if they are even seen hanging out with less "worthy" girls, that they will lose their superior status. Girls may be excluded for being "immature," for making socially inappropriate remarks or for wearing the "wrong" clothes. Smart girls may be labeled nerds, the kiss of death in adolescent society. In some cases, a girl who is favored by a popular (usually male) teacher may be excluded because the others are jealous! The world of the adolescent girl is a Byzantine one, and parents may never be able to fully grasp why some girls are "in" and others are "out."

But there are other, more valid reasons why girls may exclude, or why some girls *feel* that they are being excluded when in fact they are not. During early adolescence in particular, girls often prefer close relationships with a few, select friends over casual relationships with many friends. For this reason, these relationships appear to be impenetrable to outsiders. In reality, the girls may simply not be ready to welcome another friend into their circle until they know her better. Or they may be afraid that the newcomer will "steal" their friends away, or change alliances in a way that makes them uncomfortable.

In addition, girls are much more likely than boys not to take what is being said at face value but to try to read the nonverbal cues being emitted by others. Girls get a sense of satisfaction out of penetrating below the surface to decipher what the other person is really thinking and feeling. Sometimes an adolescent girl will read things correctly, but sometimes she won't. Adolescent girls are insecure about who they are and therefore always feel as if they are at fault. When someone whom a girl wants to befriend says she is too busy to meet her after school for a Coke, the "rejected" girl will in all likelihood assume that the other girl doesn't want to be with her. There are times when the girl's perceptions will be absolutely correct—she *has* been rejected for whatever reason—but sometimes she will jump to a wrong and hurtful conclusion. In this situation, her parents, particularly her mother, can help the girl sort out what is going on.

For example, if your daughter comes home and says, as girls often do, "Nobody likes me," or "Mary won't be my friend," you need to ask for more specific information about what went on. "Did Mary tell you she didn't want to be your friend?"

Your daughter may reply, "Well, not exactly, but she didn't want to go for a Coke after school."

You need to probe further to find out what exactly Mary did say.

Very likely, your daughter will reply something like, "Mary said that she was going over to Janet's house."

You can observe that Mary already had other plans. Your daughter may ask, "But why didn't Mary ask me to go to Janet's with her?"

At this point, you can offer some much-needed perspective. "Maybe she didn't know whether Janet wanted anyone else to come over, or maybe she's just not ready to be friends yet. It doesn't mean she doesn't like you. Ask her another time, or invite her over here to do homework next week."

Don't expect your daughter to say, "Gee, Mom, you're right." More likely she's going to dismiss your comments with, "Oh, you don't know what you're talking about," or she's going to look sullen or stalk away, as teenage girls often do. Regardless of what she says, however, keep in mind that she's taking in everything you say. Although she would never concede it, you're helping her gain some perspective on what happened, and eventually she will learn that every refusal should not be viewed as a personal rejection.

Sometimes a clique will welcome other girls when they need them, for instance, if a member of the clique is running for class president and needs the votes of others to get elected. The candidate may go out of her way to befriend the "fringe" girls whom she previously ignored. She may sit with them during lunch and act very chummy, that is, until the election is over. A girl of 12 to 13 will very likely not be able to see the other girl's true motives and will blame herself when the new class president starts ignoring her again. If she then says to her parents, "Jane won't have lunch with me anymore," her parents should reply honestly, "Isn't it funny Jane is only your friend when she's running for president?" Although the rejection may still hurt, the realization that she was being used will stop the girl from blaming herself.

HELPING THE OUTSIDER

If your daughter is on the fringe and has been unable to affiliate with a group, she may need your help. For whatever reason, some girls feel as if they are always the fifth wheel, that they don't belong in any of the established groups. Perhaps they have different interests, or perhaps they are too shy to make overtures to others. Perhaps you have recently moved to a new community and your daughter is having difficulty penetrating the existing cliques.

If you have a daughter who is an outsider, I think it is very important that you help her develop her own network of friends— it's not that hard to do and can make a tremendous difference in her life. I know of one 14-year-old girl, a talented poet, who didn't feel comfortable with girls whose main concerns were clothes and boys. Her mother came up with a brilliant plan: She suggested that her daughter invite a few of the girls in the creative writing class at school to join a literary club that would meet in her home once a week. Several of the girls were very interested, and within a short time, the daughter had found her circle of special friends. What was even more interesting is the fact that this group of talented girls began to attract a lot of positive attention, especially from boys. Instead of going through adolescence feeling lonely and "left out," this girl is establishing close friendships and developing important social skills.

Having a family that is well linked to the community can also help the fringe girl find her niche. Joining a church or synagogue with an active youth group can help introduce her to a group of potential friends. Teen programs at the local Y or community center can help expand her circle. Some museums or local colleges have special summer or weekend classes for high school students; these can put her in touch with others who share similar interests. The more the fringe girl gets out, the more likely it is that she will develop friendships.

AS FRIENDSHIPS MATURE

By about age 15, there's a marked change in the quality and style of adolescent relationships. Girls no longer rely exclusively on the group for their social support. Rather, they branch off and develop friendships on their own. At this stage of maturity, the common experience of puberty or of being in the same crowd is not enough to bind a friendship: Girls begin to evaluate their friends more critically. For example, the 15-year-old girl is sophisticated enough to determine that she may like one friend because she is a good tennis player and another friend because she knows a lot about boys. Although she may not like everything about either girl, she is mature enough to see that they each meet different needs in her life. From these observations, she gains insight into herself, her likes and dislikes, strengths and weaknesses. By age 18 or so, she will sharpen these critical skills to the point that she can reason, "Gee, Jane and I will never be close, but she sure is a great tennis player," or "Debby is a lot of fun, but boy, I can't stand all that time and attention she spends on her makeup and clothes."

As girls begin to date, the emotionality that was once invested in other girls is channeled into romantic relationships. Girls whose primary concern had been the other girls in the group are now primarily concerned about boys. Girls who used to share every thought and concern with each other are finding that boyfriends can also be an emotional outlet. Many girls of this age also discover that boys who are not romantic interests can still be good friends, and I have seen many warm platonic friendships develop among adolescents. These relationships help girls and boys better understand each other, and help demystify the difference between the sexes.

Around age 15 or 16, many best-friend female relationships break up, very often because one girl has a boyfriend and the other one may not even be dating. The nondater may become jealous of her friend's success with boys and may try to make her feel as if she has abandoned the friendship. What often happens is that the best friends drift apart and new alliances are formed. There are situations, however, when girls grow in sync, and these intense, best-friend relationships may evolve into more mature, close friendships.

As adolescent girls develop a more sophisticated worldview, they begin to see things about friends and classmates that can be quite disillusioning. A case in point is a 16-year-old high school junior who was shattered when her "best friend" stole her idea and submitted it as her own in a school art contest. To make matters worse, the girl won. The friend felt angry and betrayed, and her parents were equally shocked by the other girl's action. I wasn't. I have heard hundreds of variations on this same story: a "friend" who gets another girl in trouble at school by copying her exam word for word, a "friend" who steals her friend's boyfriend, a "friend" who passes a hurtful rumor about a friend. Although being betrayed by a friend can be painful, it is an important learning experience in that it teaches a girl that not everyone is trustworthy. If this happens to your daughter, it is important for you to point out that people are not always as they appear to be. Although most are honest and straightforward, some can be deceitful if it suits their own purposes. From this experience, and from your discussions, your daughter will learn how to be more discerning in her friendships and why it is not always wise to divulge secrets or important information to someone who has not proven her loyalty. If your daughter doesn't learn this lesson during adolescence, she is bound to pay for it later, often in more serious and painful circumstances.

Adolescent girls also learn another important lesson from peer relationships—how to disagree with a friend without destroying the friendship.

FRIENDSHIP AND FIGHTS: ADOLESCENT STYLE

Adolescent friendships are often very volatile. An adolescent girl needs to strike out and take a stand as a way of asserting her independence. Because young adolescents tend to view things in their black-or-white, all-or-nothing fashion, they have difficulty tolerating different points of view. "If you don't think like me, you're wrong" is often their way of thinking. Not surprisingly, this leads to many disagreements. Unlike childhood, when fights would be forgotten by the next encounter, during adolescence, these fights can last for days. Two girls who are engaged in a heated fight may be miserable, but neither one of them will back down because "taking a stand" may seem more important than saving the friendship.

Parents often wonder if they should intervene. The answer is no, for several reasons. First, if you innocently say, "Don't you think that you should call Mary, she's been such a good friend," it may further entrench your daughter in her position. Second, learning to work out these problems is what adolescence is all about. Learning to negotiate and compromise is an important skill for future relationships. If you as parents push the girls to "make up," they may never learn how to do it themselves. The friends may or may not reconcile —one may indeed back down, or they may find a way of reaching an agreement—but if they don't, and they really wanted to, they will understand the price of being intransigent. From this type of experience, your daughter will learn how to handle herself better the next time she finds herself in a similar situation. It's also possible that your daughter will seek out your advice, in which case it is always preferable to let her talk it out with you rather than jumping in with specific suggestions.

WHERE YOUR DAUGHTER FITS IN

Depending on her temperament and personality, every girl has her own way of finding her niche and developing friendships. Although each girl is a unique individual, there are particular styles in which girls interact during this period. Some girls will have an easier time "finding their place" than will others, but even the most outwardly self-confident and self-assured girls will have some difficulties.

The Aggressive Girl

This girl is the "born leader," other girls naturally follow her. Very often, she is the dominating force of the group, the girl whom others turn to for information and advice. The Aggressive Girl has some very positive traits: She is self-confident and self-assured and is usually not afraid to speak her mind. However, her personality can also be a drawback: Aggression is not considered to be a particularly feminine trait. Because of her strong presence, this girl will elicit sharp reactions from teachers, boys, and even other girls who want to "put her in her place."

Adolescent girls can be very fickle. The girl who is "in" one day can be "out" the next. The Aggressive Girl may become very threatened when another girl tries to usurp her authority or if the other girls in the group find someone else to admire and follow. In some cases, she may try to maintain her upper hand by becoming even more dominating and "pushy." This kind of behavior will usually alienate the other girls, and the Aggressive Girl will eventually be forced to back down. Sometimes in order to fit in the Aggressive Girl may submerge her own feelings and become very passive.

Parents of the Aggressive Girl have two jobs: First, they have to help her maintain her confidence and leadership qualities despite the fact that these are often not considered to be feminine attributes. They need to praise her when she shows initiative and imagination and encourage her to speak up. Second, they have to help her temper her aggression so that she doesn't turn people off. Her parents constantly need to remind her to consider the feelings of others. For example, when she makes an announcement about something that the group is going to do, her mother should interject, "Well, how did the other girls feel about it? It's important to listen to what they have to say." This girl needs to be reminded that other girls don't have to "obey" her commands.

The Average Girl

The Average Girl is an interesting blend of aggression and passivity: She will sometimes lead and sometimes follow. Although she doesn't want to dominate the group, she doesn't want to slavishly follow the leader, either. For example, if a friend calls and says that the others are meeting to play basketball, even though she hates the game, the Average Girl may initially agree to go along because she wants to please the others. Then, after she hangs up the phone, she may moan about how she really doesn't want to. Five minutes later, however, she may call her friend back and offer a counterproposal— such as hanging out at the baseball field where the boys are hanging out—which the group eventually follows. This girl may not always be the one who initiates group activities, but she usually cannot be coerced into doing something that she doesn't want to do.

There are times, however, that the Average Girl may not know how to assert herself appropriately. For instance, she may complain to her mother that she doesn't want to play basketball, and then instead of saying no, try to come up with an excuse as to why she can't play. Her parents may wonder why this girl simply doesn't come right out and say "I don't want to," but that can be a tall order for a still-insecure adolescent. Adolescent girls are very unsure of their own status and are fearful that going against the wishes of the group leader or a very popular girl may result in their losing membership in that group. If your daughter finds herself in this situation, in reality, she is probably blowing the entire thing out of proportion. Simply saying "I don't feel like it right now" will in all likelihood not produce the dire consequences that she fears, but nevertheless, she may go to great lengths to avoid confrontation.

In this case, her parents should steer her in the right direction by suggesting that she call her friend back and offer an alternative activity. If your daughter hesitates, remind her, "The worst thing that can happen is that they will say no; if they're really your friends, they're not going to hate you for wanting to do something else." Your daughter will not always be able to convince the group to change their plans; but there are times she will be successful. Whether or not she gets her way, your daughter will learn to be able to articulate her needs, a lesson that will serve her well in future relationships.

The Passive Girl

The Passive Girl has a quiet, easygoing personality and is perfectly content to follow the crowd—up to a point. Although she lacks the drive of the Agressive Girl, she is not a pushover. She knows how to say no and will generally not do things that are self-destructive. Often the Passive Girl doesn't have strong opinions and is usually quite agreeable, and as a result, she often makes friends quite easily.

Her greatest strength is her ability to see other people's point of view. For example, if two friends are quarreling, this girl could listen sympathetically to both of them and, with perfect sincerity, say to one, "Gee, I see your point," and to the other, "You've got a good point too."

Her greatest weakness, however, is the fact that she can be easily manipulated by others. Rather than risk confrontation, the Passive Girl will go along with the dominant forces in her crowd. At times, the Passive Girl may simply be too afraid to voice an opinion of her own for fear of alienating her friends. She may be so concerned about pleasing people and "making nice," that she keeps her mouth shut even when she wants to speak up. Unless her parents intervene, she could very well grow up to be a woman who is incapable of asserting herself at appropriate times.

The Passive Girl's parents need to continually remind their daughter that she has a right to express her own point of view. This is going to take some patience on the part of the parents. Initially, this girl may vacillate and be very reluctant to assert herself. Her parents may have to ask several times, "How do you really feel about it?" or say "I want to know what *you* think," before they get a meaningful response. With encouragement, eventually this girl can learn how to say "I feel," "I think," "I want."

True Followers and Sometime Followers

In some cases, however, extreme passivity can be a sign of real trouble. There are girls who don't know how to say no, who follow the leader without question. They never voice an opinion of their own and often have little to say. The True Follower, the girl who always listens to her peers, is a scared, insecure girl, with a poor sense of herself. She is a problem waiting to happen. She is the girl who is at great risk of drug or alcohol abuse, teen pregnancy, or even engaging in shoplifting or some other form of criminal activity. The True Follower may have started out as an Average Girl, but somewhere along the line, something caused her to change. It could be a sign that her parents have withdrawn from her—as some parents do during adolescence—and she is seeking to fill that void by turning to her friends. Or it could be a sign of another problem. Parents should heed the warning signs of extreme passivity and get professional counseling to help them cope with the situation.

There are some girls, however, who during this rocky period, become temporary or Sometime Followers. They latch on to another girl whom they greatly respect and try to imitate her every move. They dress like her, talk like her, and will often check with her first before making a decision. The girl who becomes the "clone" often feels that she is not good enough and needs to copy someone who she feels is prettier, more sophisticated, and more knowledgeable about boys in particular and life in general.

Although parents may fret that their daughter has lost her individuality, in reality, this is usually a short-lived phenomenon. It rarely lasts for more than a few weeks or months, and there is usually no cause for alarm. These girls are not the more troubled True Followers in that they are not unduly influenced by everybody, merely by their one role model.

Most parents will be annoyed and even a little bit jealous of the "other girl" who has become their daughter's "guru." Try to understand why you're so annoyed. At this age, when your daughter is looking for every opportunity to assert her independence, it will only harden her position and give her ammunition to use against you if you show your irritation. When she really wants to get a rise out of you, she will begin talking about this friend because she knows that it will annoy you. A better approach would be to repeat your daughter's words in a way that she can begin to hear what she really sounds like without ridiculing her friend. For instance, if she says, "Mary says that long skirts are coming back," you should respond, "Gee, you really think that Mary knows a lot about fashion?" If she says that Mary thinks boys like girls who wear bikinis, you should say, "Gee, you really think that Mary knows a lot about boys?"

I would also encourage this girl to express her own opinion, not simply mouth Mary's. If she starts to say "Mary says . . ." you can interject, "What do you think, I bet you have some good ideas, too." If she hesitates, you can follow up with, "You don't think that that's such a great idea?" Given this opening, she might say, "Well, I was wondering . . ." and she may begin to open up to you.

It's not going to happen overnight, but over time, your daughter will begin to hear her own words. Eventually she will begin to hear your unspoken message: Does Mary really know as much as you think she knows? Isn't your opinion as valid as Mary's?

Whether your daughter is a True Follower, a Sometime Follower, or always speaks her mind, chances are, she's spending a good deal of her time on the telephone. But before you tell her to hang up, you need to understand why she's doing what she's doing.

WHY SHE'S ALWAYS ON THE PHONE

Most parents are exasperated by the fact that their adolescent daughter tends to spend hours on the telephone—often with the same friends she sees every day—which parents typically view as a waste of time. In reality, the telephone is an important part of their daughter's life, and I believe that parents would be a bit more tolerant if they understood just how important it is.

Adolescent girls need to feel the warmth and support of their friends, even when they're apart. During the Victorian era, it was not unusual for adolescent girls to spend their evenings writing each other long and emotional letters about the intimate details of their lives. Today, for the same reasons, they turn to the telephone.

In an effort to understand their world, adolescent girls feel the need to reflect on and analyze events that adults would consider to be quite inconsequential. For instance, if your daughter told you that she ran into a boy whom she liked and he waved at her, you would probably reply, "That's nice, honey." But if she shared the same information with a close friend, her friend would have scores of follow-up questions. It would undoubtedly lead to a detailed discussion about how your daughter feels about this boy and how he may feel about your daughter and whether or not he's going to ask her out. In between, they would discuss who was wearing what, who else walked by, and where your daughter would like to go on their first date. Although this conversation seems trivial to an adult, it is very important to an adolescent who is trying to sort out the events of the day in context of her rapidly changing body and mind. I'm not suggesting that you allow your daughter to monopolize the phone every night, but she should be allowed a reasonable amount of telephone time. In an effort to maintain family harmony, you may want to designate a particular hour as the time your daughter can make and receive calls. In some cases, she may wish to use her own money, either from her allowance or from money earned from baby-sitting jobs, to pay for her own separate phone line.

Keep in mind that your daughter's need to continually talk to her friends does not make her a gossip or a frivolous person. Not at all. The desire to communicate and share feelings is very much a part of being an adolescent girl and is the same quality that will help her to grow into an empathetic and understanding woman.

FLIRTING WITH THE BAD CROWD

For some parents, the issue is not so much that their daughter is monopolizing the phone. Rather, they are worried sick about who she is talking to.

As girls get older and demand more independence, they become more difficult to control. "You can't because I say so" or "I forbid you to do it" are fighting words to a 16-year-old girl. Reason, subtle persuasion, and providing attractive alternatives are far more effective tactics. As parental control begins to diminish, some girls may wander outside of the usual acceptable crowd to see what other crowds are like. These girls may begin to hang out with the so-called bad crowd, which usually refers to kids with reputations for either drug or alcohol use or for being "fast."

However, if your daughter is a basically self-assured girl who does well at school and is not trouble prone, she may simply be experimenting by hanging out with this different crowd. It is highly unusual for a "good kid" with a good sense of who she is to suddenly get coopted by a bad crowd. Very often, a girl is not attracted to the crowd per se, but to a particular boy in the crowd, whom she hopes she can "rescue" from his bad ways. She will rarely emulate his "bad" behavior, rather, her aim is to change him. Girls initially find this challenge to be very exciting, although in the end, when they fail, they are in for a big fall.

If your daughter is in this situation, you need to point out to her what she is doing without attacking the boy directly. It's important for her to recognize her motivation, notably why she needs to spend time with someone who is not her equal. For example, you can say things like: "Gee, it must make you feel so together when you're with John; he seems so confused," or "Gee, you're not only his girlfriend, but you have to be his psychologist. What a responsibility."

She may reply, "What do you mean?" which will enable you to have a discussion about whether or not this is the type of relationship in which she is getting back as much as she is giving and whether she has taken it upon herself to give too much. As long as you keep a close eye on her for signs of problem behavior—unless you feel that your daughter is endangering herself in any way (for instance, I would not let her drive with a boy whom you suspect may have a drinking or drug problem)—you can let this relationship run its course. Usually, the "bad" boyfriend will get tired of her preaching, or she'll feel discouraged that he's not following her advice, and they'll seek out more appropriate partners.

It's also important to help your daughter to see this crowd for what it really is. Very often, because of their antics, the bad crowd comes across as stronger, more daring, and gutsier than the regular crowd. You need to help your daughter see that behind this façade are some very scared, insecure, and often neglected kids. Avoid a direct attack, instead say in your most sympathetic voice, "I really feel so sorry for Jim and Linda. Their parents couldn't care very much about them if they let them stay out all night like that. Those kids must feel terrible about themselves." Or "Boy, those kids have to be very scared and insecure to treat other people that way. Do you notice how they can't make a move without each other? They're very childish, really. It's so sad."

If, however, members of the bad crowd actually commit a criminal act, like vandalism or stealing a car for a "joy ride," you should criticize them directly and forcefully. Let your daughter know that what they did was not trivial or funny and in fact has serious consequences. "Breaking into that car was a very mean, antisocial thing to do. They destroyed that car! Can you imagine how the owners must have felt, or how Daddy and I would have felt if it were our car? Not to mention the fact that they're going to lose their drivers' licenses and may even serve some time in jail. Seems pretty stupid, doesn't it?"

Most normal, reasonably together girls will quickly lose interest in a crowd that is continually getting into trouble. Some, however, sink into deeper and deeper trouble.

ENTRENCHED IN THE BAD CROWD

When parents sense that their daughter is becoming entrenched in a bad crowd, they may not know what to do about it. For example, if your daughter is a True Follower, who rarely asserts herself with her friends, she may follow the others' lead and get into big trouble. Or, in some cases, she may have been seduced into the crowd by drugs or alcohol and may now be unable to free herself.

If you find yourself desperately worried about your daughter but unable to take any decisive action, if you feel helpless and out of control, you definitely need outside help—*you cannot handle this alone*. This is a situation where therapy, either individual therapy for you or family therapy for you and your daughter, would be very beneficial. Even if you can't afford to pay for long-term family therapy, very often a few consultations with a qualified therapist is all it takes to provide you with the tools to tackle this problem. If money is particularly tight, some agencies will offer a sliding-scale fee based on family income. In some cases, you may even be able to get some good advice free of charge from your priest, minister, rabbi, or school psychologist.

STEERING HER TO THE RIGHT CROWD

If possible, parents should try to prevent their daughter from getting involved with the wrong crowd in the first place. The first and most critical step is to avoid creating a climate at home that fosters this kind of behavior. Parental withdrawal, the "Do what you want, we can't stop you anyway" attitude, is a major culprit. Teenagers need direction, and if they don't get it from their parents, they will get it from other people who may be less interested in their welfare.

Parents need to be aware and concerned about where their daughter spends her time. I don't think that parents should allow their adolescents to routinely hang out in places such as malls or after-hours dance clubs or discotheques, all of which are uncontrolled environments in which anybody can come and go. These big, impersonal types of places seem to attract drug dealers and others who prey on teenagers.

Don't put yourself in a position in which you are constantly saying no; instead, provide alternatives. Encourage your daughter to spend time at Y's, community centers, church or synagogue youth groups, athletic clubs, or after-school activities. As a family, become involved in a number of different local organizations that provide programs for teenagers. I am often surprised at how parents who knocked themselves out to book extracurricular activities for their daughters when they were in elementary school suddenly stop when their daughters become adolescents. Although it's true that adolescents often feign lack of interest in everything, out of a wide range of activities, there are bound to be one or two that will pique your daughter's interest.

Make it a point to get to know who your daughter is spending time with. One way is to welcome your daughter's friends into your home. I have known parents who have gone so far as to install swimming pools or renovate basements into rec rooms for the specific purpose of keeping their children close to home. Those who live in smaller quarters may not be able to welcome crowds of visitors, but you can certainly encourage your daughter to invite a friend or two over for dinner once or twice a month. On occasion, you might invite a few of your daughter's friends out to a movie or to lunch.

By staying in touch with your daughter, you will not only be able to keep a better eye on her but will also create a closer and more enduring bond between you.

EIGHT: THE ACADEMIC SLIDE

There is clear evidence that the education system is not meeting girls' needs. Girls and boys enter school roughly equal in measured ability. On some measures of school readiness, such as fine motor control, girls are ahead of boys. Twelve years later, girls have fallen behind their male classmates in key areas such as higher-level mathematics and measures of self-esteem.

—*How Schools Shortchange Girls,*
American Association of University Women, 1992

Next to her family, school should be the most important part of your daughter's world. In school, she not only learns the critical academic skills she will use for the rest of her life, but other equally important lessons as well. From her teachers, she learns how to develop relationships with adults who are not family members. From her peers, she learns how to hold her own in a competitive setting. Through extracurricular activities, such as team sports and specialty clubs, she is exposed to a wide array of new interests.

School should be the place where your daughter expands her horizons and gains confidence in her ability to succeed. However, in many cases, it has just the opposite effect.

I have seen many girls begin their academic careers with high hopes and great promise. In fact, in elementary school, girls typically outshine boys in many important ways. They are generally more mature and better behaved. Girls outpace boys in verbal skills and reading and do as well or even better in mathematics and science. By junior high school, however, it's a completely different story. The same girls begin to lag, even in the areas in which they once excelled.

The girl who once achieved high test scores and outstanding report cards now often begins to falter. The girl who was once excited and enthusiastic about school often begins to talk about being "bored"—or stops talking about her classwork at all. Frequently, she has also stopped talking in the classroom.

Starting in junior high school, many girls begin an "academic slide" that is reflected in lower test scores and lower self-confidence. By the end of high school, even the highest achieving girls will not score as well as boys on college entrance exams—in either math or English—nor will they graduate from high school as prepared to meet the challenges of college or the world of work.

The academic slide for girls is particularly apparent in two traditionally "male" subjects: math and science. In the case of math, girls seem to have a built-in bias against the subject. Several girls have told me, "I used to like math, but now I don't." When I ask them why, the typical reply is, "I don't know, I'm just not good at it anymore." Ironically, many girls begin school believing that they are talented in math, but that confidence vanishes by high school. According to a recent study, about one third of all elementary school girls and one half of all boys say that they are good in math. By high school, one out of four boys—and only one out of seven girls—still believe that they are good in math. This lack of confidence on the part of girls may be the reason why nearly twice as many boys go on to take courses in higher mathematics as do girls.

Girls' feelings of inadequacy about math appear to spill over into other subjects. Throughout their academic career, they tend to shy away from courses that require a solid background in math, such as physics and chemistry. In fact, boys outnumber girls by 2:1 in advanced physics and chemistry classes.

Knowledge of math and science can mean the difference between a girl with low self-esteem and a girl with a strong sense of herself and her abilities. For an adolescent girl, there is a high correlation between achieving in math and science and maintaining her self-confidence throughout these transitional years. The ability to perform well in these subjects and to perform well in school seem to be important in terms of making a girl feel good about herself.

The academic slide is an indication that schools are somehow not meeting the needs of girls. Something is happening in the classroom that is discouraging even the brightest girls from fulfilling their potential. It is also a signal that schools are not preparing girls for life.

The lack of training in math and science means that girls are not getting a well-rounded, complete education—the kind of education they will need to feel confident and capable in a world that is becoming increasingly dependent on technology.

Unfortunately, too few girls leave school as self-assured, confident, and capable as when they began. But the academic slide does not have to happen. Obviously, not every girl—or boy, for that matter—is cut out to be a spectacular student. There are times in every girl's life when her schoolwork may suffer. Since adolescence exacts a far steeper emotional toll on girls than on boys, some girls may experience a temporary slump in their academic careers as they grapple with puberty. I believe a dip in grades for one semester is acceptable; a downward slide is not. There is no reason why girls cannot continue to do as well as or even better than boys in junior high and beyond. However, in order to prevent or reverse this slide, parents need to be aware of the particular problems that their daughters will encounter and the ways in which parents can successfully intervene.

BOYS: THE ATTENTION GRABBERS

From kindergarten on, girls may be better students, but boys dominate the classroom. Perhaps because boys are generally more active and aggressive than girls they demand and get more attention from their teachers.

In the classroom, boys are expected to behave a certain way and girls another. Observe any elementary school classroom, as I have, and you will see that boys call out answers more often than girls and usually get away with it. Boys are also more likely to interrupt other students, especially girls. However, when a girl tries the same tactics, more often than not, she is reprimanded, told to raise her hand and wait her turn. This reinforces traditional sex-role stereotypes that allow boys to be aggressive and adventurous, while girls are urged to be "good" and "ladylike."

At an early age, girls become aware of the double standard. As one astute 7-year-old noted, "The teacher always calls on the boys because, if she doesn't, they just yell out the answer anyway." Her observation is true. Boys are typically called on more often than girls, whether or not they raise their hands. Not only are they called on more often, but boys get more constructive criticism from their teachers. When a girl finally does get a chance to talk in class, the teacher usually gives her the verbal equivalent of a pat on the head —"Good" or "That's fine." Even though it's praise, it's not very helpful. The same teacher will give a boy a detailed critique of his answer and might even ask follow-up questions. Teachers may argue that since boys are not as good students as girls, they need the extra encouragement and attention. However from the perspective of the girls sitting in the classroom, it may appear as if what boys have to say is deemed more important than what girls have to say.

Even long after boys have learned not to call out and to sit in their seats without squirming, they still dominate classroom discussions. According to a recent study done in twenty-four undergraduate classrooms at Harvard, men talked up to twelve times longer than women and seemed to have no qualms about interrupting female students.

Whether they are in elementary school or college, female students are missing out on an important aspect of learning: classroom partic-ipation. As a rule, girls do not get to speak in public as often as boys and, as a result, may become more frightened and self-conscious about speaking before a group.

There are other even more insidious ways that gender plays a role in determining a student's fate.

MALE SUBJECTS, FEMALE SUBJECTS

When I encounter a girl who is good in math or science, she fre-quently attributes her talent to the fact that "I have my father's head for numbers." She is expressing a commonly held belief that certain subjects are "masculine" and certain subjects are "feminine."

From a very early age, boys and girls are tracked in different directions. Girls are given dolls and boys are given blocks. Girls play dress-up and boys spend hours constructing intricate designs with Legos. The end result is that boys are more intellectually challenged by their style of play and develop important skills that may help them later in school.

Boys are reputed to be better at subjects like math and science that require spatial skills and abstract thought. Girls are reputed to be better in liberal arts. One reason why boys may excel in more technical subjects is the fact that they have had more experience building and designing, which may help them better visualize math and science problems.

However, the male predisposition for math and science may actually be a self-fulfilling prophesy based on gender expectations. Teachers typically spend more time working with girls on reading and writing and more time working with boys on math and science. As a result, boys begin to believe that they are superior math and science students. A study of second and third graders shows that although boys were no better than girls in math they expected to get higher grades than did the girls.

Interestingly enough, the parents of boys also expected that their sons would do better in math and science than the parents of girls. Parents reinforce this belief in none-too-subtle ways. For example, a researcher at UCLA showed that the parents of gifted children were more inclined to encourage their sons to be interested in science than their daughters. These parents bought their sons science-related books and toys and discussed potential careers in scientific fields. However, parents of daughters actually discouraged them from playing with toys such as chemistry sets for fear that they would get cut or burned. The researchers noted that this seemed somewhat irrational considering that the same girls were allowed to wash dishes and cook!

Although boys and girls may be sitting in the same classroom, being taught by the same teacher, they have completely different experiences in terms of learning science. According to one researcher, by third grade, 51 percent of all boys had used a microscope, contrasted with only 37 percent of all girls. In high school, 49 percent of all boys had used an electricity meter, whereas only 17 percent of all girls had used that piece of equipment. Not surprising then, that by third grade, girls lose interest in science and begin to view it as a "male" field.

Other studies confirm that boys are much more likely to have direct, hands-on experience in science class than girls. They are encouraged to perform experiments, to take risks, and to get "down and dirty." Girls, on the other hand, are not expected to perform at the same level. A study conducted by Girls Incorporated noted that teachers tended to "rescue" girls from having to complete complicated experiments or projects. In other words, boys were expected to figure out the problem or complete the project on their own—girls watch somebody else do it.

The study concluded that when girls were given the same encouragement as boys to perform difficult tasks in science and math, they were just as interested and capable as boys. They donned laboratory coats with equal zeal, enjoyed working on algebra puzzles, and even studying snakes. However, few girls ever get these opportunities, either at school or at home.

Despite the fact that girls may not be getting an equal education in elementary school, they tend to do well. Teachers may favor girls because they appear to be so mature and articulate and are usually much less demanding than male students. However, the same factors that contribute to a girl's success in elementary school may be her undoing in junior high school.

"I USED TO BE SMART...WHAT HAPPENED?"

Jill was a gifted student who, two weeks after starting junior high school, wanted to drop out of the math honors program. Jill's parents couldn't understand why their daughter, who had always performed spectacularly at school, was suddenly saying things like "I can't do it."

Fortunately, these parents called for a meeting with Jill's math teacher and the school guidance counselor to find out what was going on. As it turned out, Jill had received a C on her first math test, and on the basis of that one mediocre grade, decided the class was simply too hard. The teacher, who was very supportive, spent an hour or two going over the paper until Jill understood her mistakes. Jill finally decided to stay in the class.

Jill's initial feelings of inadequacy are not that unusual. Like Jill, many girls are thrown by the transition from elementary school to junior high school, especially when it comes to math.

One reason why girls do so well in elementary school is that they are better behaved and are able to sit still and concentrate better in class. As a result, they are more capable of mastering the early elementary school math curriculum, which relies heavily on memorization skills.

Because girls master the work more quickly, they tend to make fewer mistakes than boys in their verbal and written work. Therefore, teachers spend less time with them and more time with the boys. The boy who makes a mistake is not simply told the right answer, rather, the teacher explains the underlying mathematical concept and has the boy redo the problem. The teacher works with the boy to make sure that he truly understands the concept.

In junior high, advanced math requires students to learn completely new skills and new concepts. The new language of algebra, geometry, and trigonometry is a complicated one; it cannot be mastered by memorizing a few basic principles and applying them to all problems. To perform well, you need to understand the basic underlying theory.

Since they more often were forced to learn the concepts behind the numbers because their teachers drilled them until they got the right answer, boys are actually better equipped to deal with advanced math. However, when girls are confronted with this strange, new math, they may respond with confusion and, like Jill, an overwhelming sense of "I can't do it."

This reaction, often referred to as "learned helplessness," may be a result of several factors. First, perhaps because of their early success, girls come to believe that intelligence is a natural gift that doesn't need to be developed. That is, you've either got it or you haven't. Thus if a girl encounters something new and doesn't "get it" the first time around, she is quick to assume that she "doesn't have it" (intelligence) and is easily discouraged. By and large, girls do not see the connection between hard work and success, as many boys were forced to.

Second, because girls are so used to getting good grades and praise, it can be quite a shock for them to get a bad grade. When asked, girls who "hate math" often confess that their dislike of the subject began in junior high school after disappointing test grades.

Girls—especially bright girls—need to be reassured that a bad grade doesn't mean that they are stupid or inadequate. Rather, it should be taken as a signal that they may not understand a particular aspect of a subject as well as they should. It's important for girls to understand that even the brightest students may at times struggle over a particular subject. And not getting it the first time doesn't man that they are incapable of understanding it, rather, it may mean that they need to work harder. They also need to be told that asking for help is not a sign of failure or weakness. Girls have told me that they find it demeaning to be singled out for tutoring and are reluctant to admit that they can't handle something by themselves. These girls should be told that if they don't understand something, asking for help is not a sign of stupidity, rather, it's the smartest thing they can do.

The new demands that are being placed on them certainly contribute to a girl's anxiety and sense of inadequacy. However, the way girls respond to change is another contributing factor to the academic slide.

THE TOUGH TRANSITION

The transition from sixth grade to junior high school is a particularly tough one for girls. For some girls, the mere act of changing schools seems to be very upsetting. One high school sophomore recalls, "I went from knowing everybody and everybody knowing me to a school full of strangers. That's when I began hating school."

A recent study in Minnesota compared the progress of girls in schools that ran from kindergarten to eighth grade to that of girls who move to different junior high schools after sixth grade. The girls who switch to junior high schools show a dramatic drop in self-esteem, as well as other signs of distress such as lower grade point averages and less participation in extracurricular activities. The K–8 girls did consistently better. In addition, the junior high school girls never caught up to the girls in the K–8 settings. Although boys experience some problems adjusting to junior high, as a whole, they tend to do better.

There are several theories as to why girls are thrown by this transition. Some experts suggest that girls thrive in the more intimate setting of the elementary school where they develop a strong relationship with one teacher as opposed to the more impersonal junior high setting where they are moving from classroom to classroom. In addition, the size and style of the school can make a real difference in a girl's ability to adjust.

A BIGGER—AND MORE DIVERSE—POND

Elementary schools tend to be smaller and less diverse than junior high schools. The switch from one to the other can result in quite a "culture shock" for many girls. Girls attending large, racially mixed schools seemed to suffer the most in terms of feeling good about themselves and participating in school life. In part, this reaction is undoubtedly a reflection of the growing problems of crime and violence in schools. Students, especially those in urban areas or in larger suburban school systems that encompass many communities, may be faced with unsafe bathrooms, unruly corridors, and a sense of danger surrounding the school grounds.

Despite the obvious drawbacks, I believe there are some advantages to attending a large, diverse school. In many ways, these schools reflect the racial, ethnic, and economic composition of the "real world," the world that your daughter will be living in after she completes school. The girl who learns to hold her own in this setting is bound to do well later on.

However, in part, I believe that the initial negative reaction to junior high school may also be triggered by the fact that for many girls, junior high is the first time that they will mix with people of other ethnic and economic backgrounds. Middle-class girls who are taught to be sedate and polite may be startled by the actions and words of girls and boys from other cultures. They may confuse aggressive talk with aggressive action, and they may be confused by their own feelings of guilt toward economically deprived students and aggressive impulses toward people who look and behave "different."

As parents, you can help your daughter better adjust to the "bigger pond" by pointing out that being different doesn't make someone bad or dangerous. Your daughter must learn to differentiate between aggressive language and aggressive action. The majority of kids in any school, including those who are loud and rambunctious, are not dangerous. They may act differently than her crowd, but they are not out to hurt anybody. However, in any school—even schools in "good" neighborhoods—there are some students who *can* be dangerous, and your daughter needs to be able to "sense" trouble before it happens. Very often, particularly with adolescents, incidents have a way of escalating. When words turn into pushing, shoving, or hitting —even if everyone is still smiling—it's important for your daughter to get as far away as possible. These are the kinds of situations in which someone can get hurt. Usually, by keeping her eyes open, the "street smart" girl will be able to avoid most potential problems.

Parents also need to become more involved in shaping the junior high school experience. For example, girls who fare the best in junior high are those who travel from class to class with the same group of students. Those who fare the worst are the ones who travel solo. In most cases, it's just as easy for a school to allow a class to stay together as it is to program each child separately, and parents should request it.

Although schools are letting girls down in any number of important ways, that is not the only factor behind the academic slide. As girls move from childhood to adolescence, they are vulnerable to new distractions that can divert their attention away from school.

PUBERTY: A NEW DISTRACTION

At this time, the typical adolescent girl has a lot on her mind. Like the boys in her class, she is concerned about school, homework, grades and her extracurricular activities, if any. But unlike the boys —who are primarily concerned with these factors—she must cope with a wide range of new pressures and distractions.

Sometime during their first year in junior high, most girls have reached puberty: That is, they have begun to menstruate and have noticeably mature-looking bodies. They are interested in boys—not necessarily the boys in their class—but certainly in the eighth- and ninth-grade boys who are also beginning to enter puberty. These boys are also very interested in them. Girls are very much aware of the fact that they are being "looked over" and judged. Every time they walk in the halls to change classes, or go down to the cafeteria for lunch, they feel as if they are on display.

The focus on appearance—the pressure to look pretty—becomes a major distraction for girls and continues throughout high school. Boys also may focus on appearance, but certainly not with the same intensity, nor is it as all-consuming a concern.

After a girl reaches puberty, she becomes aware of the fact that she is being judged by a new standard. Good grades and academic accomplishments are not enough to garner praise from her peers, or in many cases, even from her parents. In fact the girl who pursues academic success to the exclusion of everything else is often penalized for her efforts. Her peers are quick to call her a nerd, a label that can seriously hamper her social life. Even her parents may worry if she is not acting like a "normal" teenager.

In order to be noticed in a positive way, a girl has to be pretty and popular. She needs to affiliate with the "right" crowd, wear the "right" clothes, and in general, concentrate on a lot of extraneous factors that take away from her academic pursuits. As one 12-year-old put it, "What matters in my school are looks and popularity. Having a cute boyfriend will help make you popular . . . if you want to be liked, it's definitely not a good idea to act too smart."

Some girls manage to resist this pressure. As one extremely bright girl noted, "I would rather be a nerd than stupid." This girl and others like her who are able to avoid the academic slide tend to come from homes where their parents are very supportive of their academic success. Girls who don't fare as well desperately need their parents to intercede to help get them back on track, but often their parents fail to detect a problem until it gets out of hand. For example, I recently met with parents who were very concerned that their 14-year-old, Angie, was doing poorly in school. Until recently, Angie had been an outstanding student. A social Late Bloomer, Angie had channeled all of her interest and energy into her schoolwork. Although she took pride in her good grades, she felt isolated and left out of the social mainstream. By ninth grade, however, she had blossomed into a beautiful girl. Angie was thrilled when she was asked out by a very popular high school junior. Within a short time, they were "going together," spending nearly all of their free time at each other's houses. At first, Angie's parents were delighted that she was so popular and that she seemed to be so happy. Eventually, they began to worry about her plummeting grades, but whenever they tried to admonish Angie, the discussion would degenerate into a fight.

I counseled Angie's parents to help them get their daughter back on track. In this situation, the first step was to let Angie know that they believed that she was not doing as well in school as she should be. But they needed to communicate their concern in a warm, sympathetic way. "We understand that all kinds of wonderful, exciting things are happening to you that are taking your focus away from school. We know that it must feel terrific to have a boyfriend and to suddenly be so pretty and popular. But we also know that you are a smart, capable girl who should be doing a lot better in school."

After letting their daughter know that they regarded her poor schoolwork as a problem, Angie's parents followed up with some specific suggestions: "Maybe we should work with you from six to nine on Tuesday to help you finish your science project that you didn't hand in?" They also offered to bring in a tutor to help her catch up in classes in which she had fallen behind.

As it turned out, Angie herself was worried about school, but felt too overwhelmed to do anything about it. Her parents' intervention helped her see that there was a way to turn around this problem. Many girls, like Angie, would be relieved to have their parents involved in what to them may seem like an insurmountable problem. Others, however, may bristle and say, "Do you think that I'm still a baby, that I can't handle this myself?" When offered help, adolescents will often become defensive. Whenever a girl takes this stance, you can defuse the situation by saying, "I know that you're perfectly capable of handling it yourself, but why should you have to?" Follow up with, "Look, you're smart, you're capable. You can do better. What do you think should be done?" Some girls respond better to help if they believe that it was their idea.

Angie's parents in particular, and all parents, need to set limits. Angie's parents had allowed her to pursue her social life at the expense of her schoolwork. Teenagers need help in setting their priorities—they need to know that school is their primary job. Adolescents should not go on dates on school nights. Nor should they be allowed to spend hours on the telephone if they haven't finished their homework. Once Angie's parents implemented some sensible guidelines, her grades began to bounce back.

Angie's parents could have saved themselves and their daughter a lot of grief if they had recognized the problem early on, long before Angie's grades began to drop. There are warning signs pointing to the academic decline that parents often miss. Parents of daughters should be particularly careful about watching out for the following harbingers of trouble.

Red Flags

Withdrawal or lack of interest in school. Adolescents should display a healthy interest in school. Withdrawal or lack of interest in school is often the first sign that a problem may be brewing, and it may begin long before they bring home a bad test paper or a poor report card.

This is not to say that your daughter won't wake up some mornings and complain, "I wish it was Saturday," or "I can't wait for this week to be over!" On the whole, a girl should be interested and involved in what's going on in the classroom and in her school.

A girl who has a "healthy interest" in school will talk about her classes, her teachers, and activities that she may be involved in. If your daughter isn't talking about school, or only has negative things to say, it may be a sign that she is not feeling very good about school. Ask her questions about particular teachers and classes. "What did Ms. Jones cover today in American History?" or "Mr. Richards seems like a terrific teacher. Do you enjoy his class?" If she clams up, you will have to go to school and talk to her teachers yourself to find out what's going on. Ask them directly: "Kathy used to talk about school a lot and now she seems so uninterested. How is she doing in class?" If she's having a problem in a particular class, you can work with the teacher to help solve it.

If your daughter used to be involved in extracurricular activities in elementary school but no longer participates in any after-school programs in junior high, it may be a sign that she doesn't feel comfortable in her new school. As parents, you need to find out why. Is she worried about coming home from school after dark? Does she feel shy about mixing with kids she doesn't know that well? Maybe you can arrange to pick her up one day a week if she wants to stay late; maybe she can find a friend who will go to an after-school program with her. Your daughter may need a "push" from you to get her started at the new school.

What happened to math and science? Your daughter brings home a report card with two A's, two B+'s, a C, and a D. The two low grades are in math and science, her least-favorite subjects. Even though her grade point average is still good, I think that you should be concerned.

Although few people are talented in every subject, a girl who is capable of pulling A's and a B+ should also be capable of performing reasonably well in math and science. If she says things like "I hate chemistry" or "I just don't understand what's going on in algebra," you need to take immediate action.

First, you need to communicate to your daughter that you feel that she can and should do better. Very often, girls may not see a connection between their future aspirations and subjects such as math and science. Your daughter may respond, "Well, I want to be a lawyer, what do I need to know chemistry for?" Point out that lawyers work on all kinds of cases, including lawsuits involving toxic wastes or harmful medicines. Let her know that developing good skills in math and science will be critical for life in the twenty-first century, and if she doesn't obtain this knowledge, she will be severely limiting her options.

Don't just lecture, offer help. If you are good in math or science, you may be able to review the material with her yourself. If you're not, many schools provide tutoring for students who need help. If your budget allows, you may want to hire a private tutor.

Whatever you do, don't let the slide continue. Early intervention can mean the difference between a girl who catches up with the rest and one who falls hopelessly behind.

She's doing everything but her schoolwork. Your daughter may talk about school and seem perfectly happy, but you begin to notice that you never actually see her sit down and do any homework. She's always on the go, meeting her friends or going to another activity.

As girls become more and more distracted by normal adolescent pursuits, their schoolwork often falls by the wayside. An average junior high school student is going to be assigned at least an hour or two of homework every night. In addition, she's going to need to devote some time to studying for tests.

If you suspect that your daughter is not devoting enough time to her schoolwork, you need to become more vigilant. She needs more direction. Set a specific time during the afternoon or evening when you expect her to do her homework. To emphasize how important you think this is, tell her that neither you nor other family members will bother her during this time. Review her homework with her every evening. Don't do it in a punitive way. Simply tell her, "Gee, I'm really interested in what you're learning and I'd like to keep track of what's going on in your school."

She's not getting what she needs. Parents often assume that teachers are the experts and that what they say is right. This is not always the case. Even the most well-meaning teachers may misread your daughter, or they may be so overwhelmed by overcrowded classrooms that they don't know anything more about their students than their test scores. It's up to you to make sure that your daughter gets the attention she needs.

There are specific signs that your daughter is not getting what she needs. When you talk to her teachers, you may get a sense that they don't really know her. They may say things like "Well, she seems to be doing well, but she doesn't say much in class." When you review her test papers or other assignments, you see only letter grades, or a single word such as "Good" or even "Excellent," with no other comments. Even though your daughter may be doing well, she may not be getting what she needs in terms of feedback from her teachers.

If you hear from a teacher that your daughter doesn't raise her hand in class, you should ask, "Well, do you ever call on her anyway? I don't know why she's not raising her hand, maybe she needs a little encouragement." Some girls may be more shy than others, some may think that it's not "cool" to appear too smart or too eager. The fact is, very often, once a girl knows that the teacher is going to call on her anyway, she'll start raising her hand on her own. In addition, if a teacher knows that you expect your daughter to be an active participant, he or she will find a way to get her involved in class discussions.

Sometimes it's the teacher who needs to talk more. If your daughter brings home papers with few or no comments, I would ask her to get further information from the teacher. Tell her, "I don't understand what 'good' means. Does it mean that you covered this topic well? Does it mean that you left out some important things, and, had you included them, you would have gotten an 'excellent'? You really need more clarification from Mr. Marks."

At the next parent-teacher conference, I would ask the teacher to include more specific comments on my daughter's papers.

KEEPING HER INTERESTED

Maintaining your interest in your daughter's education will help to keep her motivated and interested. I asked several high-achieving girls to describe their parents' attitude toward school. To a girl, they responded with answers such as, "My parents believe that school is very important," and "They don't push me, but they show me that school should be a top priority."

How do these parents communicate these feelings to their daughters? By staying involved and offering support when they need help. As one 16-year-old explained, "We talk about what went on at school at dinner. If I need help with some of my courses, my mom will try to help me find the answer in the textbook. If she can't figure it out, we wait for my dad to get home, and he tries. If he doesn't know, we'll ask my older brother."

If this girl doesn't do well on a test, she and her parents discuss what went wrong. "They never yell, but they tell me that they expect me to do better. My dad might say, 'You were up late watching TV the night before the test, and you should have been studying harder. Next time, stay in your room longer and study harder.' "

Concerned parents also resort to innovative approaches to encourage better study habits. For instance, Kelly, 14, desperately wanted a telephone in her room. Her parents, however, were upset because they believed that their daughter was not reading enough. They struck an interesting bargain: If Kelly would read a 150-page book each week for the next four months, until her birthday, she would be given her own telephone as a present. If she stopped reading, however, the telephone would be removed from her room. Kelly earned her present but continued to be a voracious reader. "Not just to keep the phone, I actually enjoy it," she said.

What the parents of successful students have in common is the fact that they consider school to be a number-one priority, and their feelings are reflected in their actions.

DIFFERENT GIRLS, DIFFERENT PROBLEMS

Up until now, I've discussed problems and situations that could apply to any type of girl. However, girls with particular personality types and social styles are going to encounter different kinds of problems. The following section describes girls with different temperaments and personalities and the specific problems they may encounter.

The Aggressive Girl. Of all the personality types, the Aggressive Girl—the girl who raises her hand as often as the boys and who refuses to be interrupted or cut off—is going to encounter the most difficulty at school, with teachers and with other students.

Teachers who adhere to sex-role stereotypes are going to be uncomfortable with a girl who doesn't conform to their concept of "femininity." Other students may find her behavior off-putting, and she may even earn the dreaded nerd label.

The Aggressive Girl has as competitive spirit that will help her succeed later in life, and her parents need to see that this spirit is not crushed at school. Very often, in order to "fit in," when she reaches adolescence, the aggressive girl switches gears and becomes very quiet at school. Parents can prevent this from happening by preparing their daughter for the reactions of others. They can say, "We want you to talk up in class and we want you to do as well as you can, but you know, a lot of girls prefer to just sit there and let the boys do the talking. Some teachers may like you because you talk up and speak your mind, but some may feel that girls should be quieter and less aggressive. We love you the way you are, but you have to realize that some people have some very old-fashioned ideas."

I would also make sure that my daughter understood that the same personality traits that may make her life more difficult today will serve her well in the future. Whenever you can, show her examples of women on the news or in public life who are not afraid to speak up and whose voices are making a difference.

I would, however, caution my daughter about interrupting other students and speaking out of turn: There is a difference between being aggressive and being abrasive. "Even though some boys may call out or interrupt other kids when they're speaking, it's not the right thing to do. Although you may not mean anything by it, you could end up offending people or hurting their feelings."

The Passive Girl. The Passive Girl may be a good student, but she is at serious risk of falling into the cracks. This girl will be lost in a large classroom and will have a great deal of difficulty in raising her hand and speaking before a crowd.

I have seen a Passive Girl blossom in a warm, personal setting, with small classes where every student gets a good deal of individual attention. Unfortunately, unless you can afford a private school, this environment may not be available. Most public schools are big and often overcrowded. Therefore, parents have to make sure that their daughter isn't being overlooked in the classroom. If your daughter is intimidated by a crowd, let her teachers know. Tell them that your daughter may appear to be very quiet, but nevertheless has some interesting things to say. Ask them to encourage her to speak up in class. The first few times may indeed be terrifying for her, but after a while, she will get used to talking in public.

I would also encourage the Passive Girl to get involved in an after-school activity or club where she can meet in a small group with other students in an informal, noncompetitive setting. This kind of girl makes friends more easily on a one-to-one basis.

The Gifted Girl. The girl who has been labeled a "gifted" student will face her own particular challenges in junior high. First, as I discussed earlier, this type of girl may be more susceptible to learned helplessness than other, so-called average, students. When she is confronted for the first time with a difficult task or assignment that requires her to learn new concepts, she may fail because she is not used to having to apply herself in that way. The parents of the Gifted Girl have to keep a close eye on her schoolwork during the transition from elementary school to junior high. They need to be especially vigilant about making sure that she is keeping up in math and science. This doesn't mean that you should badger your daughter about her schoolwork, but you should keep tabs on her progress. Unfortunately, very often, the parents of a Gifted Girl are not used to having to monitor their daughter's work. They have grown accustomed to her doing well and assume that she always will.

The Gifted Girl may also feel that the "gifted" label is a social liability. During early adolescence, girls desperately want to be like everybody else, and anything that sets them apart from the crowd may be upsetting. If your daughter is in a program specifically geared to gifted students, she may have an easier time because she will blend in with her peers. If she is at the top of her class, she may feel embarrassed by her academic success.

Parents need to make sure that the Gifted Girl is given an opportunity to relate to her peers in a nonacademic setting where she will fit in. This girl should be encouraged to pursue a team sport or a hobby that will help her develop friendships in an arena in which she is just another member of the club or team.

The mediocre student. Not every girl is going to be an outstanding student. Some will make average grades, and some will fall below average. There are some girls who, no matter how hard they try, always achieve only mediocre grades. This doesn't mean that they're not intelligent—in some cases, mediocre students may simply not have the interest or the drive to do better. In other cases, the academic arena is not their forte.

If your daughter is only a mediocre student, don't despair. Not everyone who does well in school does well in life and vice versa. There are people who barely squeak through school and who nevertheless manage to build interesting, productive lives for themselves. In addition, many people who do miserably in lower school may be academic Late Bloomers who go on to do very well in college or professional school.

The mediocre student is at risk of feeling bad about herself. She may feel that she is not as smart or as capable as others. These feelings will be exacerbated if her parents continually chide her to try harder and to do better. This girl needs love and support, not lectures. Offer to help her with her work, or, if you can afford it, get her a tutor if she is having particular difficulty with a subject or two. If you have a choice of schools, the mediocre student does better in a less competitive, more personal atmosphere.

Find reasons to praise her. Although she may not be an academic whiz, home in on her particular strengths and talents. Perhaps she is a wonderful cook, a talented musician, or works particularly well with children. Make sure that she knows that you are aware of her special qualities and are not judging her solely by her report cards.

Whatever type of daughter you have, the transition to junior high will be a difficult one, so difficult in fact that experts are beginning to look at different ways of educating girls. One of the "new" and "innovative" suggestions that is frequently discussed is the old-fashioned all-girls school.

COED OR SINGLE SEX?

Up until the 1960s, single-sex schools were not that unusual: There were many public and private schools throughout the United States geared specifically for either boys or girls. The most prestigious colleges and universities were also single sex. Harvard, Columbia, and Princeton were for men; Radcliffe, Barnard, and Vassar were for women. Although these schools kept the sexes separate, they weren't always equal. Very often, more resources were allocated to the "brother school" than the "sister school," or the school curriculum reflected gender bias.

By 1970, discredited as outmoded and old-fashioned, most single-sex schools had become coed. For the first time, women were sitting side by side with men in the Ivy League and just about everywhere else.

THE ACADEMIC SLIDE 167

Today, the few remaining single-sex junior high and high schools are usually either private or affiliated with religious institutions. There are only a handful of public single-sex schools in the United States. However, educators are beginning to have second thoughts about whether the rush to coeducation was a mistake, especially for girls.

A recent study of all-girls Catholic high schools showed that their students actually fared better than girls in coed schools in many important ways. The study noted, "Girls' schools evidenced consistent and positive effects on students' attitudes towards academics. These students were more likely to associate with academically oriented peers and to express specific interests in both mathematics and English."

The study also noted that girls in single-sex schools did more homework and exhibited less role-stereotype behavior than girls in coed schools.

As these studies suggest, girls' schools may indeed be more attuned to the needs of girls. In addition, girls may feel less self-conscious about themselves and their bodies in an all-female environment and thus may be more focused on their schoolwork. "You really don't worry about what you look like when you go to school," noted one 15-year-old in a girls' Catholic high school. "My friends in coed schools spend hours dressing up before school. I don't have to worry about impressing anyone."

In addition, girls in girls' schools often feel more comfortable about talking in class. "You definitely feel much freer to express your opinion. In a coed school, you'd be worried about what the guys will think about you if you raise your hand to answer a question or to ask one. In a girls' school, you raise your hand without thinking twice about it."

I believe that a girls' school can be a haven for the right kind of girl. The academically oriented girl who is excited by school will do well in this environment because she will be shielded from the social pressures that she might feel in a coed environment. The Passive Girl may also do very well in a classroom setting where she will not be overshadowed by the more aggressive male students.

Many girls thrive in an all-girls setting, but there are some who may resent being in a school without boys. Some parents may believe that a girls' school will prevent their daughter from becoming preoccupied with boys, but nothing is further from the truth. All-girls schools are not convents; if a girl is determined to meet boys, she will find them—probably at the all-boys school down the block. If you have an option to send your daughter to a girls' school, do so because you feel that it will give her a fine education. Don't send her to a girls' school for the sole purpose of keeping her away from boys.

THE OLDER ADOLESCENT

The younger adolescent may be overwhelmed by puberty and other distractions, which may affect her schoolwork, but the older adolescent has her own particular set of problems.

Boredom. Some girls at around 16 or 17 complain of being "bored" by school—in fact, this condition is so common that it has been dubbed "junioritis," or "senioritis," depending on the grade in which it strikes. The symptoms are fairly common: A formerly good student may suddenly bring home a poor report card, or may begin cutting classes or cutting school altogether. Many girls snap out of this slump after one bad semester, but others remain stuck in it.

Chronic boredom is a symptom that a teenager is not being sufficiently challenged at school. I would try to talk to my daughter to find out why she is so bored. Does she find all of her teachers to be boring, or is it one particular teacher? Does she dislike all of her courses, or just some of them? Talk to her teachers about making the work more interesting for her. If her school allows it, perhaps she can change her curriculum to include some new types of courses. Some of the more innovative schools may allow a student to devise an independent study project on a topic that she finds to be particularly intriguing. Becoming engaged in one interesting project at school may be all she needs to get her motivated again.

In some cases, however, she may need to be taught in a different setting. Perhaps there is another school nearby that would better suit her needs. If you can afford it, you may want to consider sending her to a private school.

Grades and competition. As your daughter moves closer to college, there is increasing emphasis on grades and test scores. PSATs (Preliminary Scholastic Aptitude Tests) and SATs—the college entrance exams—become of paramount importance. Girls of 16 and 17 are made to feel as if one test, or one grade, can make or break them. Many girls feel terribly pressured during this time, and there are many things that parents can do to help them.

First, parents need to put grades and scores in perspective. Liking school and doing well at school are very important, but not just because you get a numerical rank at the end of the year. Second, and even more important, is teaching your daughter how to accept a challenge and accomplish a specific goal.

Parents who are truly interested in motivating their daughters do not push them to achieve, nor do they stress competition with others. These parents teach their daughters that the best form of competition is competing with oneself. They encourage their daughters to strive for steady improvement over past performance. If your daughter brings home a B in math, it is perfectly all right to say, "Gee, that's great. Last year, you got a B-minus, and now you're up to B. So do you think that maybe next year you could get up to a B-plus? I bet you can do it." By teaching her to strive to be a little bit better, you will be giving her an invaluable lesson in how to compete in the outside world.

Parents can also help their daughters by stressing that the college entrance exams are simply one more task to be mastered. Parents should tell their daughters, "These exams are just like any other job —you prepare for them. You work hard, and chances are, you will do well." Be sure that your daughter has at the very least taken the sample exams in the SAT review books—there are several excellent ones available at bookstores. If your daughter does not do well on the PSATs—which are usually given early in the junior year—it's not the end of the world. Suggest that she take a special review course to prepare for the second set of tests. I've known many girls who were able to raise their scores in this way. Let your daughter know that for every important endeavor in life, planning and preparation can pay off.

NINE: DATING AND SEXUALITY

Among the basic tasks of adolescence is learning how to be comfortable with your own sexuality and how to be comfortable with the opposite sex. Toward this end, dating serves several purposes: It teaches a girl how to relate to boys and gives her a chance to become familiar with and learn about her own sexual stirring.

Dating enables a girl to learn about herself and her needs: What kind of person is she compatible with? What does she want from a relationship? What is she willing to give? These early dating experiences provide the foundation on which she will build her adult relationships.

Dealing with the intense sexual feelings of adolescence is not easy. Adolescent girls desperately need the right kind of advice and guidance from their parents. Unfortunately, parents today are very confused about these issues themselves, and even the most enlightened parents dread having to discuss them with their daughters. Embarrassment and ignorance about what to say and how to say it often results in parents saying very little, if anything at all. To compound the problem, many girls may feel uncomfortable discussing these highly personal issues with their parents.

Consequently, adolescent girls learn about sex and dating in bits and pieces from a wide variety of sources ranging from the books their mothers conveniently leave around the house, to their "more experienced" peers, to the all-too-explicit love scenes on afternoon soap operas. As a result, they often get a very skewed and unrealistic view of relationships between men and women, which can be very harmful.

THE NEW FACTS OF LIFE...AND DEATH

Although adolescent girls spend a great deal of time thinking and talking about sex—which is perfectly normal—there are enormous gaps in their sex education, which is reflected in their behavior.

About one third of all teenage girls do not use contraception the first time they have intercourse (many really do believe that you can't get pregnant the first time!), and about 20 percent of all sexually active teens don't use contraception at all.

The "hit or miss" attitude toward contraception that is reflected in these figures also means that these girls are having intercourse with partners who are not using condoms, their only protection against sexually transmitted diseases (STDs) such as AIDS, which is fatal, and herpes and chlamydia, which can wreak havoc on their reproductive systems. With the AIDS epidemic increasing at an alarming rate among the teenage population, the stakes are extremely high; one mistake can be the mistake of a lifetime, especially for a girl.

The chance of contracting AIDS through heterosexual contact is sixteen times greater for females than for males—any girl who has intercourse without a condom is playing Russian roulette with her life.

The rate of unintended pregnancy among teens is soaring, and although it is not life threatening, it can certainly be emotionally wrenching. By age 18, nearly one fifth of all white and 40 percent of all minority teenage girls will become pregnant at least once.

As sex is getting riskier, girls are having sex at younger and younger ages, way before they are emotionally or physically prepared for it. By age 15, 27 percent of all teenage girls will have intercourse as compared to only 19 percent ten years ago. Many middle-class parents would like to believe that the 15-year-old Fast Trackers who are having sex are not *their* daughters. However, most of the increase in teenage sexual activity was among white teenagers in upper-income families.

What's even more alarming is that many of these girls are not choosing to have sex, rather, they are being pushed into it. According to a recent Harris poll, 17 percent of young teenage girls who had sexual intercourse said they were pressured to have sex by their boyfriends, and 34 percent said they did it because they had succumbed to peer pressure. In college, coercion often takes on the more ominous form of date rape: Studies show that about 15 percent of all college women have been raped while on a date.

The adolescent girl who has sex before she is ready because "everybody else is doing it" or to keep her boyfriend from breaking up with her, is at serious risk of thwarting her emotional growth by skipping the appropriate stages of adolescent dating. She will emerge from adolescence less prepared to form meaningful relationships than girls who moved at a slower pace, *but* who established a firmer sense of themselves and their own wants and needs before having to attend to the emotional needs of others.

All of these problems stem from one undeniable fact: Parents are not providing their daughters with the critical information and emotional support they need to protect their health and their psyches as they enter the world of sex and dating.

WHAT SHE NEEDS TO KNOW

- The emotional and physical components of sex
- The mechanics of intercourse
- How to get pregnant . . . and how not to
- The dangers of sexually transmitted diseases (STDs)

Sex education should be an ongoing process that begins in early childhood and continues throughout adolescence. The parent should be the primary sex educator: This important job should not be left to an impersonal book or too-clinical explanation by a junior high school hygiene teacher or a gynecologist. If a parent relegates this role to a professional, a child will think that this is a "forbidden" topic that cannot be discussed directly with her parents. Therefore, she won't go to her parents when she needs to ask a question or if she has a problem.

Although many people are competent to give an adequate description of the basic "facts of life," sex is not merely a physical act— there is an equally important emotional component. Part of sex education is teaching a girl how to evaluate a relationship; how to differentiate between good ones and bad ones and how to determine what kind of relationship is right for her. This information is best explained to a teenage girl by someone who can connect to her on a warm, loving level.

By the time a girl is menstruating, she should understand the mechanics of sexual intercourse, how to prevent pregnancy, as well as the risk of contracting AIDS or another sexually transmitted disease from her partner. Parents can do their daughters a great service by "de-romanticizing" sex; too many girls believe that sex is something that just "happens" in the heat of passion. To teenagers, romantic sex is spontaneous sex—however, spontaneous sex can be very dangerous. A girl should know from the start that sex should be something that she and her boyfriend think about and plan for ahead of time.

Many parents may feel that informing a girl about "safer sex" is tantamount to giving her permission to have sex. Nothing could be further from the truth. Alerting your daughter to the dangers of pregnancy and sexually transmitted diseases is not going to encourage her to embark on a sexual relationship. In fact it may make her think twice before she does.

There are many parents who may want to talk to their daughters about sex, but who may feel uncomfortable bringing up the subject, or may be worried that their daughters may feel uncomfortable discussing it with them. Many parents are surprised to find that when they finally do break the ice, their daughters more than meet them halfway. Just because their daughters are not talking about sex with them doesn't mean that they don't want to.

From around age 11 on, girls are consumed with questions about sex—they talk about it with their close friends, they have a great deal of anxiety about sexual issues—many would jump at the chance to have some of their questions answered by an adult. Even the social Late Bloomer who may not yet be interested in boys is very curious about what is happening to some of her friends and is filled with wonder and apprehension about what lies ahead.

There are some girls who may disguise their discomfort, or who may want to appear as if they "know it all," who will say in exasperation, "Oh, Mom, I know all about that."

No matter how much your daughter protests—or how sophisticated she appears to be—don't take her word for it. Ask her directly, "Well, tell me what you know." You may be surprised at just how little the "know it all" girl really does know.

When I've asked 12- to 13-year-old girls to explain how you get pregnant, first, they usually dismiss my question with an, "Oh, everyone knows that." End of conversation. Then, when I push for a fuller explanation, they often answer in very vague terms.

"The boy sticks his thing in the vagina."

When I question further, "What do you mean by 'thing,' a finger?" I'm often greeted by silence. These girls desperately need some straightforward, honest answers—using straightforward, honest language—and they need it from their parents.

Some girls may be very resistant to discussing these issues with their parents and may simply clam up. They may prefer to turn to their friends for information on sexual issues. They may not want to discuss dating with their parents. I would certainly respect a girl's privacy—there is no need for her to divulge the intimate details of her social life if she doesn't want to. However, I would still try to communicate with her on a more general level.

These girls may respond to a more indirect approach. One technique that I've used quite successfully is to depersonalize the conversation by focusing on an imaginary relationship portrayed on television or in a movie or book.

For instance, if you and your daughter are watching a television show together that presents a relationship between a man and a woman, you might ask her casually, "What do you think of that couple? Do they really love each other? Is he treating her the way he should?" The shy or more private girl may feel more comfortable talking about other people's feelings than her own, but in the process, she will be learning what she needs to know and eventually may begin speaking in the first person.

BASIC VALUES

Sex education should not be simply about sex. It should include an ongoing dialogue about the basic values pertaining to sexuality.

Although the pendulum may swing back and forth on sexual issues, the basic values—the core beliefs that underlie a girl's actions and behavior—should remain the same. Whether a girl opts for virginity until marriage or chooses to become sexually active, the same rules apply: A girl needs to be brought up to believe that she is worthy of being cared for and cared about. She needs to feel that she is an important person and that her needs are as important as anyone else's—and she also needs to feel good about herself whether or not she has a boyfriend.

Unfortunately, in our culture, girls and women are often made to feel that they are worthless or incomplete without a man. To a large extent, girls derive their status and self-worth from their boyfriends. Some girls are so desperate to have a relationship, that they will do almost anything to keep a boyfriend—even risk their lives. For example, I recently saw a segment on the TV newsmagazine *20/20* which explored why, despite the rise in AIDS, many unmarried couples still don't use condoms. The segment included an interview with a young woman who taught a class on "safer sex" at a community center. This young woman noted that men were much more resistant to using condoms than were women. She even admitted that she could not get her own boyfriend to use one! Nevertheless, knowing the risks, she continued to have sex with him because she did not want to lose him.

Her confession is a very sad commentary on the state of relations between men and women and on women's need to please men, regardless of the cost. A girl who is raised to respect herself and her body will not do anything to hurt herself, either physically or emotionally. She will not risk her health or emotional well-being because of peer pressure or the desire to keep a boyfriend.

As a parent, your fundamental job is to instill in your daughter a strong sense of self-worth and self-respect that will help her come to relationships from a position of strength.

A WORD ABOUT ABSTINENCE

Many parents are encouraging their daughters to remain abstinent. There are certainly some very good reasons for teenagers to delay sexual intercourse for as long as possible. As far as we know, abstinence is the only foolproof method of avoiding AIDS and other STDs —even condoms aren't risk free.

Although I believe that encouraging abstinence is a good idea, I think that parents have to be careful about discouraging any form of sexual outlet. We don't want to make girls feel bad or uncomfortable about their sexual needs, or unduly frustrated, either. Teenagers need a release for their sexual feelings, and when we talk about abstinence we need to clearly state, "Sexual intercourse, particularly with many partners, or with someone who has had many partners, is very dangerous these days. And that's one of the main reasons why I'm telling you not to do it."

Masturbation is a common and safe sexual outlet for teenagers. Most teenage girls would be very embarrassed to talk about it with their parents, but if the subject does come up, parents and their daughters need to know that it's normal and widely practiced.

THE PASSAGES OF DATING AND SEXUALITY

In order to educate your daughter effectively about sex and prepare her for this new role, you have to tailor your discussions to her particular stage of emotional and physical development. You need to speak in language she understands about issues that she cares about. The following section describes the different stages of dating and sexuality, what is normal and usual to expect from your daughter, and the different problems that may crop up.

Late Childhood—Preview of What Is Yet to Come

During middle childhood, from about ages 6 to 9, boys and girls tend to divide up into same-sex groups at school and at play. The typical 7-year-old will invite only girls to her birthday party and may have few, if any, male friends.

In our "hurry up and grow up" society, however, at around age 10, boys and girls begin to "rediscover" each other. It's not unusual for 9- to 10-year-old girls to have a coed party where they will try to mimic what they think is typical teenage behavior. For instance, boys and girls may dance together, and some Fast-Track preadolescents may even play "kissing games" such as Post Office and Spin the Bottle.

Many girls find these games to be tantalizing and are very curious about what it feels like to actually kiss a boy on the mouth or to have a boy put his arms around them. However, Late Bloomers and even many On-Time girls may feel uncomfortable or may simply not yet be interested in the opposite sex. These girls may wonder what in the world is going on.

The Primary Message: You're Beginning to Change

If your 9- to 10-year-old girl is going to a coed party, try to prepare her for what may happen. The girl who knows what to expect is going to feel more confident and self-assured. It's very important for parents to bring up the possibility that some of the kids may play kissing games and that these games are a preview of the new way that boys and girls will begin to feel about each other sometime down the road.

PARENT: You're starting to grow up and you're going to begin to feel a special way about boys. This is just the very beginning of these feelings. As you get older, these feelings get stronger. We've talked about how grown-ups fall in love and have children. It's all related to these new and exciting feelings. But right now, at 10 years old, you may enjoy holding a boy's hand or even playing a kissing game. Some of the kids may do this, if you don't want to, you don't have to, you're still very young and have lots of time for this later.

During these early discussions about dating, I would try to establish a reasonable level of expectation by stressing that boys and girls really don't begin to go out on dates until they are real teenagers.

PARENT: We don't feel that you should go out on a date alone with a boy until you're 14. Dating is fun, but it can get very complicated, and you need to be ready for it. But you can certainly enjoy seeing boys at parties or in mixed groups.

Don't get into a long argument about this. This should be presented as one of the "house rules" that doesn't change: You wouldn't let an underage teenager drive a car, no matter how much she badgered you, and you shouldn't let an underage preteenager date.

The Late Bloomer who is still more interested in playing with Barbie than playing kissing games with boys may feel uncomfortable at coed parties and may wonder what all the fuss is about. I would reassure the Late Bloomer that her feelings are quite normal—when the time is right, she will become interested in boys—but for now, she should pursue her other interests.

It's also important for parents to be aware that although girls of this age may have a basic understanding of how babies are made and how AIDS is spread, they may be unnecessarily fearful about doing things like hugging and holding hands. It won't stop them from doing them, but they may worry about it after the fact. It would be very helpful for parents to remind them, "You can't get pregnant from hugging a boy, or holding his hand, or even from kissing him."

Parents should also make sure that their daughter clearly understands that the AIDS virus cannot be spread through casual contact. It can be spread through blood, through sexual intercourse, and by sharing dirty needles. Some doctors think that AIDS can be spread through saliva. French kissing (tongue kissing) may be dangerous if your partner carries the AIDS virus and you have an open sore in your mouth. This doesn't mean that you can't make out, but doctors do advise against French kissing if you have sores in your mouth or if you're wearing braces. AIDS absolutely cannot be caught from toilet seats or by hugging.

Unless a girl asks specifically, I would not get into a detailed conversation with a preadolescent about condoms—it really won't mean anything to her, and I think it's unnecessary.

Young Adolescence: The Era of the Crush

Boys and girls between the ages of 11 to 13 tend to admire each other from afar, usually from the safety of a group. Most of the socializing takes place at school, or community center dances, church or home parties.

Although some may have one-on-one dates, this is a rarity, and in my opinion, is encouraging the girl to grow up too fast. There are some Fast-Track girls as young as 12, however, who may want to go out on dates with older boys. Very often, a physically developed girl may attract the attention of older boys and may have older friends. I would definitely not let her go out on a "real date" alone with the boy, such as to a movie. If she's dating that seriously now, what's left for her to do when she's a real teenager?

Parents should stick to their guns and say, "Girls your age don't go out on dates, and we don't want you to until you're a bit older."

Undoubtedly, there will be one girl in your daughter's crowd who *is* dating, and your daughter will be quick to say, "But Sally goes on dates."

Your reply should be, "Well, I think that Sally's parents are wrong, because Sally is too young." Parents of a 12-year-old do have the right, and I believe the responsibility, to prevent their daughters from rushing through childhood.

Most girls this age don't want to date: At this point they're too busy falling in and out of "love." Crushes—transient, passionate feelings about boys—are very common among young adolescent girls. When a girl of this age says she's in love, despite the intensity of the proclamation, very likely she will be focused on somebody else by the end of the week. It's possible for a girl to have a crush on someone that she hasn't even met, such as a celebrity, a boy she passed in the hall at school, or even a photograph of a friend's older brother who may be away at college.

When groups of boys and girls get together, they may experiment with each other by holding hands and kissing, and some Fast-Track 13-year-olds may even neck or make out. Girls are very concerned about such fundamental issues as what to do if a boy wants to hold hands and their hands are sweaty, or if a boy wants to kiss them and they're not sure if they should let him, or they're not sure how to kiss.

Before a girl goes off into a social situation, she will be feeling a great deal of anxiety, which her mother can help alleviate. For instance, if a girl is invited to a coed birthday party, her mother can ask, "Do you think they'll be playing Spin the Bottle?" The girl will probably reply, "Oh, no, Mom, that's baby stuff," at which point her mother can ask, "So what do bigger kids do? Do they hold hands, do they kiss?" And the girl will probably say, "Yeah, sometimes," and this will give her an opportunity to describe what goes on and to talk about anything that might be on her mind.

It is the rare young adolescent girl who goes any further than necking—most limit their sexual activity to a quick kiss and hand holding. In fact, girls of this age are often scared of intercourse because they think that it's going to be painful or that there's going to be a lot of bleeding. Some girls may ask their mothers to explain what it feels like. Be truthful. Let her know that in some cases, there may be some discomfort and minor bleeding. I think, however, it's important to stress to your daughter that when she is emotionally and physically ready, sex will be a wonderful experience. Although you want to discourage her from embarking on a sexual relationship too soon, you want her to know that it is expected and desirable that she will one day enjoy her mature sexuality.

The Primary Message: Take Care of Yourself

First and foremost, as girls begin to develop women's bodies, parents need to get a basic message across to their daughters: They must assume responsibility for their own health and safety. I would begin a discussion on how to take care of your body by saying something to this effect:

PARENT: Mom [or Dad] and I try to steer you in the right direction, but we can't watch you every second of the day. You're the one who has to watch out for yourself. You have only one body to last you for your entire life: It's very precious. What you do to your body now can affect your whole life. You need to do everything you can to take care of it. Your body is as important as your emotions and as your mind, and you should never put it at risk.

This opening could lead to a discussion about abstinence, the risks of unprotected sex, and the importance of always using a condom. Before puberty, you may have discussed these issues in very general terms. Now it's time to be more specific.

PARENT: Do you know what a condom is?

DAUGHTER: I think it's something boys use for birth control.

PARENT: That's right. But it's even more important than that. A condom is a sheath that goes over the penis, and it's particularly important because it can help prevent the spread of AIDS, and we've talked about how dangerous that is. When I was younger, our main concern was not getting pregnant, and a girl could take the Pill or use a diaphragm to prevent that. But today, we're in an epidemic. Do you know what an epidemic is?

DAUGHTER: Like AIDS?

PARENT: Yes, like AIDS. An epidemic is when a disease is spreading very quickly. We are in the middle of an AIDS epidemic now, and what makes it so serious is that there is no cure. So far, everybody who gets AIDS will eventually die. And it's not only AIDS we have to worry about; there are still other serious diseases that can be spread sexually that may not kill you but can make you very sick and even hurt your chances of having a baby many years from now when you really want to. That's why condoms are so important. And that's why it's so important to wait until you're older to have sex, when you're really in love with someone, and you both understand the risks, and you're experienced enough to know how to protect your precious body.

The early adolescent years are a time when your daughter may ask direct—and often unexpected—questions about sex. During dinner, she may blurt out, "Are rubbers the same as condoms?" Or out of the blue, she may ask, "Can you get AIDS from oral sex?" As surprising or embarrassing as these questions may be, don't react with shock or say, "Not at the dinner table." First, she may never ask you again, and moreover, you don't want to communicate a sense that there is something secretive or mysterious about sex. There is always the danger of making the "secretive" aspect of sex too alluring, which may indirectly propel some girls into engaging in activities that they might not have otherwise.

Therefore, my advice is that you answer these questions directly and honestly. Take any opportunity your daughter gives you to discuss sexual responsibility and safer sex. Always ask, "Any other questions?" Make sure she knows that you will listen to whatever she has to say.

There are times that you may have to postpone the discussion. If there are small children at the table who are too young for this conversation, you can say, "Let's discuss this after dinner when we can talk in private," and make sure that you have that talk.

Middle Adolescence: Thoughtful Crushes

Middle adolescence ushers in a new phase of early dating, which sets the stage for the more serious dating of late adolescence. During the years 14 to 16, boys and girls typically begin to date one on one and may go to a movie or to a party together, or even out to dinner. For both boys and girls, early dating is highly experimental; because they are unsure of who they are and which types of people best suit their needs, they tend to go out with a variety of different people.

Early dating relationships are often very transient—they break up after a few dates when one or the other partner decides to search for greener pastures. A "long term" relationship may last a few months. Girls tend to take all relationships more seriously than boys—but especially romantic relationships. As a rule, girls spend a great deal more time thinking and talking about their boyfriends than boys do about their girlfriends. They invest more of themselves in these short-lived relationships. As a result, girls tend to be more upset about breaking up and assume that they were somehow responsible for the demise of the relationship. I have seen girls simply shattered over the breakup of a relationship that had lasted for only two or three dates. I think that one of the reasons that this happens is that they had been poorly prepared for this stage of dating.

The Primary Message: Don't Get Too Serious

From the start, parents should instill in their daughters an understanding of the temporary nature of these relationships. In no way should parents suggest that these are enduring bonds that are going to last beyond the next few weeks or months. For example, when a girl asks her mother, "Isn't John wonderful?" her mother should reply, "Yes, he certainly is nice."

She should not say, "What a lucky girl you are to have such a wonderful boyfriend," or "Gee, I hope you two stay together." To make anything more out of the relationship is a mistake because it will be setting her daughter up for a huge disappointment.

It's also a good idea to gently remind a girl in the throes of first love that she is experiencing these emotions for the first time.

PARENT: You're having some wonderful and exciting feelings now—this is all very new for you. As you get older, you'll feel them more often and about lots of different boys. Eventually you'll fall in love, and that will feel even better.

When the inevitable breakup occurs, the girl will still be hurt and upset, but she will have a sense that this is the normal course of events, and she won't be blaming herself for her failure to sustain this relationship.

When a girl is hurting over a breakup, parents should be warm and sympathetic and allow their daughter a brief period to "grieve" over her loss. Remember, she is in pain. Don't make light of her situation. Tell her, "I know that you're hurting, that's perfectly normal. It can be painful to lose someone that you care about."

Let her cry on your shoulder if she wants to.

However, though a few days or even a week of moping around the house is reasonable, after that, I would certainly try to get her mind on other things. Take her out to dinner, take her to a movie. Try to get her interested and involved in other activities. Nature will take its course, and before too long, she should be back to normal.

Her Boyfriends

Although she still gets "crushes," the middle adolescent girl is more mature than the young adolescent in that she can begin to articulate the specific quality in a boyfriend that she may find appealing. She may be "in love" with someone because she finds him "smart" or "fun to be with," but her emotional range is still rather limited—adult love is still far off.

Because this stage of dating is highly experimental and to some degree superficial, a girl may choose to date someone on the basis of his looks or because she's curious to see what he's like. She may make completely inappropriate choices, and you may wonder, "What in the world does she see in this kid?"

There will be times when you will not like her choice of boyfriend —you may find him dull, or sloppy, or lacking a sense of humor. You may think that she can do a lot better. If she asks you what you think of him, I wouldn't lie and say I liked him, but I wouldn't go out of my way to find fault with him, either. I would simply reply, "John's a nice boy, but I think you may meet someone down the road whom you might have more in common with."

I would certainly not prevent a girl from dating someone just because I didn't think that he was right for her, unless I had a good reason to think he might be dangerous to my daughter. Given the rebellious nature of these teen years, parental disapproval can make even the most unattractive date seem very desirable.

Sometimes a girl may be reluctant to terminate an inappropriate or unfulfilling relationship because she feels too guilty about leaving her boyfriend. In some cases, she may feel that she is deserting her boyfriend at a time of need, or that he may do something drastic if she leaves, either to himself or to her. If her parents push her to break up, it may have the opposite effect by putting her in the position of the boyfriend's defender. Therefore, parents need to handle this situation with kid gloves. The best approach is to talk to her about her guilt feelings and how hard it is to leave someone who may care about her, but who nonetheless is not appropriate. In time, the gentle guidance and support that she receives from her parents may help her end the relationship.

I would, however, take stronger measures to prevent her from dating someone I felt could imperil her physically or psychologically.

For instance, if I knew that a teenage boy had a drug problem or had been caught drinking and driving, I would not allow her to go out with him. I would explain my reasons very clearly and try to get her to see that my main concern was her safety. Your daughter may or may not understand your point of view. Although she may be very upset when you say no, parents' fundamental job is to keep their child free from harm, even if they have to take some flak for doing so. Given the transient nature of these crushes, within a short time, your daughter will probably be interested in someone else. However, if she is hell bent on entering into a potentially destructive relationship or makes a habit of fixating on inappropriate choices, I think it's a sign that she needs help, and you should consult with a therapist.

"Safer" Sex

Given the fact that about one third of all girls experiment with sex by age 16, your 15- or 16-year-old may tell you that one of her friends is having sex. I would avoid saying things like "Oh, that's terrible" or "What kind of girl is she, anyway?" which really won't accomplish very much except to prove to your daughter that you have no concept of what's really happening in her world. Instead, I would initiate the following conversation:

MOTHER: Janet and Brad are having sex? Are they using condoms?
DAUGHTER: I don't know, we've never talked about it.
MOTHER: You've never talked about it? Boy, you'd better talk about it with her, because Janet is really putting herself in jeopardy.
DAUGHTER: I think Janet's on the Pill.
MOTHER: So she won't get pregnant. What about AIDS?
DAUGHTER: Brad doesn't use drugs. I don't think that anything will happen.
MOTHER: Look, you never know who he's slept with, or whether he'll sleep with anyone else, and he doesn't really know who she's slept with. Sounds to me like Janet's rushing into this without really understanding what she's getting herself into. Certainly, I don't think she understands the physical risks or the responsibility that she's taking on.
DAUGHTER: But it's embarrassing talking about condoms with a boy. And a lot of boys don't want to use them.

MOTHER: First, if a boy really cared about you, he wouldn't want to put you at risk. Second, better you lose him than get AIDS and lose your life. You know I think that girls your age are too young for sex because it is so complicated. But I know it can get hot and heavy, and I know that sometimes things can happen even if you didn't plan on it. If I were Janet's mother, I would want her to protect herself with a condom, no matter what. I hope that if you ever find yourself in that situation, you won't forget that your life is more important than anything.

Although this mother is not telling her daughter it's okay to have sex, she is stressing that if the girl does, she must take the proper precautions.

Chaperons and Safety

By 15 or 16, many girls notice a real difference in their maturity and begin to push for concrete signs that they are growing up. Very often, they want to show how sophisticated they are by giving or attending parties without adult supervision. Their argument is usually, "Don't you trust me?" and your answer should be, "Yes, I trust *you*—but I don't trust everybody else."

Make it clear that your primary concern is your daughter's safety, and for good reason. Illegal drugs are an ever-present threat in the lives of teenagers. One person with marijuana, crack, or cocaine can change the entire tone of a party.

In addition, teenage parties often involve alcohol—it's so common these days that many parents "compromise" by allowing their teenagers to serve beer instead of the hard stuff. Some kids may bring alcohol with them. Although I don't think that adolescents should drink before it's legal, unfortunately, it is a widespread practice. In addition, in some states, the drinking age is 18, and therefore a 16-year-old girl may indeed be dating someone who can legally drink.

Your daughter needs to be told that alcohol and drugs can seriously impair someone's ability to function and think clearly. They can also change someone's personality—not necessarily for the better. Although some kids may have a few drinks or a few puffs of pot and get a bit silly or giddy, others may get rough and abusive. Indeed, many of the highly publicized date rape trials have involved men and women who were drinking or using drugs.

Parents also need to be aware that there is a good chance that their daughter will be driving home with someone who has had a couple of drinks or may have been using drugs. They must say to their daughters, "I want an adult to be present in that house to make sure that no one is getting behind the wheel of a car who shouldn't be."

I don't think that an adult needs to be present at the party, but a nonintrusive adult should be a "benign hovering presence" in the house while the party is going on to keep an eye on things.

Too Much, Too Soon

Most middle adolescent girls will "make out" with their dates, and some of the older girls may progress as far as "feeling up" or even petting. Some may even have experienced sexual intercourse, but out of this group, few are in what adults would consider to be a real "relationship"—that usually doesn't happen until around 17 or 18.

What very often happens now is that the more sexually experienced girl may, usually on the spur of the moment, decide to "go all the way." Many girls find their initial sexual experience to be a lot less than they expected. They may feel pain, and most don't experience an orgasm their first time. Although the girl may feel that she has a very special bond with this boy, he may not reciprocate her feelings, or even if he does, he may not be the slightest bit interested in pursuing a serious relationship at this point. It can be a tremendous blow to the girl if he doesn't call her again, but it can also be a signal to her that she is in over her head.

I've talked to many girls who have had sex too early and have decided to postpone further sexual intercourse for another two or three years. In an ideal situation, this girl feels free to talk to her parents about her experience so that they can help her sort out her feelings.

Parents need to explain that the boy's not wanting to pursue a real relationship should not be taken as a personal rejection, nor does it mean that he's a bad person or that "all boys want from girls is sex." Rather, the girl needs to understand that in all likelihood the boy is simply not ready to make an emotional commitment, and that few boys his age would be. In fact, the girl herself is probably too young and inexperienced to commit to any one person. At this stage, she needs the freedom to meet and get to know lots of different boys. In reality, the strong emotional feelings of a sexual relationship may be too overwhelming.

Parents also need to communicate that "Sex is a wonderful thing if you're ready for it. If you're not, and if your boyfriend isn't, it can be a terrific heartache, and maybe this is a sign that you need to slow yourself down."

Promiscuity

There are some girls who, for lack of a better word, are "promiscuous" in that they have had several sexual partners. When a 14- or 15-year-old girl starts "sleeping around" it's a sign that something is amiss.

Some girls use promiscuity as a way to get their parents' attention, but many girls use sex as a way to get affection. During adolescence, some parents—especially fathers but some mothers too—pull away from their daughters. The intense bond between parent and child is weakened, and these girls respond to the loss by searching for a replacement. Instead of blaming the "promiscuous" girl for her behavior, parents need to examine her possible motivation and the ways they may be contributing to it.

In some cases, parents can intervene and turn the situation around. Those who have managed to intervene successfully are not the parents who punish and blame, but those who take a sympathetic but firm approach. The girl who is desperately seeking any kind of relationship needs her parents to say, "We love you, we care about you. We're upset that you're treating your body so badly, that you're not giving yourself the respect that you deserve. We're very worried about AIDS and the other risks that you're exposing yourself to. We need to talk about why you're doing this and what we can do to help."

If the relationship between the girl and her parents has deteriorated to the point where they're not even talking, family counseling by a trained therapist may be very helpful.

There is a sizable minority of girls who may be coerced into sex because they don't want to lose their boyfriends. I think a girl who understands the fleeting nature of these encounters may be less inclined to be pushed into sex on the mistaken notion that this will help keep the relationship going.

Girls need to be told quite directly that having sex with someone doesn't mean that the relationship will last any longer than if you don't. In fact, it could have just the opposite effect. A boy could be so overwhelmed by the intensity of the relationship that he might simply move on.

Girls also need to understand that having sex doesn't automatically make people closer. The feelings of warmth and love have to be there first or the relationship will not grow, no matter what you do.

Finally, parents need to communicate that a relationship based on fear and insecurity is doomed from the start.

I also feel that a girl who can derive a sense of accomplishment from other aspects of her life is less likely to fall into this trap. She may indeed feel bad if her boyfriend moves on or if she wants to call it quits, but it will not be the end of her world—she has other interests to pursue.

Helping the Nondater

By age 14 or 15, most girls have at least gone out on their first date or two and are more or less part of their group's social scene. A minority of girls, however, remain bystanders. For a variety of reasons, they have not made it into the social mainstream. The nondater in the crowd of daters—the girl who is never asked to the school dance and has never been out with a boy—feels terrible about herself. She can't help wonder "What's wrong with me?"

There may be nothing wrong with her at all—she may simply be shy, or lack the social confidence to attract a boy's attention, or be a Late Bloomer. At this age, boys are often as insecure as girls about making the first move, and they often look for a sign from the girl that their advances would be welcome. In some cases, a girl may discourage a boy from asking her out because she is embarrassed by her inexperience. Some girls—especially those whose parents have not talked with them openly about sex—may be apprehensive about what really happens on a date and how a girl should handle herself. Some parents may be indirectly discouraging their daughter from dating because they have difficulty letting go, or they may simply feel that it is unimportant.

For instance, I recently worked with a 16-year-old girl who was distraught about her lack of a social life. This girl, however, was a spectacular student, bringing home straight A's every semester. Her parents simply couldn't understand why their daughter was so upset about not dating since she was so successful in other ways.

When she came home from a party upset because no one had asked her to dance, her father told her, "Don't worry about it, you've got brains, and that's much more important."

I certainly place a high value on academics, however, I also feel the goal of every person should be to live a well-rounded life. Although I don't think that parents should act as if it's a tragedy that their daughter isn't dating, they need to realize that she is missing out on an important part of adolescence.

I advised these parents to help their daughter develop the social skills she obviously lacked. For instance, when she came home from a party upset because no one had asked her to dance, her parents should ask some questions.

PARENT: Gee, honey, that must have been rough. Did you know anyone there?

DAUGHTER: Well, I knew a few kids from school, but they had dates.

PARENT: Wasn't your friend Mary there?

DAUGHTER: Yeah, she was there.

PARENT: What was she doing?

DAUGHTER: She was dancing—she knows everybody.

PARENT: Did you ask her to introduce you to anybody?

DAUGHTER: No, not really.

PARENT: Maybe next time you can ask her to introduce you to a few of the guys? Wasn't there anyone without a date you could have danced with?

DAUGHTER: Well, maybe.

PARENT: Yeah, I bet some of them felt as funny as you did.

Whatever the reason their daughter is not being included in the social scene, parents need to intervene. Very often, these social Late Bloomers require a push to get them going. Parents should find ways to get their daughter involved in social situations outside of school where she will have an opportunity to meet new people. A girl may feel less inhibited in exploring this new side of life in a setting where she has not been labeled or stigmatized as the "nondater." Parents should insist that their daughter attend any socials or dances at their church, country club, or community center. If possible, they should arrange dates for their daughter with the sons of their friends. Even if their daughter balks, they should not take no for an answer. It may take just one date or one enjoyable evening at a dance to help break her into the social world. I have seen many wallflowers flourish under this benevolent "strong-arm technique," and at the very least, it will give her some social confidence.

The Older Adolescent: "I think I'm in love . . ."

The older adolescent intellectually understands the difference between love and infatuation, a crush and "the real thing." She is more thoughtful and critical in her analysis of her relationships. She will no longer say, "I'm in love with this terrific guy," she will more cautiously say, "Well, I think I'm in love, but I'm not really sure." The mature girl understands that love is not merely an intense emotion, but brings with it a feeling of commitment.

By 17 or 18, an experienced savvy girl will have a better sense of which type of boy is best suited for her. A girl of this age might say a bit wistfully, "Gee, he's an attractive guy, and going out with him would be very exciting, but I don't think that it can go anywhere." Although she is probably not interested in marriage or a long-term commitment, she is ready for a relationship that lasts for more than a few dates. The Late Bloomer who is just starting to date, however, will still be in the experimental phase and will not have yet reached this degree of dating savvy.

By 19, more than half of all girls are sexually active, and out of that group, about 60 percent have had more than one sex partner. Only half of these sexually active girls will have used condoms. Given these statistics, it's a good idea for parents to continually review the principles of safer sex with their daughters and to make sure that they are protecting themselves. No girl should be sent off to college without this basic information.

The Primary Message: Don't Be Pushed

Due to a handful of highly publicized trials involving celebrities, college athletes, and professional sports figures, we have heard a great deal about so-called date rape, or acquaintance rape, in recent years. Studies show that as many as 15 percent of all women on college campuses say that they have been forced to have sexual intercourse by men whom they were dating. Given this shockingly high statistic, I feel that it's very important for parents to make their daughters aware of this potential threat.

First, parents have to bring the issue to their daughter's attention by making sure she understands what date rape is all about. Because of all the publicity surrounding the date-rape cases, your daughter has probably heard about it but still may be a little confused.

It's up to you to bring this issue to your daughter's attention. She needs to understand what date rape is and what it isn't. Date rape is not a clear-cut situation in which a woman is attacked by a rapist who secretly follows her home or pulls her into a secluded area or a car; rather, it is an act committed under more ambiguous circumstances by someone whom the young woman knows and may even like, whom she has willingly spent time with.

Although accounts of date rape vary—many men attack without any warning, for instance—the typical scenario usually involves some prelude leading up to the sexual overtures. The couple may have dinner and a few drinks together, he may suggest that they go for a ride in his car or back to his apartment. They may begin to neck, and then suddenly he unzips his pants. She protests, but he doesn't listen and forces her to have intercourse. After the incident, the young woman is often conflicted about what happened. Was it rape? Did she lead him on? The woman feels angry, ashamed, helpless, and very confused.

Parents need to make their daughters aware of the possibility of rape, even by someone who seems to be a "nice guy." A young woman needs to understand that her date may have something else in mind when he suggests going for a drive to a secluded area or back to his apartment for coffee. She may have something in mind, too, in which case their feelings are mutual. But if she doesn't, she should be extremely careful about spending time alone with someone who could misinterpret her actions.

There will be men who will try to use guilt ("I took you out to the best restaurant in town") or coercion ("If you don't, you can forget about our date next Saturday") to get a woman to go back to their apartment or for a drive to a secluded area. Parents should make girls aware of these ploys, and tell them to hold their ground. A girl should understand that no one who really cares about her will ever force her to do anything that she doesn't want to.

I know that there are people who would accuse me of putting the onus on the girl. Nothing could be further from the truth. This is not about blame. Any man who overpowers a woman and forces her to have sex is the guilty party. However, rhetoric will not protect a girl from his horrible and demeaning experience. Education, or "sexual savvy," is her best defense.

Parents also need to tell their daughter in no uncertain terms that if she is raped on a date, she should call the police immediately and then call them. They should make it clear that they will always be there to help her—no young woman should have to keep this crime a secret.

TEENAGE PREGNANCY

More than a million teenagers get pregnant each year—this problem is widespread and cuts across racial and socioeconomic lines. Whether a girl lives in an urban ghetto, on a farm, or in a posh, sophisticated suburb, if she is sexually active, she is at risk of unwanted pregnancy.

How the problem is handled, however, very often depends on race and class. Black girls from poor or lower-middle-class homes are more likely to carry their babies to term than are white girls from middle- to upper-middle-class homes. The more affluent the girl, the more likely it is that she will opt for an abortion.

As a result, in the white community, teenage pregnancy is a hidden problem: Most parents don't like to acknowledge that it exists, or that it could possibly affect their daughters. There is far too little discussion of this problem among well-educated, well-meaning parents and their children. There are far too many unintended pregnancies in a community that has the resources to do something about it.

The high rate of teenage pregnancy is a reflection of our failure as parents to provide adequate sex education for our children. It is also a reflection of a breakdown in trust and communication between parents and their children. If a girl comes home pregnant, I don't think that she should be punished or blamed for her predicament. I do think that her parents need to take a long, hard look at whether or not they have let their daughter down by not providing her with the information she needed. If the parents have indeed done their job, but their daughter has not heeded their warnings, they need to examine why they failed to "connect" with their daughter on this important issue. At the very least, an unwanted pregnancy should be taken as a sign that more parental guidance is warranted.

Many parents deal with their daughter's pregnancy by rushing her to the doctor for an abortion and then never speaking about the incident again. I think that they are making a terrible mistake. The girl needs to be periodically reminded in a gentle but firm way that if she is sexually active, she must use contraception. Her mother should say, "I hope that you're using your diaphragm [taking your pills] and your partner is using a condom. I don't want you to go through that again, and you certainly don't want anything else to happen [like AIDS] that we can't fix as easily."

This is one of those times when "Don't tell Dad" is completely unacceptable. When a girl is going through an emotionally difficult event such as an unwanted pregnancy or an abortion, both parents should be concerned and involved in the decision-making process. Although a girl may be embarrassed initially at having to tell her father, in the long run she will benefit from having the support of two loving parents. If the relationship between the daughter and the father is such that she is terrified at the thought of him finding out, it is a sign that the family should seek outside counseling.

Although under the "right" set of circumstances, unintended pregnancy can happen to anyone, it is more likely to happen to some girls than to others. The following is a discussion of the kinds of girls who are most likely to get pregnant. Read this section carefully, even if you don't think that your daughter is sexually active or is ever likely to have intercourse in her teens, because that is precisely the kind of girl who heads the list.

The Inexperienced Girl

The scenario is simple: A girl and a boy are on a date. They start to make out—it feels good—they remove some clothes and begin to pet—it feels even better—and then in the passion of the moment, they have intercourse—which may feel a bit strange, or may feel terrific. Then, it's over. The girl never really acknowledges what happened—in some cases, she may not even be sure exactly *what* happened, but at the end of the month, she misses her period. Another month goes by, and she misses another period. By now, she's beginning to worry and tells her mother. The mother is stunned to learn that her sweet, innocent daughter is pregnant. The daughter is terribly embarrassed and humiliated by her own ignorance and can't help but wonder, "How did this happen to me?"

This scenario is more typical than we would like to think. Many girls who get pregnant are so sexually naïve and inexperienced that they may not even know exactly what intercourse is, and they certainly have never thought about getting pregnant. Some fall prey to myths such as:

"You can't get pregnant if your periods are irregular."

"You're safe if he withdraws."

"You only can get pregnant on one or two days in your cycle."

The culprit is ignorance, which can best be overcome by better sex education. Parents have to give this inexperienced girl a crash course in everything she needs to know to protect herself from this ever happening again.

Every girl needs to know that unless she is using contraception, she runs a high risk of getting pregnant, at any time of the month. Every girl needs to know that as long as she is sexually active, she runs the risk of pregnancy.

The Needy Girl

This girl may sense a deterioration in her relationship with her parents and, as a result, may feel unwanted and unloved. She misses the closeness and the intensity of love that she used to feel from her parents. Although she may try to fill the emptiness with a variety of boyfriends, this proves to be unsatisfactory. Swept away by the passion of the moment, the needy girl often "forgets" to use contraception. Before too long, she gets pregnant. This "unplanned" pregnancy is often a reflection of her desire to have a child who will love her in a way in which her parents no longer make her feel loved.

The Competitor

The girl who is locked in a competitive struggle with her mother has to prove that she is the better woman. Typically, she dates a lot of different boys to show that she is the more attractive of the two. But in order to win this contest, she has to "outdo" her mother by getting pregnant and having a baby—her way of saying "Anything you can do, I can do better." This particular scenario often occurs with a mother who had her daughter in her early teens and now must deal with her adolescent while she is still in her twenties—barely out of her own adolescence. The competition between the young adult and the young adolescent is incredibly intense and closely resembles sibling rivalry.

. . .

Although teenage pregnancy is a very serious problem, it is nearly 100 percent preventable. Eradicating unwanted pregnancy, however, will require parents to take more of a leadership role in transmitting important and potentially life-saving information to their daughters.

HOMOSEXUALITY

Up until this point, I've focused solely on heterosexual relationships. We know, however, that around 5 percent of the population is gay, which means that some parents will have daughters who will grow up to be lesbians.

Although harboring homosexual feelings is considered a normal phase for adolescent boys, and in fact, a sizable number of heterosexual males have at least one homosexual encounter in their teenage years, there is very little discussion about homosexuality among teenage girls. I believe that girls also harbor homosexual feelings, but they may manifest themselves in subtle ways.

Being attracted to and excited by a peer of the same sex is a normal developmental step. Young adolescent girls frequently get "crushes" on other girls whom they admire. They may copy their way of dressing or their mannerisms and may feel happy or excited when they're around them. By age 14 or so, these feelings are usually directed toward boys. However, some girls may still be feeling this way toward other girls and may think that they are actually in love. They may be very worried about having homosexual feelings and even more worried about your reaction.

If a 14- or 15-year-old girl professes her love for another girl, her parents should treat it the same way as they would any other crush. Instead of looking shocked and saying, "No daughter of mine can feel that way," a better approach would be, "That's nice, she's such a nice girl, and you're going to meet many other people like her whom you may love even more."

No one at this age is emotionally ready to choose a lifetime sexual partner, and 14- or 15-year-olds are certainly not in touch enough with themselves to be certain that their homosexual feelings are permanent and not fleeting. For now, I would assume that this was a "crush on another girl phase" and leave it at that.

I also think that it's imperative for you to let your daughter know that you will love her if she is gay or straight. There is a high correlation between suicide and homosexuality among teenagers—in fact, according to one recent study, 30 percent of all teenagers who attempt suicide are gay or lesbian. It's understandable why the girl who feels "strange" or "different" and who feels that she has no one to turn to would be driven to such desperation. If you come down hard on your daughter in the belief that you can "change" her, you not only run the risk of driving her to the edge, but you can be assured that she will never talk to you about her feelings again.

If your 18- or 19-year-old daughter, however, tells you that she is in love with another girl, that's a different story. The older adolescent is capable of making those kinds of decisions, and her pronouncement of love should be taken more seriously. However, keep in mind that even at 18 or 20, sexual preference can change. I know of several girls who had lesbian relationships in college, then went on to get married and have children. This is not to suggest that all of them will. There are girls who will be lesbians for their entire lives. But even they may not know their true feelings until they are well out of adolescence.

If you're very disturbed by your daughter's claim to be in love with another girl, I think that you should get some counseling to help you cope with the situation. There are many people who may be perfectly willing to tolerate homosexual behavior in other people's families, but are intolerant when it comes to their own families. In order to preserve your relationship with your daughter, you need to get some professional advice from a qualified therapist.

III

SPECIAL SITUATIONS

TEN: SELF-DESTRUCTIVE
BEHAVIORS

There is nothing that causes parents more anguish than watching their daughter engage in dangerous or self-destructive behaviors. When a child is in pain, parents typically feel helpless and ineffectual. Parents of a troubled girl often feel isolated and lonely—that they are the only parents in the world with this problem. Nothing could be further from the truth.

Adolescents can be very self-destructive in a variety of ways, for a variety of reasons. Some forms of self-destructive behavior are more lethal than others. An adolescent who is abusing drugs, has attempted suicide, or has a severe eating disorder (see Chapter 6) is in serious and imminent danger. Other forms of self-destructive behavior, such as smoking or even shoplifting, may not be life threatening or pose an immediate threat, but may have long-term consequences. In the end, any form of self-destructive behavior is dangerous and requires parental intervention.

Self-destructive behavior is a sign of extreme distress or an underlying emotional problem. Adolescents are not good at articulating their needs. They may be in a great deal of pain and not know why. Very often, the self-destructive girl may be responding to a troubled home. However, even the best of kids, from the best of homes, can be insecure and unhappy or can be goaded into doing dumb and dangerous things. Adolescents—even "good kids"—can be immature and impetuous. Adolescents—even from stable homes with understanding parents—can be overwhelmed by the emotional roller coaster of puberty and can seek solace in unhealthy outlets. Teenagers looking for a "quick fix" or immediate relief for their pain can do things that are desperate and dangerous.

You may be tempted to skip this chapter in the belief that it does not apply to your daughter. I urge you to read it anyway. Very often, parents are the last ones to spot signs of distress in their own children. They are simply too close to the situation, too emotionally involved, and too steeped in denial to accept the fact that their daughter may have a serious problem. When they finally do recognize it, it is often very late, long after the girl first began showing signs of self-destructive behavior. In the case of the thousands of adolescent girls who commit suicide each year, it is too late.

Parents who overlook problems are not necessarily neglectful or uncaring. For one thing, girls often internalize their feelings of anger or distress. Parents, schools, and society in general encourage girls to stifle their aggressive impulses. Displays of anger are considered to be unfeminine. An unhappy boy will typically call attention to his plight by resorting to "acting out" behavior: He will be disruptive at school, come home roaring drunk from a party, or commit an act of vandalism that lands him jail. In contrast, an unhappy girl will often hide her feelings, directing her anger against herself. She will feel worthless and inadequate, but she will respond to this very quietly. When she engages in self-destructive behavior, more often than not it is a cry for help. She is pleading, "Pay attention to me. I may not be able to tell you what's wrong, but please make it okay."

This is not to say that girls never engage in acting out behavior. Some do, but it is not as common as among boys and often takes on different and more subtle forms. Sexual promiscuity and shoplifting are classic female acting out behaviors. However, these forms of acting out are not always obvious to parents, and often the only way that parents discover the problem is when their daughter gets caught, that is, she gets pregnant from careless sex or arrested for stealing.

Parents also miss signs of need because they are genuinely confused by adolescent behavior. I'm often asked, "Adolescents are so moody and volatile so much of the time, how can I tell problem behavior from normal behavior?" Although it may be true that normal adolescents can behave in what adults may consider an abnormal manner, there is a real difference between the normal angst of adolescence and behavior that results from serious emotional problems.

SIGNS OF THE TROUBLED GIRL

Adolescence is a time of intense emotions and frequent mood swings. A "normal" adolescent girl can be ecstatic one minute, and close to tears the next. She can spend the day moping over a boyfriend and the evening giggling on the phone with her friends. Despite the highs and lows, a normal adolescent is a reasonably happy, well-adjusted person.

There is a big difference, however, between a "normal" girl and a troubled girl, in both mood and behavior. The following outlines some of the signs of emotional distress.

Depression. Although few adolescents would meet the diagnostic criteria for a true clinical depression, troubled girls often show at least some of the signs of depression. They include:

- Loss or change in appetite
- Insominia and early rising
- Lack of interest in normal activities
- Obsessive or repetitive self-destructive thoughts such as "Life is not worth living," "I am worthless."

The troubled girl who is showing signs of depression often functions on a very flat emotional level. This girl usually doesn't go from tears to giggles, she seems to be "stuck" in a sad, unhappy mood.

Impulsive behavior. The troubled girl often acts in an irrational, erratic manner. This girl is out of control. She's the girl who in a moment of anger, will pick up a knife and point it at her mother or a sibling. She's the girl who "just meant to give my little brother a little slap" and sends him flying halfway across the room.

Looking for thrills. A troubled girl is more likely to drive in a reckless fashion and is more susceptible to criminal behavior such as shoplifting. On the surface, this girl is looking for the "high" of courting danger or the perverse excitement of doing something wrong and not getting caught. On a deeper level, thrill seeking is a sign of a far more serious problem. The girls whom I have treated for this kind of behavior almost always feel ignored and neglected by their parents. They are seeking "thrills" as a way to fill their emotional void. If a girl is caught engaging in this kind of behavior it should not be dismissed as a teenage "prank." Her parents need to take an honest look at their family situation to see what would drive their daughter to such dangerous behavior.

Self-destructive behavior. The troubled girl is more likely to develop a life-threatening eating disorder or to abuse drugs and alcohol. Girls who engage in this kind of behavior are not "experimenting" or "going through a phase," they are deeply disturbed.

If the troubled girl comes from a troubled family, the situation is all the more difficult. One or both parents may deny or ignore their daughter's emotional problems for fear of exposing their own. However, even parents from stable homes may be concerned that they're going to be blamed for their daughter's problem. I've known many good, well-meaning parents who were afraid to seek outside help because they felt guilty that they were responsible for their daughter's behavior.

I don't believe that parents should torment themselves over past mistakes—not only is it counterproductive, but it could actually hurt your daughter. Even if you missed signs of need in the past, it's not too late to do something about it. The best thing that you can do is to seek professional counseling as quickly as possible, from a qualified therapist who works with teenagers. Letting the problem go untreated could lead to some serious and deadly consequences.

TEEN SUICIDE

It's estimated that as many as a half million teenagers attempt suicide each year and nearly 5000 succeed. Although girls are four to five times more likely than boys to attempt suicide, more boys actually succeed in killing themselves. As a rule, boys choose violent methods, such as handguns, which are both deadly and precise. Girls who try to kill themselves typically take a bottle of tranquilizers or painkillers, which may be enough to require that they have their stomachs pumped, but not quite enough to kill them.

In my experience, many of the girls who attempt suicide really don't want to die, rather, they are desperate to get themselves out of a painful situation. They look to suicide as a way of ridding themselves of their problems, but few actually understand the finality of death. In some cases, the suicide is a desperate cry for help, often because their other, less-dramatic cries have fallen on deaf ears.

Suicide is not the act of a normal girl who is driven over the edge

by a particular incident. Suicide is the act of a seriously troubled girl
—usually from a troubled home—who becomes completely overwhelmed by a difficult situation, and it's not always the situation she
attributes it to. For example, a girl who attempts suicide may blame
her actions on the fact that she recently broke up with her boyfriend,
but fails to say that she and her parents are distant and estranged.
Certainly the breakup with her boyfriend was painful. However, if
this girl had a solid emotional base at home, she would have been
better able to cope with it. Any girl who attempts suicide, or who
even talks about suicide, should be in treatment. A girl who says,
"I'm so unhappy, I could kill myself" is not simply blowing off steam.
At the very least, she is telling you that she is in pain, and her threat
needs to be taken very seriously. Parents may be tempted to dismiss
such talk with, "Oh, she's only looking for attention," but even if
that's true, they should wonder why their daughter feels that she
has to resort to such desperate talk to *get* their attention.

SUICIDE PREVENTION

Teen suicide can be contagious. When a teenager kills herself (or
himself), the entire community feels the shock wave. The story of
the tragic death is highlighted on the nightly news and in the local
newspapers. Very often, the next day or the next week, another
teenager kills herself, and the story receives even more attention.

Teenagers tend to romanticize death. In the world of a teenager,
death does not appear to be final—somehow people continue to live
on. Teenage heroes, such as Jimmy Dean and Elvis Presley, are
talked about as if they were still living. When a teenager kills herself
and is "immortalized" on the news, it feeds into the belief that the
dead continue to be part of this world. A vulnerable teenager who is
on the edge of killing herself, may get so caught up in this fantasy
that she decides to go ahead and do it.

After a suicide occurs in a community, it's very important for the
local schools and for parents to deal with this issue in a realistic,
unromantic way. The school should arrange for a specialist to come
in and conduct a suicide prevention program. Parents should discuss
the death in an open, frank manner. Teenagers need to be reminded
that death is final—that the teenager who killed herself has been
cremated or embalmed and is now in a coffin six feet under the

ground. The dead girl will never see her parents or her friends again and, in reality, will probably soon be forgotten by all but a few people.

Teenagers also need to know that suicide is not the act of a normal person. Normal people, even unhappy people, don't kill themselves. Suicide is aberrant behavior and a sign of profound problems.

Suicide is not a solution—it's a quick way out of a problem. Similar to drugs and alcohol, it offers immediate relief, but it also exacts an enormous toll. When teenagers are made to truly understand the price they must pay for this relief, I believe that many would not view it as a viable option.

SUBSTANCE ABUSE

Suicide is the ultimate form of self-destructive behavior, but there are other ways that teenage girls inflict damage on their physical and emotional selves.

Substance abuse is a crutch that adolescents often turn to as an escape from their problems, or to make themselves feel better, without recognizing the long-term and potentially lethal consequences of their actions. The teenager who is looking to numb the pain, or the teenager who is looking for instant acceptance and popularity, can often find it by taking a drink or smoking a cigarette.

Cigarette Smoking

Although adults are quitting smoking in droves, more and more teenage girls are taking up the habit. In fact, today more teenage girls than teenage boys are puffing on cigarettes. A recent study noted that 18.1 percent of all high school senior girls smoke, as compared to 17.4 percent of all senior boys.

In the adult population, for the first time, there are as many women smokers as male smokers. If the present trend continues, within a few years more women will be smoking than men.

Parents should be very concerned about these statistics. Smoking is not a "harmless phase" or a habit that your daughter will outgrow. It is a deadly habit, especially for women.

In 1987, lung cancer became the number one cancer killer of women, surpassing even breast cancer. Smoking is also a major culprit in heart disease, the leading cause of death among women.

Cigarettes are linked to high blood pressure, various other forms of cancer, stroke, bronchitis, emphysema, osteoporosis, and premature menopause.

Although the effects of cigarette smoking may not hit until adulthood, smoking is very much a teenage problem. Roughly 90 percent of all smokers start before age 18, with the majority lighting up for the first time between ages 11 to 13. A national survey of junior high and high school students showed that by eighth grade, 44 percent had experimented with cigarettes and 14 percent had lit up within the past thirty days. Although many of these kids are not hard-core smokers yet, many will be in time.

Teenage girls may begin smoking because of peer pressure or because they think it is sophisticated and "adult." But there's another reason why girls become so attached to their cigarettes—they believe that smoking keeps them thin. The overwhelming number of teenage girls who smoke cite weight control as the primary reason, and the cigarette companies play up to this belief by marketing brands like Virginia Slims. All too often, when a teenage girl is hungry, she reaches for a cigarette instead of food and thus learns to control her eating by smoking. In addition, nicotine may have a mild effect on metabolism, helping to burn calories faster, which is why many smokers begin to gain weight after they quit. (Eventually, the metabolism normalizes and the weight gain stops.)

If you want your daughter to live a long and healthy life, you must make sure that she doesn't start smoking, and the earlier you begin emphasizing the downside of smoking, the better. One or two discussions citing the risks of smoking are not sufficient. You need to engage your daughter in an ongoing dialogue about smoking long before she would even consider trying a cigarette. But in order to be effective, you need to know how to talk about smoking in a manner that your daughter can relate to.

Reasons Not to Smoke

The health risks. Telling an 11-year-old not to smoke because she will get lung cancer in thirty years, or that she will keel over from a heart attack at age 50, is not going to have the desired effect. The typical adolescent has a great deal of difficulty projecting herself as an adult and is more focused on the present than the future.

This is not to say that children and adolescents should not be told about the health risks involved in smoking. They certainly should be made aware of the potential hazards of lighting up, but keep in mind that this alone will not stop them from doing so. To be successful, parents need to focus on their daughter's more immediate concerns.

If your daughter is athletically inclined, point out that smoking will interfere with her endurance and will hamper her athletic performance. By lighting up, she will lose her competitive edge.

In addition, many studies have shown that adolescents are very concerned about dental health. Many teenagers would be surprised to hear that cigarette smoking can cause severe damage to teeth and gums. I believe that most adolescents would be very turned off at the prospect of one day having to spend hours in the dentist's chair having their teeth drilled and gums scraped, all because they smoked.

Cosmetic concerns. Adolescent girls care about their looks, and parents should capitalize on this concern in presenting arguments against smoking. Cigarettes stain the teeth a yellowish color that is so unattractive that there are toothpastes on the market that promise to bleach the teeth back to their natural color. Let your daughter know that none of these products can ever restore the teeth to their original state and in fact can cause damage to tooth enamel.

Tell your daughter that smoking also causes bad breath, which can be a turnoff to boys—especially when it comes to kissing. Point out that although smokers are constantly using breath spray or chewing gum, it never fully camouflages the odor. The smell of smoke also sticks to hair and clothing. In addition, smoking can cause the fingers on the smoking hand to turn a yellowish color.

The social stigma. Let your daughter know that smoking is fast becoming a social liability. Point out signs in public buildings and restaurants that don't allow smoking or isolate smokers in specific sections. Tell your daughter that many employers ban smoking in the workplace.

It's important to point out that there are many boys who will not date a smoker.

Smoking limits contraceptive choices. Teenage girls need to know that women who smoke cannot take birth control pills. Studies show that women who smoke and take the Pill run a 40 percent greater risk of developing a serious cardiovascular problem, which may lead to stroke or heart attack. A responsible doctor will not let a smoker take the Pill. Therefore, by smoking, your daughter is limiting her choices of contraception.

It's harder to quit during pregnancy. If your daughter is thinking about having children one day, you can point out that she'd better not start smoking. Smoking during pregnancy poses a severe risk to the fetus, can complicate the pregnancy, and can cause birth defects. Women who get pregnant are routinely advised to quit. However, this is a lot easier said than done. Under the best of circumstances, it's difficult for women to quit, but it can be a real ordeal during a stressful situation such as pregnancy. Therefore, tell your daughter she's ahead of the game if she never starts smoking.

Weighty issues. If your daughter already smokes, chances are if you talk to her about stopping, she will say, "Well, if I stopped I'd get so fat." You need to point out that although some women may gain a few pounds temporarily, she doesn't have to. Women who are careful not to overeat generally don't gain that much weight. Furthermore, exercise can provide the same benefit as cigarettes in terms of weight control, but with none of the lethal consequences. In addition, exercise actually helps prevent many of the same diseases that cigarettes can cause.

Let her know that she's being used. Make your daughter aware of how cigarette ads are actually targeted toward the young. When you see a billboard depicting an attractive, athletic couple in ski clothes, puffing away on cigarettes, you can say something to the effect of, "Gee, the way they're smoking, I don't think they'll make it down the slope." Then ask your daughter, "What do you think this ad is saying about cigarettes? What are they trying to make you think? Do you think they're telling the truth?"

This kind of discussion with a 10- or 11-year-old can be very effective in terms of teaching her how to decipher the hidden messages in ads. In addition, no adolescent is going to feel good about being manipulated and lied to.

Tips for Parents Who Smoke

Ideally, all children should be raised in smoke-free homes. However, a third of all American adults still smoke, therefore, it is likely that many teenage girls live in homes where one or both parents smoke.

If you or your spouse smoke, you may feel powerless to stop your daughter from smoking for fear of her saying, "Well, if it's so bad, then why do you [and/or Dad/Mom] do it?"

Therefore, to spare themselves the pain of confrontation, many parents may tacitly condone their daughter's smoking. I feel that this is a terrible mistake. It is simply not fair to condemn your daughter to the potential hazards of smoking simply because you don't want to quit or are unable to. As a parent, it's your responsibility to speak up. If your daughter tries to turn the tables and confronts you about your smoking, I would deal with her very honestly. I would say, "Well, it's true that I smoke, however I started years before we knew how dangerous it is. I really want to stop, but boy, it's very hard to do. Each time I stop, it's very painful. One day, I hope to quit. But just because I smoke, it doesn't mean that it's right or that it's smart. I love you, and I just want to spare you the pain that I've gone through."

Rather than admit that they can't control their cigarette habit, many parents may be tempted to say, "I'm an adult and I can smoke if I want to. You are a teenager and you cannot." Teenage girls smoke so that they can be adult. A girl doesn't need to hear that smoking is an acceptable adult activity—that will make it all the more alluring. What she does need to hear is that smoking is an unacceptable activity at any age.

Alcohol: The Drug of Choice

Alcohol is the number one drug used—and often abused—by teenagers. Ironically, most teenagers, and even parents, don't think of alcohol as a drug.

Unlike other mood-altering drugs, such as marijuana, alcohol is legal—at least for adults. However, despite the fact that it is illegal for teenagers under 18 (in some states under 21) to drink, that doesn't seem to stop them. According to recent studies, 92 percent of all high school seniors have used alcohol, and 20 percent of all 14- to 17-year-olds are considered to be "problem drinkers." Many are girls. We know that 5 percent of all women are problem drinkers, and a good number began drinking during adolescence.

The fact that alcohol is so easily available may be the reason why it is literally impossible to keep it out of the hands of adolescents. Many homes have well-stocked liquor cabinets and refrigerators full of beer or wine. At every social occasion, from weddings to bar mitzvahs to graduation parties, the alcohol flows freely. Unlike illegal drugs, in many states alcohol can be purchased everywhere from supermarkets to convenience stores.

In some families, teenagers are permitted to drink at home in the mistaken belief that by doing so, they will learn how to handle alcohol. However, studies show that just the opposite is true. Teenagers who are given access to alcohol, that is, who are allowed to mix drinks for company and even pour a few for themselves, are more prone to develop drinking problems than those raised in homes where drinking is strictly off limits.

Some parents may be somewhat casual about drinking because they tend to underestimate the risks associated with alcohol abuse. When a parent hears that his or her child has been caught drinking, the initial reaction is often a relieved, "Well, at least she's not using drugs." Nothing could be further from the truth. Alcohol is a drug, and a potent one at that. It can be a lethal drug for teenage girls.

The Risks

Alcohol is a drug the chemical name of which is ethanol. It works by depressing the central nervous system. One or two drinks may make an adult woman feel "high," that is, slightly euphoric. In many cases, more than two drinks may cause changes in mood and behavior, compromising judgment and ability to perform such tasks as driving. Teenagers in general cannot handle liquor as well as adults. However, due to their smaller size, teenage girls will feel the effects of alcohol even faster than boys.

A girl who is high or drunk is not going to be able to make intelligent decisions at appropriate times. She may risk her life by getting into a car driven by a friend who is in no shape to drive. In fact the leading cause of death among teenagers is automobile accidents, most involving a driver who has been drinking.

A girl who is not thinking clearly may also make other serious mistakes. She may engage in risky sexual behavior, that is, having intercourse without using a condom, or lacking the wit to say no, engaging in sex when she doesn't want to at all.

In addition, boys under the influence of alcohol may behave quite differently when they are drunk than when they are sober. After a few drinks, some boys can become very aggressive and violent.

Given the prevalence of alcohol, it is very likely that your daughter will encounter drinking in a social situation. Even if you forbid your daughter to use alcohol, she will undoubtedly see her friends using it at parties or be at someone's house when a group decides that it would be fun to raid the liquor cabinet. Therefore, you have to prepare your daughter for the likely event that one day she will have to make a choice between drinking or abstaining.

The Rules of Drinking

At what age can she drink? I would absolutely not condone drinking before it is legal to do so in your state. First, you don't want to communicate the message that it is okay to break the law. Second, teenagers physically cannot handle alcohol.

If your daughter balks and says, "Well, you and Mom (or Dad) drink," you need to point out the differences between an adult and a teenager. You can say, "Yes, it's true that on occasion I may have a glass of wine with dinner or a drink when we go out. But my body has stopped growing, alcohol doesn't affect me the same way that it affects you. And because I am an adult, I know my limits. I know when I've had enough, I know when to stop. And you will too when you're my age."

At what age can she go to a party with drinking? The younger adolescent (from age 11 to 15) should be given strict instructions that if alcohol is being served at a party, you expect her to leave—it is simply not the proper environment for a young teenager. It may be easier if you can get two or three of her friends' parents to establish the same rule. That way, your daughter won't be the only one who has to leave. (You also want to find out who was responsible for serving alcohol at that party and have a forceful conversation with them about what a foolish action that was.)

From your daughter's point of view, you must recognize that having to admit that her mother won't let her stay at a party where there is drinking is going to be very difficult for her. Let her know that you understand her dilemma. "I know it's hip to drink, and some kids think it's cool. I know that it's very hard to say, 'My mother won't let me.' But the reason that I won't let you is that I care about you too much to put you in danger."

It may actually make it easier for your daughter to say no if you threaten to impose a specific punishment. For example, you can tell her that if you ever hear that she was at a party with drinking, she's going to be grounded for two months. That way she can tell her friends, "I've got to leave because if my mom finds out, I won't be able to go out for two months, and it's just not worth it."

I think that you need a different approach with a 16- or 17-year-old. In her case, there may be older teenagers at the party who can drink legally, and it is unfair to expect her to leave. Therefore, you need to make it clear that she can party with people who drink, as long as she herself doesn't.

Educate her about the effects of alcohol. It's important for a teenage girl to understand the physiological effects of alcohol. She needs to know that when she's drunk, she's not herself; she may say and do things that she wouldn't if she were sober.

Girls should be told that the drunken state is actually very unattractive; you look sloppy, your speech becomes slurred, your breath is bad, and you are generally out of control. A girl who is concerned about her appearance will not like the prospect of looking so disheveled.

Alcohol is fattening. One of the most effective ways to get teenage girls not to drink is to stress how fattening liquor can be. Girls who are watching every calorie are going to be put off by the fact that there are a 100 calories in a mere 3.5 ounces of wine, and a mixed drink such as rum and Coke, a favorite of teenagers, has a whopping 350! Stress the fact that there is no nutritive value at all in alcohol, and in fact, there is evidence that it may actually slow down your metabolism.

The driving connection. Boys are usually the ones who drive on a date, and therefore, your daughter has to know that it's not enough that she doesn't drink, but she needs to make sure that her date remains sober and clearheaded. Tell her that teenagers killed in car accidents typically have a much lower level of alcohol in their blood than do adults who are involved in similar accidents. Even if after a few drinks her boyfriend says, "Oh, don't worry about me, I know what I'm doing," or "I drive even better after a few drinks," she should either call a cab or call you to take her home.

Some of the more responsible teenagers select one member of their group as the "designated driver" for the evening, that is, the one who agrees not to drink so she or he can drive the others home safely. I would encourage my daughter to work out a similar arrangement with her friends.

Be sure to let your daughter know that she can always call you to drive her home if her date or "ride" has had too much to drink. Make sure that she knows that you won't be angry, rather, you would be proud of her maturity.

Learning her limits. I would stress to my daughter that even when she is legally eligible to drink, it is not a license to get drunk. She needs to know that part of growing up is learning to set limits for herself and learning how to drink responsibly. One or two drinks during the course of an evening—when she is also eating—will in all likelihood not have an adverse affect. Five or six drinks will definitely interfere with her judgment and can even make her sick.

Your daughter also needs to know that alcohol should not be a prerequisite to having fun. If she can't enjoy the company of a group of her friends without drinking, then she is becoming overly dependent on alcohol, and it is becoming too important in her life.

If a teenage girl is abusing alcohol, she should be treated as soon as her parents become aware of her problem. If your daughter comes home drunk once, I would not immediately assume that she was alcohol dependent. I would, however, discuss her actions with her, carefully pointing out the risks that she was taking, and would then implement some form of disciplinary measure. However, if she comes home drunk as frequently as once a month, I would get her into an alcohol treatment program, preferably one that was geared to teenagers. I would not dismiss it as a lark or something that all teenagers do. Call your local hospital or chapter of Alcoholics Anonymous to find an appropriate treatment program.

Other Drugs

Marijuana

If alcohol is the drug of first choice among adolescents, marijuana runs a strong second. About 3 million 10- to 17-year-olds have used this drug. Although alcohol and to some extent cocaine have eroded marijuana's following among high school students, studies show that nearly half of all high school seniors have used the drug at least once.

Marijuana is a derivative of the common hemp plant and has been used as a mild intoxicant for about 5000 years. Marijuana is usually smoked in the form of a cigarette. For the occasional user, the risks of marijuana are not that great. However, as does alcohol, marijuana can impair judgment and coordination. Therefore, driving under the influence of marijuana is every bit as dangerous as driving under the influence of alcohol.

Although there is some controversy over whether or not marijuana is addictive, I do believe that people can become dependent on this drug. In fact I have treated teenagers who couldn't make it through a day without using marijuana. Excessive use of marijuana can result in general fatigue, apathy, and an inability to function normally. Preoccupation with marijuana is particularly bad because it takes an adolescent's focus away from the more important things in life—her schoolwork, her friends, and her family.

When marijuana was first rediscovered by the baby boom generation in the late 1960s, teenagers were barraged with reports about the drug's potential dangers. Most of those stories turned out to be false. Marijuana does not make you sterile, or make you crazy, or turn you into a heroin addict. The overly hysterical propaganda was completely ineffective. It did not deter kids from smoking pot, but it made it difficult to talk sensibly about the very real risks posed by this and other mood-altering drugs.

I recommend that you talk to your daughter in a thoughtful, rational way. First, I would express concern for her safety. Make sure she knows that someone who has been smoking marijuana should not drive. Marijuana can have a subtle effect on thought processes and reflexes, and the person who has been smoking pot may not realize the drug's potent effect. Warn your daughter, "You wouldn't get in a car with someone who's drunk, and you should not get in a car with someone who's stoned, even if he swears up and down that he's fine, because chances are, he's not."

Second, I would emphasize that marijuana is illegal. Tell your daughter that if she is caught smoking marijuana, she may have to face the legal consequences, which vary from state to state. In addition, whether or not she is caught, using marijuana may haunt her in the future. Recently, a nominee to the Supreme Court had to take his name out of consideration because he had been seen smoking marijuana earlier in his career. The public mood has swung strongly against drug use, and there is simply no telling how a history of drug use may affect a future career.

Finally, I would discuss why it is so damaging to rely on drugs to elevate your mood or to drown your sorrows. Tell your daughter: "If you have friends who are interesting and who care about you, it shouldn't be necessary to use marijuana or alcohol to liven up the party or to make you feel better. It's so much better—and so much more fulfilling—to get real emotional support from real friends and, of course, your family."

Cocaine

As marijuana use has declined among high school students, an even more potent illegal drug is gaining in popularity—cocaine. About 800,000 adolescents have tried this deadly drug. Cocaine is a stimulant found in the leaves of the coca plant, genus *Erythroxylon*. The leaves are dried and ground into a fine, white powder, which can be inhaled, or injected intravenously.

Cocaine creates an immediate euphoric high that can be very alluring—and very deceptive. Once the drug wears off, the cocaine user can feel extremely low and depressed.

A new and more deadly form of cocaine known as crack, which is smoked, has infiltrated the cities and even the suburbs of America. Crack is one of the most additive substances in the world. Whereas it takes a heroin addict two to three years to become physically hooked, crack takes a mere six months. Some people become addicted after just one or two tries.

Cocaine is not a social drug; it is a serious and potentially lethal substance, especially for girls and women. The drug can cause serious damage to the heart, which can lead to heart attack or a fatal arrhythmia. Every girl and every woman should know that if she uses cocaine, she is taking a terrible risk with her life. Women's bodies are particularly vulnerable to cocaine's lethal affects. Even if you've used the drug already, there's no way of knowing whether that next snort or puff will be the one that gets to your heart.

I would also stress that people who care about each other do not ask each other to do dangerous things. Say, "Remember, if someone really cares about you, they would never ask you to do anything that could hurt you. Anyone who wants you to use cocaine is no friend."

There are some girls who may protest, "Well, what do you think, that I'll become an *addict*? I can handle it . . . really I can." At that point, you need to have a serious discussion about the perils of addiction.

Most teenagers tend to regard drug addicts as somehow subhuman —they simply cannot imagine that they would ever end up in that state. You need to set them straight by explaining, "No addict started out in life thinking that she or he was going to become an addict. No one starts with drugs or alcohol believing that he or she is going to become enslaved to them. Everybody—even the addicts that you turn up your nose at—believed that they could handle it. But you reach a point where you lose control, and for everybody that point is different. You begin relying more and more on the drug. Maybe you start by using it so you can loosen up at a party. Then you turn to it when you're depressed. And pretty soon, you're miserable if you can't have it. It's not that hard to become an addict."

I think that every girl who is considering experimenting with drugs needs to be told that she is not immune to addiction, and that people just like her can and do get hooked.

Designer Drugs

Also known as "boutique" drugs, these substances are chemical concoctions produced in home or private laboratories. Depending on their ingredients, these mood-altering drugs may be stimulants or depressants.

You can never really be sure what's in so-called designer drugs. There have been cases of designer drugs causing severe neurological damage as well as other physical harm. If you use these drugs, you are literally taking your life in your hands.

Make sure your daughter is aware of designer drugs and their potential danger. Tell her, "Never take any pill or medicine that someone tells you will make you 'feel good,' because it may be a very dangerous drug. It's not going to feel very good to end up in the hospital in a coma."

To emphasize my point, I would add that you would never dream of buying an opened bottle of painkillers from the drugstore because you would worry about whether anyone had tampered with it. "Using a designer drug is a risk like taking painkillers from a bottle that had already been opened by someone else at the store. You could end up dead."

Deadly Combinations

As if designer drugs weren't bad enough, parents must now deal with a new style of substance abuse that can be equally deadly. Teenagers looking for an amphetamine-type "rush" are combining alcohol with diet pills. Taken in large amounts, this combination can cause brain hemorrhage and death.

For some people, even legal, over-the-counter diet pills by themselves can be lethal. A chemical known as phenylpropanolamine (PPA) used in some diet pills can cause irregular heartbeat and stroke in susceptible individuals.

The teenager who experiments with mixing alcohol and drugs may not understand the potential lethal consequences of her actions. She is looking for a quick high, she is not looking for a quick death. Parents have to make sure that their daughters know their bodies are simply too valuable—and too vulnerable—to be subjected to that kind of abuse.

There are certain values that parents need to instill in their daughters, and one of the major ones is the responsibility of every individual to take care of her body. Teenagers need to be reminded that the body they were born with is the only one they will ever have. Tell your daughter, "You have only one body, and if you don't take care of it, you will pay a price down the road. In some cases, if you take unnecessary risks and use drugs, particularly dangerous combinations of drugs—you may have to pay for it a lot sooner. You have only one heart and only one brain, and playing with drugs is like playing Russian roulette. You wouldn't put a gun to your head or your heart. Like a bullet, these drugs can permanently damage these organs."

There are some teenagers who, no matter how much you try to educate them, simply will not listen. They will use drugs anyway, and many will get into trouble.

GIRLS WHO ARE PRONE TO SUBSTANCE ABUSE

The girl who feels worthless. To a certain extent, all teenage girls suffer from periods of low self-esteem, however, some girls have an especially poor sense of self. These girls generally come from homes where they do not get the love and emotional support they need to make them feel confident and secure. Because they are so vulnerable to peer pressure, these girls are at special risk of developing a drinking problem or succumbing to another form of substance abuse.

The girl who provides her parent(s) with vicarious thrills. Parents who come from homes that were particularly rigid in terms of discipline often react in just the opposite way with their own children. They develop a laissez-faire attitude in which their children are allowed—and I think encouraged—to do whatever they like. These parents are actually reliving their fantasy of their own missed adolescence through their children. They revel in their children's wild antics and are secretly pleased when they are caught drinking or using drugs.

Teenagers are always testing and pushing the limits, but unfortunately, in these kinds of homes, there are none. Therefore, girls raised by these parents are out of control and are very likely to become problem drinkers or marijuana or cocaine abusers.

The parent with a problem. The parent with a drinking or drug problem is going to be the last one to reprimand his or her child about drinking or using drugs. Chances are, he or she is too busy denying and covering up his/her own problem.

Children who are raised in these homes often react in one of two ways: Some are so disgusted by the sight of drunkenness or drugged behavior that they stay as far away from liquor and drugs as possible. However, others may begin drinking or using drugs themselves.

If a parent has a problem with alcohol or drugs, it is incumbent on his or her spouse, or other adult members of the family, to get him or her into treatment, if not for his/her own sake, then for the sake of the children. Very often, family members join with the substance-dependent person in trying to hide or make excuses for the addiction. This is a terrible mistake and is terribly unfair for any children condemned to live in that household.

DOES YOUR DAUGHTER ABUSE DRUGS OR ALCOHOL?

If your daughter confesses that she's smoked marijuana once or twice, or had a drink, I would not assume that she is drug dependent. I would review all the reasons why she should avoid using illegal drugs and hope that she listens.

However, there are times when kids really do get into serious trouble with drugs, and often their parents are the last to know, because they are missing the telltale signs. Here are some warning signs that could suggest that your daughter has a problem with drugs.

Secretive behavior. Does your daughter seem unusually aloof or secretive? Has she begun locking the door to her room? This is often a sign that she is involved in something that she knows is wrong and is troubled by it. The obvious way in which she tries to shut you out is her way of calling for help.

A change for the worse in behavior. A teenager who is drug dependent may exhibit a marked change in behavior and/or outlook. The girl who was once happy may seem extremely moody and depressed. The girl who enjoyed getting out and doing certain activities may seem lethargic and uninterested.

Poor academic performance. Drugs and academics don't mix, and the girl who is abusing drugs will probably begin losing ground at school. If your daughter's grades suddenly plummet, and you're hearing things from teachers like "She seems so bored, she can barely stay awake in class," it's time to think about the possibility that she may be using drugs.

Hanging around with the wrong crowd. If your daughter has begun spending time with a group rumored to drink or use drugs—or both —it's definitely time to take action. If you ask your daughter whether she is drinking or doing drugs, she'll deny it—few people with a substance-abuse problem ever admit it, often not even to themselves. Instead, say firmly, "I know that you're hanging out with kids who have a reputation for using drugs [drinking], and I'm not going to ask you what you're doing personally, but I've made an appointment with a substance-abuse counselor for next week, and we're going together." Period, no discussion. If your daughter swears up and down that she doesn't have a problem, you can say, "Well, we want to keep it that way, so we're going to see the counselor anyway."

A skillful counselor will be able to recognize problem behavior and will advise you about further action.

TREATMENT

If there is a drug or alcohol problem, it is absolutely critical for parents to get their daughter into treatment as fast as possible. I recommend a program that is specifically geared for teenagers. Programs that are geared for the hard-core adult addict are very restrictive and often require participants to live on site, sometimes indefinitely. Depending on the level of drug dependency, this may be completely unnecessary for an adolescent.

In many cases, your daughter may be able to be treated in a less restrictive program held after school or on weekends. For information on programs for teenagers, see the Resources section on page 238.

PREVENTING PROBLEMS

Parenting is not a precise science—there's no magic formula that will insure that a girl grows up to be healthy, happy, and drug free. However, there are many things that parents can do to lessen the odds that something will go wrong.

Be attentive and concerned. Parents should make it their business to know what's going on in their daughter's life. The best way for parents to do this is by spending time with their daughter—there is no substitute for love and attention.

Adolescents need parental supervision. Despite their protests, they also want it. At the same time they are striving for independence, they need to feel cared about and watched over.

Do you know where your daughter is? Adolescents should not be left night after night to fend for themselves while their parents work late or pursue their own activities. An occasional night out for parents is okay—but on most nights, at least one parent should be at home.

Adolescents should not be allowed to disappear on the weekends without their parents knowing where they are and that they are being properly supervised. Parents should know their daughter's friends and should know how and where she spends her free time.

Despite your best efforts, your daughter may get into trouble. If this happens, the best thing you can do is talk to her, and if necessary, get help. Appropriate intervention at the right time can help get a troubled girl back on track. It might even save her life.

ELEVEN: DIVORCE AND STEPFAMILIES

I try very hard not to do anything to upset either of my parents. If I buy something that's too expensive, my dad will call my mother and complain, "Oh, she doesn't really need it," and they'll start fighting over it. If my dad says I can do something that my mother doesn't like, she'll call him up and scream at him. I'm stuck in the middle. It's not fair.

—Danielle, age 13

In an ideal world, every girl would come of age in an intact family, with two loving, devoted parents. However, the reality is quite different for millions of adolescent girls.

With roughly one out of two new marriages ending in divorce, more and more families are fitting into a nontraditional mold. About 23 percent of all children in the United States live with one divorced parent, usually their mothers. Even children who reside with two parents may not be living with two biological parents. Today, more than 20 percent of all married-with-children households include a stepparent.

Changes in marriage and family have profoundly affected the lives of children. We know from several recent studies that the effects of divorce on children can be both devastating and long lasting. Children of divorce often blame themselves for their parents' breakup and suffer from a terrible loss of self-esteem. As adults, they often have difficulty forming permanent relationships.

Depending on the timing of the divorce, girls can be especially hard hit. Young adolescent girls in particular have a great deal of difficulty coping with their parents' marital problems. This is not surprising considering that puberty itself can be a difficult adjustment for most girls. In addition, girls are more sensitive to the interpersonal nuances between their parents and may find them more disturbing. Young adolescent girls also have more trouble adjusting to the remarriage of a parent.

However, being raised by a divorced parent or with a stepparent does not automatically mean that a girl will fare poorly, either during her adolescence or later in life. In fact, girls can emerge from these experiences as strong and happy as girls who are raised in more traditional settings. Whether or not a girl is scarred by her parents' divorce, however, often depends on a number of factors, but the most important one is her relationship with her parents and their relationship with each other.

In the best-case scenario, both parents have mutually decided that they would be better off living apart, and without any malice or rancor, go their separate ways. Although they may be living apart, they are keenly aware of their responsibility to their daughter and have her best interest at heart. Unfortunately, this rarely happens. Very often there is anger and lingering resentment between the divorced parents that can fester for years. Wrapped up in their own problems, they miss important signs of need on the part of their daughter. Sadly, their daughter gets caught in between and is often used as a pawn by her parents to hurt each other. As a result, the girl feels conflicted and torn between her parents and suffers untold hurts herself.

Sensitive, concerned parents who are determined to put the needs of their daughter first can avoid many of these pitfalls. But to do this, parents need to be made aware of the particular dynamics that emerge between a daughter and her divorced parents and the ways that they may be unwittingly hurting their daughter. They also need to understand the ways that they can cushion the blow for their daughter, and timing the divorce correctly is one of them.

TIMING THE DIVORCE OR SEPARATION

Coping with a divorce is never easy for children, but there are times when it may be more difficult than others. That's why I feel that, if possible, parents should try to time a divorce or remarriage to occur during a period of growth when their daughter will be hurt the least.

Of course, there are exceptions to the rule. If one parent is physically or verbally abusive to the other, or has a serious problem such as substance abuse, separation at any time is preferable to keeping the family together.

However, if the situation is not intolerable, parents should try to avoid breaking up the family during a time when it would have the most detrimental effect on their daughter. Children around the ages of 5 to 6 have a tremendous amount of difficulty coping with divorce. During these years, children make tremendous developmental leaps; they begin "real school" and start to develop a separate identity outside of their homes. In order to accomplish these tasks well, they need security and stability.

Ages 11 to 13 are equally critical, especially for girls who must cope with the onslaught of puberty. Because young adolescent girls are so overwhelmed at this time with their own concerns, I feel that it is important not to burden them with a split between their parents. Breaking up a household, having one parent move out of the house, or moving with a parent into a completely new home, can be quite a jolt for an adolescent. Therefore, I advise parents to avoid a formal separation or divorce during the 11 to 13 years.

Young adolescent girls are very self-absorbed with their own feelings and problems, which is a perfectly normal part of the maturing process. During this unsettled period, they especially need their fathers—an adolescent girl does not need to be burdened by the belief that she somehow has driven him away. If her parents force their daughter to focus on their marital problems, it will distract her from her basic adolescent tasks of establishing her own identity and moving toward independence from her parents. This is not only terribly unfair but can actually thwart an adolescent girl's emotional growth and development.

I'm not saying that parents have to lie and act as if they are happy. They don't need to pretend that they love each other, nor do they have to spend a lot of time together. I am saying that the shock and finality of a divorce should be postponed until a girl has passed this early adolescent stage.

BETWEEN DIVORCED MOTHERS
AND DAUGHTERS

After a divorce, unless the couple specifically opts for joint custody, child custody is usually awarded to the mother. The mother bears the responsibility of raising the children, and in addition, usually has to work outside the home whether she wants to or not. Generally, after a divorce, a husband does better economically than his former wife, and this causes a great deal of contention between the two.

The mother is typically left with less money, but more work. It is the mother who spends the most time with her daughter, and it is the mother who most often must deal with her daughter's adolescent mood swings and behavior. It is the mother who is left with the tougher job.

Although many adolescent girls and their divorced mothers develop close, supportive relationships during this time, very often the added burdens placed on the mother can adversely affect her relationship with her daughter. The following section reviews the troublesome modes of behavior that mothers can get locked in and their potential risks to the adolescent girl.

The Angry Mother. This mother is simply furious at her former spouse and is so blinded by her anger that she tries to turn her daughter against her father. The Angry Mother may resent her ex-husband for sins committed during marriage, for his lack of generosity during the divorce settlement, or may even become enraged when he remarries. Very often, the Angry Mother rationalizes her behavior by believing that what she is doing is actually good for her daughter. Under the guise of telling her daughter "the truth," this mother looks for every way to knock her ex-husband. "Oh, he manages to find time to date that woman, but he can't seem to send the support checks on time." Or "He knew you were having an important test tomorrow, he should have called to wish you 'good luck.' " If the girl has strong feelings for her father, she's going to feel compelled to defend him, and that's going to lead to a fight with her mother. If the girl's relationship with her father is fragile, she may join forces with her mother, which will only further alienate her father. No matter how you look at it, the daughter of the Angry Mother loses in a big way.

The Angry Mother has to step back from the situation and look at the harm that she is inflicting on her daughter. She needs to honestly reexamine her motives and to ask herself: "I know I hate him, but am I punishing my daughter with my hate?"

I know one Angry Mother who, when she became aware of the devastating effect her anger was having on her daughter, decided that the best solution was to move away from the city in which her husband lived. The mother and father agreed that the girl would spend the school year with her mother, but would spend all of her holidays and summer vacation with her father. The mother found that she was better able to cope with her anger when she did not have to deal with her husband on a frequent basis. The daughter also preferred this arrangement because she no longer had to deal with her mother's wrath or incessant questions after her weekends with Dad.

Although moving thousands of miles away may be impractical for some, it is possible to emotionally distance yourself from your former spouse. You don't need to fuel your anger by demanding that your daughter report back everything going on in his home, you don't need to know who he's dating or what he's spending his money on. In fact, very often, the less you know about his personal life, the better, and the quicker you will get on to developing a personal life of your own.

The Overwhelmed Mother. It's hard enough for women to work and raise children when they have a husband who can share in the responsibility, but it can be a bone-crushing task for the single mother. The Overwhelmed Mother feels worn out and exhausted. Very often, she turns to her adolescent daughter to help ease her burden. Although it's perfectly all right to ask a daughter to help out around the house, the Overwhelmed Mother expects her daughter to shoulder much of the housework and care for younger siblings. However, her daughter, who is absorbed by her own adolescent concerns, is not particularly interested in serving as coparent with her mother. When the daughter fails to meet the mother's expectations, the mother becomes very resentful of her daughter. The daughter senses her mother's disappointment and disapproval and feels that she must be at fault. If a mother finds that she is very resentful of her daughter, it's a sign that she may be expecting too much. It is unfair to expect a teenager to act like an adult or assume adult responsibility. The Overwhelmed Mother needs to come to terms with her feelings and to admit to herself, "Yes, I have a lot to do. Yes, I sometimes feel like I can't handle it, but it's not my daughter's fault. It's not fair to expect her to pick up the slack."

It is fair, however, to ask your ex-husband for more help, and I'm not just talking about money. Perhaps he can pick up the kids one evening a week from their after-school activities, maybe he could take them out to dinner on nights when you have to work late. Don't assume that he'll refuse; ask him. Many men do want to remain part of their children's lives and really do understand that they have an important role to play. In addition, many men feel inept regarding child rearing, particularly with girls, and believe that mother knows best. When a woman expects more from the father of her children, very often he is pleased to do his part.

The Distracted Mother. This mother is trying so hard to get on with her life and function independently after her divorce that she loses sight of her parenting responsibilities. The Distracted Mother is often wrapped up in her job and her social life. Although she may have every good intention toward her daughter, her primary concern is herself. Very often, she is jolted back to reality when her daughter, in a desperate attempt to get her mother's attention, begins to act out in dangerous or unhealthy ways. Hopefully, this mother recognizes her daughter's signs of need before she has harmed herself physically or emotionally.

If a mother finds that she is so preoccupied with other aspects of her life that she is not thinking about her daughter as much as she used to, or feels that she is losing touch with her daughter, it's a sign that she should consider reordering her priorities.

Although mothers may assume more of the child-care responsibilities after a divorce, fathers may also find themselves overwhelmed and confused by their new situation. The father who used to leave the rearing of the children up to his wife must now spend holidays and weekends alone with a daughter with whom he may not feel all that comfortable. Even a father who was very much involved in his daughter's life may find it difficult to develop a "normal" relationship on such a temporary basis. However, if he devotes enough time and energy, more often than not he finds the experience to be a rewarding one.

BETWEEN DIVORCED FATHERS
AND DAUGHTERS

Similar to divorced mothers and their daughters, divorced fathers may develop particular modes of behavior in response to their new situation that pose risks to their daughters' well-being.

The detached father. Even in an intact family, fathers often react to a daughter's adolescence by withdrawal—they become emotionally distant and remote. The father who is not living with his daughter on a daily basis may be even more prone to this kind of behavior. The Detached Father may simply not know how to handle his daughter and therefore finds ways of avoiding contact. The Detached Father may also be acting out his anger at the mother on his daughter. He may view his daughter as a surrogate for the mother and may resist any meaningful contact with her for fear of being sucked back into his past life.

Although he may give lip service to wanting to see his daughter, somehow this father is always too busy to keep their appointments. Even if he adheres to a visitation agreement, he may park his daughter in front of a television set to avoid conversation or even leave her alone a good deal of the time. In some cases, he may constantly invite friends over so that he doesn't have to spend time alone with his daughter. The daughter senses what's going on and, sadly, feels that she must be a worthless human being because even her own father is uninterested in her.

Very often, the Detached Father doesn't realize the pain he is inflicting on his daughter. In fact he may not even recognize what he is doing. He may indeed rationalize his actions by thinking, "Gee, I'd love to spend more time with Susan, but I'm just too busy right now," or "Gee, I just don't know what to do with Susan on the weekends." If you find yourself thinking these kinds of thoughts, or if you find that you're hardly spending any time alone with your daughter, it's a sign that you need to reexamine your motives and behavior.

The Overindulgent Dad. This dad, who more often than not is a "weekend, holiday dad," tries to show his love by buying his daughter things—lots of things. He may feel so bad—or guilty—about moving away from his daughter that he seeks to compensate by giving in to her every whim. In addition, constantly shopping and going out to nice places can be an easy way to fill the time without having to discipline or act like a true parent.

Initially, the daughter allows herself to be "seduced" by her father's lavish presents. In fact, she may play this for what it's worth by imploring Dad to buy her things that her mother has refused to get her. Eventually, however, the daughter of Overindulgent Dad is going to feel guilty about taking so much from her father and will also recognize that, in many cases, Dad is trying to substitute "things" for true affection.

The girl's mother may be very annoyed by Overindulgent Dad, especially if he ignores her wishes. It would be a mistake, however, for this mother to call her former husband and complain. It would probably just lead to a fight, and the problem would remain unresolved. The best approach would be to help the daughter deal with this situation on her own. If possible, the mother should try to engage her daughter in a dialogue. For example, the mother could say in a warm, nonthreatening manner, "Boy, Dad's been buying you a lot of nice things lately. Why, do you think?"

The daughter may reply somewhat defensively, "Well, I guess he loves me." At which point the mother could say, "Is buying things tantamount to telling someone that you love them?"

This will give your daughter an opportunity to think about her situation, and she may begin opening up to her mother: "Sometimes I feel a little uncomfortable about taking all these things." Her mother should then note that it must be difficult to have someone buying you everything that you want, because you know deep down that it's not really giving you what you need. If the mother is able to reach her daughter, she may help the girl discuss the situation with her father. Hopefully, the girl will be able to say, "I love you, Dad. You don't have to buy my love. Just start acting like a real dad."

The User Dad. The User Dad expects his daughter—and probably women in general—to be subservient. He is only concerned about his own needs. On her weekend visits, he expects his daughter to do his laundry and clean his apartment. He may even ask her to babysit for his girlfriend's children—free of charge, of course. This father usually neglects his daughter for most of the weekend and goes on with his life as if she wasn't there. The User Dad was probably estranged from his family long before the divorce and never viewed his children as anything more than burdens. Although the User

Dad's daughter is going to feel very hurt and confused by his behavior, she will rarely protest. She is much too insecure about this relationship and is so desperate to maintain it that she is fearful of making waves.

Her mother, however, may suspect what's going on and may be simply furious. As tempting as it would be to get on the phone and scream, "How dare you treat my daughter this way?" a far better approach would be to empower the daughter to handle it herself.

First, Mother has to make her daughter aware that she is being treated unfairly. "Why are you doing all that housework?" The girl may defend her father by saying, "Well, Dad works so hard during the week, it isn't fair that he has to do housework on the weekend." The mother can counter with, "Well, why doesn't he hire somebody to do it for him?" The daughter will quickly say, "Oh, he can't afford it." At which point the mother can point out that Dad has enough money to live in a nice apartment and go out on dates and wear nice clothes, he can certainly find the money for a housekeeper.

I think the mother should ask the girl if she feels that she can stand up for herself with her father. If the girl says yes, the mother should say, "Well, I'll support you in whatever you want to do." If the girl confesses that she can't, the mother should offer to "forbid" her from visiting Dad as long as he treats her like a maid. This will relieve the girl from her household "duties" without forcing her to confront her father.

WHEN A PARENT DESERTS

There are few things as traumatic for a child as when a parent simply disappears, severing all contact with his or her family. The remaining parent is left with the job of having to comfort a hurt, confused, even shell-shocked child.

There are several reasons why a parent will desert his or her family, but very often they revolve around other serious problems such as drug or alcohol abuse, or compulsive gambling. People who fall prey to these types of addictive behavior lose control over themselves and their lives and, inevitably, hurt the people who love them. If a spouse who deserts his or her family has this kind of problem, the other parent should let his or her daughter know the truth. Let her know that "Mommy is addicted to alcohol, and it's taken over her life," or "Daddy is deep into drugs and can no longer handle his responsibilities."

There are some parents who may be simply overwhelmed by the responsibility of supporting or caring for a family. In this case, the most comforting thing you can say is, "Yes, Mommy [Daddy] may have cared about us, but she [he] couldn't handle taking care of us. I think that she [he] is very immature, because her [his] own problems were more demanding than caring for her [his] child."

It's very important that the remaining parent not make excuses for the parent who left. The daughter who has been abandoned is going to feel very angry, and she needs to know that her anger is absolutely justified. The girl will also be relieved to hear that the parent who left has a serious problem, and that she is not responsible for the parent's actions. All too often, an adolescent girl will think, "If only I had been nicer to him," or "If only I hadn't acted up the way I did, this wouldn't have happened." Nothing can be further from the truth, and the girl should be told that it has nothing to do with her.

If the parent deserts for another man or woman, the daughter will ask, "Doesn't Mommy [Daddy] love me anymore?" I would not say yes unless I was sure that it was true. Perhaps due to their own inadequate parenting, some parents may remain detached from their families and may not connect with their children in normal ways. Once again, I would tell the truth: "When you were younger, I didn't think you'd understand what I have to say, but now I think you will. Daddy [Mommy] never seemed to be very close to us. It has nothing to do with us, I don't think that he [she] knows how to love in a normal way. When you really love someone, you just don't walk out and not see them anymore."

If you're not sure whether or not the other parent has feelings for your daughter, I would also express my confusion: "I'm not sure how Daddy [Mommy] really feels. You'll find that out for yourself later on. You'll see if he [she] tries to stay in touch with you, and you can sort out your feelings later. I know that you're hurting right now, but I can't give you a definite answer."

If the girl is very upset by her parent's disappearance, I would certainly get her into some kind of professional counseling. In this case, a support group with other children who have had similar experiences may be very comforting.

THE "GOOD ENOUGH" DIVORCE

Parents who care about their daughter need to understand that although they may want to divorce, they can't ever sever their mutual tie completely: They are bound together through their child. Once they accept this fact, they can go on and create a better environment for their daughter.

Even though a couple may not have had a good marriage, they can strive for a "good enough" divorce. By that I mean that they are able to rise above their differences for the sake of their daughter.

When it comes to child custody, sharing should be the operative word. A mother who is so enraged at her former husband that she tries to avoid any contact with him is making a terrible mistake. Ironically, after the divorce, she may need him even more than before. Being a single mother is a tough job, and a savvy woman would accept whatever help she can get from her former spouse. In addition, a father who is included in his daughter's life is less likely to become distant or detached, no matter where he is living.

I generally support joint custody agreements in which child care is shared fifty-fifty by both parents. Ideally, your daughter should spend equal amounts of time with both. I not only think that this arrangement is fair, but I think that the girl benefits by having two equally involved parents. It's important for your daughter to know that if she has a problem, she can turn to her mother *and* her father, who are both equally concerned about her welfare.

Even if your daughter does not spend equal amounts of time with both parents, she should feel equally wanted in both households. It's imperative that she have her own space at both homes and not be made to feel like a visitor in either one.

Despite their differences, divorced parents need to be able to make decisions together about their daughter. They also need to realize that there will be times when they disagree on child-rearing issues, and they must learn how to resolve these issues without forcing their daughter to take sides. They should deal directly with each other and never use their daughter as a go-between. For example, I knew one divorced couple who were at odds over whether or not to allow their 14-year-old daughter to work as a counselor at a summer camp. The father, who had some friends who raved about the camp, thought that the job would be a terrific experience for his daughter.

The mother, however, had heard stories from other parents that the camp director overworked the staff and didn't provide enough supervision. In the worst-case scenario, each parent would have tried to get the daughter to side with him or her. However, in this "good enough" divorce, these parents did not want to put their daughter in the painful situation of having to choose between them. Rather, united in concern over their daughter, they decided to try to understand each other's point of view. The father agreed to speak with the parents who were unhappy with the camp, and the mother agreed to talk with the camp director, as well as parents who were pleased with the camp. When they finished their research, neither parent was certain that the camp was appropriate for their daughter. The parents ended up selecting two other camps that were acceptable to both of them and left the final decision up to their daughter.

These parents are to be commended for their restraint and concern for their child. However, if divorced parents find that discussions about their daughter usually degenerate into accusations and name calling, I feel that they need outside counseling. There are special divorce mediators who deal with these kinds of problems, and their input can be very helpful.

Parents need to remember that although they may be wrapped up in their own problems after a divorce, they should not overlook the needs of their adolescent. Because her parents no longer love each other, the daughter may feel unloved and unwanted. She may ask, "Why did you ever have me, anyway?" The parents should be able to find it within themselves to say, "At the time we conceived you, we loved one another, and we were so thrilled when you were born. Things changed over time between your dad [mom] and me, but we never regretted having you." She needs to be reassured that although they may no longer love each other, they both still love her very much.

Since an adolescent girl tends to blame herself when things go wrong, she also needs to be told that she was not responsible in any way for her parents' divorce. Her parents need to reassure her: "You're a terrific girl. And we're sorry that this has to be going on around you. But our problems are our problems, and they have nothing to do with how we feel about you."

DATING AND THE SINGLE PARENT

Although I am the first one to remind single parents of their responsibility to their children, I understand that you also have a responsibility to yourself. You are entitled to make time in your life for your own friends, and some of these friendships may develop into romantic relationships. However, the rules of dating as a divorced parent are much different from dating as a single person. For your daughter's sake, it's important for you to understand the difference.

As a parent of an adolescent girl, your social life is no longer a private matter between you and the people you date. Whether you like it or not, you have an audience.

Your daughter is watching your every move. As she begins to enter the dating arena herself, she is looking to you as a role model. You can't preach one line to your daughter and behave in a completely different manner yourself. Your daughter will emulate your actions, not your words. Therefore, you need to comport yourself in a way that sets a good example.

First, you expect your daughter to introduce you to the boys she is dating, and therefore, you should introduce her to the people that you go out with. If a date picks you up or brings you home, you can invite him or her in to meet your daughter. I wouldn't make a big deal of this, I would treat it in the same manner as if I was introducing her to a good friend. It is also perfectly reasonable to invite your date in for a drink or coffee when you get home.

If you're a noncustodial parent who only sees your daughter every other weekend or on occasional weeknights, I would try not to go out without her during her visits. This is your special time together, and you owe it to her to give her your undivided attention. If you happen to be involved in a serious relationship, you don't have to banish your boyfriend or girlfriend when your daughter comes. However, at least initially, don't expect your daughter to be too happy at the prospect of a threesome. If your daughter objects to "sharing" you with another person, you can help soften her position by suggesting that the three of you do something very special that your daughter particularly enjoys. An activity such as swimming or going to a movie may seem less threatening to your daughter than the prospect of sitting through a two-hour dinner, having to make pleasant conversation with someone she may not even like. Gradually, over time, she may get used to having someone else around. I would still make sure that you and your daughter have a chance to spend a large chunk of time alone.

Whether your daughter is living with you or not, there are times when she may develop an intense dislike of someone you are dating. If the relationship is casual, you can handle the situation by seeing the person outside of your home, without your daughter. If you are becoming serious about that person, you need to have a heart-to-heart talk with your daughter. First, you can try to find out what she finds so objectionable about this special friend. She may have some legitimate reasons: "Bob is so condescending," or "Betty never seems to want me around." If you feel that your daughter has a point, you need to talk to your friend about making your daughter feel that she is wanted. However, in many cases, your daughter will not be able to articulate what she dislikes about your friend. She may feel that you are rejecting her for somebody else. Or she may simply reject the person you care about out of loyalty to her other parent. You have to let your daughter know that although you care about her, you are not going to give up this relationship for her. Tell her directly, "I love you, but I also care a great deal about Diane, and we're planning on staying together for a long time." In this way, you are letting your daughter know that she is going to have to adjust to this situation. Very often, once an adolescent sees the "other woman" or "other man" is here to stay, she begins to accept her or him, albeit grudgingly at first.

SEX AND THE SINGLE PARENT

For many people, dating often leads to a sexual relationship. Normally, the decision to become intimate with someone else is a very personal one, but as a single parent, you now need to consider your daughter's welfare.

You should not have a date sleep over in your bedroom unless you are certain that this is a serious, long-term relationship. If you are casually involved with someone, but want to have sex with him or her, don't bring him or her home. Be as discreet as you can. Casual sex is not an example you want your daughter to follow.

If you are convinced that you have found the person with whom you want to share your life for a long time to come—and the feeling is mutual—you should give your daughter time to adjust to this new situation. You might invite the person over for dinner and then suggest, that since it is late, he or she could spend the night on the couch. I know that this sounds a bit contrived, but it will give your daughter an opportunity to get used to seeing him or her around the breakfast table without having to deal with the sexual issues.

If you are serious about someone and don't want your former spouse to know, don't expect your children to keep your secret. It is extremely unfair to ask children not to tell their other parent about significant events in their lives. This will make them feel very torn and conflicted. Once you tell your children, you should simply accept the fact that your former spouse will also know.

A serious relationship can lead to marriage, and that can lead to a whole new batch of problems.

STEPFAMILIES

To an adolescent girl, a parent's remarriage to another person finally makes the divorce a reality. Up until then, she may have harbored secret fantasies that, somehow, her parents would get back together. Now she knows that it will never happen.

Initially, a girl will often resort to acting out behavior in protest of the new union. She will be surly and hostile to a stepmother. She may be equally nasty to a stepfather, or she may try to be sexually provocative in an effort to entrap him in a relationship that will infuriate her mother. However the adolescent chooses to provoke the new stepparent, the best response is a calm and firm disapproval of her behavior. Don't get locked into a struggle; simply tell her, "I don't like this kind of behavior. I hope that we can start to get along and you won't find it necessary to act this way. But I'm not going away, whatever you do."

Another reason why a girl may resist liking a stepparent is that she may view it as being disloyal to her mother or father. In many cases, an attractive, nice stepparent can be more threatening to a girl than one she can legitimately dislike. She will inevitably be comparing this person to her biological parent, who may or may not have the same attributes, and this can make her even more uncomfortable. That's why I feel that it's important not to push your daughter to be too warm or loving to a new stepparent; she needs time to sort out her feelings.

If the new stepparent has children of his (or her) own, he will be in a better position to understand the feelings of his stepdaughter. If he doesn't, he'd better educate himself quickly about adolescence. I have seen many stepfamilies crumble because the stepparent was so poorly prepared for his or her new role. These stepparents often feel that their adolescent stepdaughters are just whiny, spoiled brats, when in fact, they are merely acting like normal adolescents. A stepparent may find it very useful to take a parenting class geared to the adolescent years, or to seek counseling from a group such as the Stepfamily Foundation.

The girl's noncustodial parent can help ease the transition by making sure that the daughter still feels very much wanted. The parent should go to extra lengths to spend time alone with her and should make it clear that he or she is not deserting her but, rather, wants to include her in his or her new life.

If the noncustodial parent is remarrying, he or she must be very certain that the daughter feels welcome in the parent's new home, particularly if there are other stepchildren. The daughter should be given a special place where she can keep her things, and her own bed to sleep in—she shouldn't be made to feel like an unwelcome guest each week as her parents scout around for a place for her to sleep.

With planning and understanding, stepfamilies can work. In the best-case scenario, your daughter can enjoy being part of two families and can gain from both sets of parents. However, this won't happen overnight, and just like everything else involving your adolescent girl, it's going to require a great deal of time and patience.

THE LESSONS OF DIVORCE

The lessons that your daughter learns from your divorce do not have to be negative ones. Your daughter can learn that people can make mistakes—serious mistakes—and still survive and create a new life for themselves. Your daughter can learn that not all relationships will work out, and this knowledge may make her more discerning in her own choice of a long-term partner. Your daughter can also learn something about her own inner resources—that, if need be, she can adapt to new and often difficult situations and overcome major disappointments.

Finally, if you and your ex-spouse are determined to make your divorce work for your daughter, your daughter will learn that your love for her transcends any problems you may have with each other. This is the most important lesson of all.

RESOURCES

CHAPTER 6: BODY IMAGE AND SELF-ESTEEM

For information on nutritional counseling, contact:
The American Dietetic Association
216 W. Jackson
Suite 800
Chicago, IL 60606
312-899-0040

For information on eating disorders, contact:
Anorexia & Related Disorders, Inc.
P.O. Box 5102
Eugene, OR 97405
503-344-1144

American Anorexia & Bulimia Ass'n, Inc.
418 E. 76th St.
New York, NY 10021
212-734-1114

For information on support groups, contact:
Overeaters Anonymous
World Service Office
P.O. Box 92870
Los Angeles, CA 90009
310-618-8835
(You can also check in your local directory under *O* for the nearest O.A. branch.)

CHAPTER 9: DATING AND SEXUALITY

For information on contraception, sexually transmitted diseases, and other reproductive issues, contact:
Planned Parenthood
National Headquarters
810 Seventh Ave.

New York, NY 10019
212-541-7800
(Check your telephone directory for a local chapter.)

American College of Obstetricians and Gynecologists
409 12th St., SW
Washington, DC 20024-2188
202-638-5577

CHAPTER 10: SELF-DESTRUCTIVE BEHAVIORS

For support and information on alcoholism, contact:
Alcoholics Anonymous
(Check local directory under A for your nearest group.)

Family members and friends of alcoholics can get support and information
from the following:
Al-a-non & Al-a-teen
1-800-344-2666 (U.S.)
1-800-443-4525 (Canada)
1-800-245-4656 (New York City)

For information on cocaine abuse and recovery programs, contact:
1-800-COCAINE

To find a specialist in treating substance abuse, contact:
The American Society of Addiction Medicine
12 W. 21st St.
New York, NY 10010
212-206-6770

For referrals for therapy and/or counseling, contact your local mental health
association.

SELECT BIBLIOGRAPHY

Baker, D. P., and Entwisle, D. R. "The Influence of Mothers on the Academic Expectations of Young Children: A Longitudinal Study of How Gender Differences Arise." *Social Forces* 65:670–95 (1987).

Bauman, K. E., and Fisher, L. A. "On the Measurement of Friend Behavior in Research on Friend Influence and Selection: Findings from Longitudinal Studies of Adolescent Smoking and Drinking." *Journal of Youth and Adolescence* 15:345–53 (1986).

Billy, J. O. G.; Rodgers, J. L.; and Udry, J. R. "Adolescent Sexual Behavior and Friendship Choice." *Social Forces* 62:653–78 (1984).

Blos, P. *On Adolescence.* Glencoe, Ill.: Free Press, 1963.

———. "The Second Individuation Process in Adolescence." *Psychoanalytic Study of Children* 22:162–86.

Blyth, D.; Simmons, R.; and Zakin, D. "Satisfaction with Body Image in Early Adolescent Females: The Impact of Pubertal Timing Within Different School Environments." *Journal of Youth and Adolescence* 14(3):207–25 (1985).

Brooks-Gunn, J. "Antecedents and Consequences of Variations in Girls' Maturational Timing." *Journal of Adolescent Health Care* 9(5):1–9 (1988).

Brooks-Gunn, J., and Petersen, A., eds. *Girls at Puberty: Biological and Psychosocial Perspectives.* New York: Plenum Press, 1983.

Brown, B. B. "The Extent and Effects of Peer Pressure Among High School Students: A Retrospective Analysis." *Journal of Youth and Adolescence* 11:121–33 (1982).

Brown, B. B.; Lohr, M. J.; et al. "Early Adolescent Perceptions of Peer Pressure." *Journal of Early Adolescence* 6:139–54 (1989).

Brunberg, J. J. *Fasting Girls: The Emergence of Anorexia Nervosa as a Modern Disease.* Cambridge, Mass.: Harvard University Press, 1988.

Butcher, J. "Longitudinal Analysis of Adolescent Girls' Aspirations at School and Perceptions of Popularity." *Adolescence* 8(81):136–43 (1986).

Contraceptive Services. The Alan Guttmacher Institute, New York, 1991.

Covey, S. L., and Tam, D. "Depressive Mood, the Single-Parent Home, and Adolescent Cigarette Smoking." *American Journal of Public Health* 80:1330–33 (1990).

Dornbusch, S. M., Carlsmith, J. M., et al. "Sexual Maturation, Social Class and the Desire to Be Thin Among Adolescent Females." *Developmental and Behavioral Pediatrics* 5(6):308–14 (1984).

Dornbusch, S. M., Carlsmith, J. M., et al. "Sexual Development, Age & Dating: A Comparison of Biological and Social Influences Upon One Set of Behaviors." *Child Development* 52:179–85 (1981).

Eagle, C. J., and Schwartz, L. *Psychological Portraits of Adolescents: An Integrated Developmental Approach to Psychological Test Data.* New York: Lexington Books, in press.

Entwisle, D. R., and Baker, D. P. "Gender and Young Children's Expectations for Performance in Arithmetic." *Developmental Psychology* 19:200–9 (1983).

Erikson, E. H. *Childhood and Society.* New York: W. W. Norton & Co., 1950.

Feldman, S., and Elliot, G. *At the Threshold: The Developing Adolescent.* Cambridge, Mass.: Harvard University Press, 1990.

Fischer, G. "College Student Attitudes Towards Forcible Date Rape: I. Cognitive Predictors." *Archives of Sexual Behavior* 15(6):457–66 (1986).

Freud, A. *Normality and Pathology in Childhood: Assessments of Development.* New York: International Universities Press, 1965.

———. *The Ego and Mechanisms of Defense.* New York: International Universities Press, 1934.

Gilligan, C. *In a Different Voice: Psychological Theory and Women's Development.* Cambridge, Mass.: Harvard University Press, 1982.

Gilligan, C.; Lyons, N.; and Hanmer, T. *Making Connections: The Relational Worlds of Adolescent Girls at Emma Willard School.* Cambridge, Mass.: Harvard University Press, 1990.

"Girls Talk, Boys Talk More." *The Harvard Education Letter* Jan/Feb 1991.

Gjerde, P., and Block, J. "Preadolescent Antecedents of Depressive Symptomatology at Age 18: A Prospective Study." *Journal of Youth and Adolescence* (20)2:217–32 (1991).

Greif, E., and Ulman, K. "The Psychological Impact of Menarche on Early Adolescent Females: A Review of the Literature." *Child Development* 53:1413–30 (1982).

Gunnar, M. R., and Collins, W. A. *Development During the Transition to Adolescence: The Minnesota Symposia on Child Psychology,* vol. 21. Hillsdale, N.J.: Lawrence Erlbaum Associates, 1988.

Hall, R. "The Classroom Climate: A Chilly One for Women?" Project on the Status and Education of Women, Association of American Colleges, February 1982.

How Schools Shortchange Girls. Commissioned by the American Association of University Women Educational Foundation, Washington, D.C., and researched by the Wellesley College Center for Research on Women, 1992.

Jordan, J., Kaplan, A., et al. *Women's Growth in Connection: Writings From the Stone Center.* New York: The Guilford Press, 1991.

Kopp, C., ed. *Becoming Female: Perspectives on Development.* New York: Plenum Press, 1979.

Krosnick, J., and Judd, C. "Transitions in Social Influence at Adolescence: Who Induces Cigarette Smoking?" *Developmental Psychology* 18(3):359–68 (1982).

Lee, V., and Bryk, A. "Effects of Single-Sex Secondary Schools on Student Achievement and Attitudes." *Journal of Educational Psychology* 78(5):381–95 (1986).

Lee, V., and Marks, H. "Who Goes Where? Choice of Single-Sex and Coeducational Independent Secondary Schools." University of Michigan. Photocopy. Revised 28 November 1990.

Leinhardt, G.; Seewald, A. M.; and Engel, M. "Learning What's Taught: Sex Differences in Instruction." *Journal of Educational Psychology* 71(4):432–39 (1979).

Lerner, R., and Foch, T., eds. *Biological-Psychosocial Interactions in Early Adolescence*. Hillsdale, N.J.: Lawrence Erlbaum Associates, 1987.

Miller, A. *Prisoners of Childhood*. New York: Basic Books, 1981.

———. *Thou Shalt Not Be Aware: Society's Betrayal of the Child*. New York: New American Library, 1986.

Montemayor, R. "The Relationship Between Parent-Adolescent Conflict and the Amount of Time Adolescents Spend Alone and with Parents and Peers." *Child Development* 53:1512–19 (1982).

Mosher, W. "Contraceptive Practice in the United States, 1982–1988." *Family Planning Perspectives* 22(5):198–205 (1990).

Muehlenhard, C.; Friedman, D.; and Thomas, C. "Is Date Rape Justifiable? The Effects of Dating Activity, Who Initiated, Who Paid, and Men's Attitudes Toward Women." *Psychology of Women Quarterly* 9(3):297–310 (1985).

Nottelmann, E. D. "Competence and Self-Esteem During Transition From Childhood to Adolescence." *Developmental Psychology* 23(3):441–50 (1987).

Paikoff, R., Brooks-Gunn, J.; and Warren, M. "Effect of Girls' Hormonal Status on Depressive and Aggressive Symptoms Over the Course of One Year." *Journal of Youth and Adolescence* 20(2):191–215 (1991).

Petersen, A. "Adolescent Development." *Annual Review of Psychology* 39:583–607 (1988).

———. "Adolescent Depression: Why More Girls?" *Journal of Youth and Adolescence* 20(2):217–47 (1991).

Piaget, J. *The Construction of Reality in the Child*. New York: Basic Books, 1954.

———. *The Origin of Intelligence in Children*. New York: International Universities Press, 1952.

Rubin, J.; Provenzano, F.; and Luria, Z. "The Eye of the Beholder: Parents' Views on Sex of Newborns." *American Journal of Orthopsychiatry* 44(4):512–19 (1974).

Simmons, R., and Rosenberg, F. "Sex, Sex Roles and Self-Image." *Journal of Youth and Adolescence* 4(3):229–58 (1975).

Sports Nutrition: Eating Disorders. Report by the United States Olympic Committee, 1987.

Steinberg, L. "Transformations in Family Relations at Puberty." *Developmental Psychology* 17(6):833–40 (1981).

———. "Impact of Puberty on Family Relations: Effect of Pubertal Status and Pubertal Timing." *Developmental Psychology* 23(3):451–60 (1987).

Stone, L. J., and Church, J. *Childhood and Adolescence.* New York: Random House, 1957.

Teenage Sexual Reproductive Behavior in the United States. The Alan Guttmacher Institute, New York, 1991.

The Explorer's Pass. Girls Inc. National Resource Center, Girls Inc., Indianapolis, Ind., 1991.

Thornton, J. "Feast or Famine: Eating Disorders in Athletes." *The Physician and Sportsmedicine* 18(4):117–22 (1990).

"Two-Earner Families May Produce Sexist Sons." *The Wall Street Journal,* B1, 15 July 1991.

Yates, A. "Current Perspectives on the Eating Disorders: I. History, Psychological and Biological Aspects." *Journal of the American Academy of Child Adolescent Psychiatry* 28(6):813–28 (1989).

INDEX

Abortion, 192–93
Abstinence, 175–76
Abstract thought, 151
Academic performance, 28, 68
    drugs and, 218
    See also School(s)
Acne, 58
Acquired immune deficiency
    syndrome, *see* AIDS
Acting out, 21, 200
    by parents, 33
    in stepfamilies, 234
Addiction, 214–15
    See also Alcohol abuse; Drug abuse
African Americans, 22, 29
After-school activities, *see*
    Extracurricular activities
After-school jobs, 69, 74
Aggressiveness, 21, 139
    in school, 156, 163–64
Aging, physical aspects of, 83
AIDS, 27, 31, 171, 173, 175–78,
    180, 181, 184, 185, 187, 193
Alcohol abuse, 15, 30, 121, 141,
    144, 199, 202, 208–12
    combined with drug abuse, 215–
    216
    by parents, 228–29
    at parties, 185
    risks of, 209–10
    signs of, 217–18
    treatment for, 212
Alcoholics Anonymous, 212
Algebra, 154
Allowances, 66
Amenorrhea, 114
American Association of University
    Women (AAUW), 21, 22,
    148
Anemia, 112
Anger, 21, 61, 90
    dealing with, 62–64
    at deserting parent, 229
    internalized feelings of, 200
    of parents, 17, 32–33, 35–36, 40,
    43–44, 223–24, 226
Angst, normal, 200
Anorexia nervosa, 25, 49, 108, 113–
    116
    prognosis for, 114–15
    risks of, 114
    treatment for, 122–23
    warning signs of, 115
Apathy, parental, 36
Appearance, *see* Looks
Appetite
    voracious, 50
    See also Eating disorders

Assault, vulnerability of women to, 26
Athletic clubs, 146
Athletics, 68
    eating disorders and, 121
    smoking and, 206
Attractiveness
    to boys, 62
    See also Looks
Authoritarianism, 40
Authority, challenging, 25
Automobile accidents, 209, 211
Autonomy, 17, 23, 67, 74
Average Girl, 139–40

"Baby fat," 49
Bad crowd
    entrenchment in, 145–46
    flirting with, 144–45
    steering daughter away from, 146–147
    substance abuse and, 218
Barnard College, 166
Behavior, change in, 218
Best friend
    mother as, 86
    See also Friends
Betrayal by friends, 137
Birth control pills, 206–7
Bizarre eating habits, 115
Blood pressure, 117
    dangerously low, 114
    high, 205
Body hair, 51–52
Body image, 23–24
    distorted, 115
Body odor, 57–58
Body preference, values reflected in, 109
Boredom in school, 168
Boundaries, appropriate, 95
Boutique drugs, 215
Boyfriends, 183–84
    See also Dating

Breast cancer, 204
Breast development, 47, 50–51
Breast implants, 126
Breast reduction surgery, 126, 128
Bronchitis, 205
Bulimia, 25, 107–8, 116–19
    prognosis for, 118–19
    risks of, 117
    treatment for, 122–23
    warning signs of, 118

Calcium, 112
Camps, weight-loss, 125
Cancer, 204–5
Careers, 77
    math and science and, 28, 29, 161
Carroll, Lewis, 46
Cars, 76
    accidents, 209, 211
Catholic high schools, 167
Chaperons, 76, 185–86
Chemistry, 149
Chin implants, 126
Chlamydia, 27, 171
Church youth groups, 136, 146
Cigarettes, see Smoking
Classroom participation, 151
Cliques, 65, 72, 132
    outsiders and, 135–36
Clothes, picking out, 66
Cocaine, 30, 185, 214–15
Coercion, sexual, 171–72, 187, 191
Cognitive development, 64
College, 78, 166
    date rape at, 171–72, 190
    entrance exams for, 149, 168–69
    single sex, 166
    for sons, 102
Columbia University, 166
Communication
    hostile, 68
    improving, 42–43
    strained, 15

Competition, 169
  maternal, 85–86, 194
Compromise, 72
Compulsive behavior, 117, 118, 121, 122
Condoms, 171, 175, 178, 180, 181, 184, 185, 190, 193
Confidence, lack of, 14
Confrontation, avoiding, 140
Contraception, 27, 171, 193, 194
  smoking and, 206–7
Control freak, father as, 96
Copycat tendencies, 14
Crack, 30, 185, 214
Cramps, menstrual, 56
Crimes
  in schools, 156
  victims of, 26
Criminal activity, 141, 145
Criticism
  constructive, 151
  excessive, 85
Crushes, 178–79
  on other girls, 195
  thoughtful, 181
Curfews, 26, 72, 76
Curse words, 61
Custody, 223, 230

Dances, 178, 189
Danger, sense of, 156
Date rape, 172, 185, 190–92
Dating, 27, 170, 176–77
  academic slide and, 158–59
  in bad crowd, 144–45
  in early adolescence, 65–66, 178–179
  friendships and, 136–37
  in late adolescence, 76–77
  in middle adolescence, 72–73, 181–84, 188–90
  mother's memories of, 83
  by single parents, 232–33
  See also Sex

Deals, making, 71–72
Decision-making skills, 74
Deodorant, 58
Dependency, 67
Depressants, 215
Depression, 14, 16, 21, 41, 123, 201
  anorexia and, 116
  in good girls, 100
  smoking and, 30
Desertion, parental, 228–29
Designer drugs, 215
Destructive relationships, 15
Detached Father, 226
Diaphragm, 193
Dieticians, 125
Dieting, 24, 111, 113
  long-term consequences of, 111–112
  overzealous, 119
Diet pills, 216
Distorted body image, 115
Distracted Mother, 225
Diuretics, abuse of, 117
Diversity, importance of, 129
Divorce, 29, 220–31
  father-daughter relationship after, 226–28
  "good enough," 230–31
  lessons of, 235–36
  mother-daughter relationship after, 223–25
  timing of, 221
Dress code, family, 104
Drinking
  rules of, 210
  See also Alcohol abuse
Driving
  drinking and, 186, 209, 211–12
  under the influence of marijuana, 212–13
  See also Cars
Dropping out of school, 22, 66
Drug abuse, 15, 30, 66, 121, 141, 144, 199, 202, 212–16

Drug abuse (*cont.*)
  dating and, 184
  by parents, 228–29
  at parties, 185
  signs of, 217–18

Eating disorders, 14, 25, 31, 108,
    109, 199, 202
  treatment of, 122–23
  vulnerability to, 119–22
  See also Anorexia nervosa;
    Bulimia; Obesity
Eating habits, bizarre, 115
Economics, 74
Emotional battering by siblings,
    99
Emotional changes, 60, 130
  in early adolescence, 62
  friendships and, 132
  in late adolescence, 76
  in middle adolescence, 69–70
  sex and, 171, 172
Empathy, parental, 42
Emphysema, 205
Empowerment
  physical development as source of,
    24, 110
  sense of, 21
Endorphins, 116, 119
Estrogen, 50
Exercise
  excessive, 116
  See also Athletics
Extracurricular activities, 146–48,
    160
  reduced participation in, 155

Family therapy, 187
  for eating disorders, 123
Fast Trackers, 19–20, 23, 52,
    54
  breast development of, 51
  body odor in, 57

dating by, 65–66, 178
eating disorders in, 120
friendships of, 131
growth spurt of, 50
menstruation in, 53–54
negative feelings about their bodies
    by, 109
parents as, 41
popularity of, 133
preadolescent, 176
sexually active, 171, 179
Fathers, 89–98
  "demystifying" other sex by, 91–
    92
  divorced, 226–28
  expectations of, 90
  "good enough," 98
  midlife conflicts of, 94
  "most wonderful dad in the
    world," 97–98
  as negative models, 91
  in pubertal triangle, 92–93
  roles of, 90–91
  "ruler of the roost," 96–97
  seeking approval from, 91
  sexual tension with, 93
  withdrawing, 94
Fat phobia, 111
Fertility problems, 112
Fights with friends, 138
Followers, 141–43
  in bad crowd, 146
Food, attitudes toward, *see* Eating
    disorders
Frank, Anne, 52–53, 92
Friday, Nancy, 82
Friends, 65, 72, 130–32
  bringing home, 147
  fights with, 138
  interactions styles and, 138–
    143
  maturing relationships with, 136–
    137
  phone calls with, 143–44
Frustration, parental, 17

Galen, 116
Gambling, compulsive, 228
Gender expectations, 152
Geometry, 154
Gifted students, 165
Girls Incorporated, 152
"Glass ceiling," 15
Goals, plans for achieving, 77
"Good enough" divorce, 230–31
"Good enough" father, 98
"Good enough" home, siblings in,
    103–4
"Good enough" mother, 89
Grades, 168–69
Grounding, 211
Growth spurt, 49–50
Guilt by association, 133
Gypsy (musical), 88

Hair, body, 47, 51–52
Hand holding, 179
Hands-off mothers, 87
Harvard University, 151, 166
Heart disease, 204
Helplessness, learned, 154, 165
Herpes, 171
High blood pressure, 205
Hispanics, 22
Homework, 161, 167
Homosexuality, 195–96
Hormones, 49, 58, 114
Hospitalization for eating disorders,
    122–23
Hypothalamus, 50

Identity, quest for, 69
Immune system, 114
"I'm not you" phase, 61
Impulsive behavior, 201
"In crowds," 133
    See also Cliques
Independence, 16, 17, 23, 67
    for boys, 25

daughter's bid for, 84
difficulty asserting, 43
Individual therapy for eating
    disorders, 123
Inexperienced girls, pregnancy in,
    193–94
Infertility, 114
Intellectual changes, 60
    in early adolescence, 64–65
    friendships and, 131
    in late adolescence, 75–76
    in middle adolescence, 70–71
Ipecac, 117
Iron, 112
Ivy League, 166

Jealousy, maternal, 85
Jobs
    after-school, 69, 74
    dead end, 15
    of mothers, see Working mothers
Jocks, 121
Joint custody, 223, 230
"Joy riding," 145

Kissing games, 176, 177

Language, offensive, 61
Lanugo, 115
Late Bloomers, 20, 54, 109
    academic, 166
    breast development, 51
    breast implants for, 127
    dating by, 77, 188–90
    friendships of, 131
    menstruation in, 53–54
    parents as, 37
    preadolescent, 176
    in school, 158
    sex and, 173
Laxative abuse, 111, 117, 119
Learned helplessness, 154, 165

Lee, Gypsy Rose, 88
Legs, shaving, 52
Lesbians, 195–96
Liberal arts, 151
Limits
    setting, 71–72, 76, 159
    testing, 217
Liposuction, 126
Loneliness, memory of, 38
Looks, 62
    cultural preoccupation with, 112
    de-emphasizing importance of,
        128
    drinking and, 211
    focus on, 157
    obsession with, 24, 108–10
    school performance and, 158
    smoking and, 206
    and societal pressure to be pretty,
        110–11
Love, 68
    starving for, 119–20
    unrealistic notions of, 104–5
Lung cancer, 204, 205

Macrobiotic diet, 113
Marijuana, 185, 208, 212–14, 217
Marital problems, 105
    See also Divorce, 176
Math, 14, 69, 148–50
    in all-girl schools, 167
    and career options, 28, 29, 161
    feelings of inadequacy about,
        149
    gifted students in, 165
    in junior high school, 154
    low grades in, 160
    as "male" subject, 151–53
    test scores in, 28
Maturity, concrete evidence of, 66
Medication for eating disorders,
    123
Mediocre students, 165–66
Menarche, 52

Menopause, premature, 205
Men's movement, 29
Menstruation, 16, 20, 24, 26, 48,
    52–57
    cessation of, 114
    communicating right message
        about, 56–57
    concerns about, 55–56
    disorders of, 112
    explaining, 54–55
    growth spurt and, 50
Midlife conflicts, 16
    of fathers, 94
    of mothers, 83
Mistakes
    allowing for, 77
    avoiding, 40–41
Mood swings, 61
Mothers, 82–89
    as best friends, 86
    competitive, 85–86
    divorced, 223–25
    "good enough," 89
    hands-off, 87
    at midlife, 83
    overprotective, 84–85
    in pubertal triangle, 92–93
    stage, 88–89
    working, see Working mothers
Movies, 16
My Mother/My Self (Friday), 82

National Centers for Disease
    Control, 24, 111
National Collegiate Athletic
    Association (NCAA), 121
Necking, 179
Needy girls, pregnancy in, 194
Negative models, 61, 65
    fathers as, 91
Negotiation, art of, 72
Nerds, 133, 157, 158, 163
Nondaters, 188–90
Nonverbal cues, 134

Nose, cosmetic surgery on, 126,
127
Nuclear family, 29
Nutritional counseling, 123

Obesity, 123–26
Obsessiveness, 36
Odor, body, 57–58
On-Time Girl, 19–20
breast development in, 51
preadolescent, 176
Opinions, expressing, 73
Options, exploring different, 73
Organ damage
in anorexia nervosa, 114
in bulimia, 119
Osteoporosis, 112, 114
Outsiders, helping, 135–36
Overeaters Anonymous, 123
Overindulgent Father, 226–27
Overprotectiveness, 42
of fathers, 95
of mothers, 84–85
Overweight teenagers, 123–26
Overwhelmed Mother, 224–25

Pain, unacknowledged, 40
Parental relationship, 104–6
Parent-teacher conferences, 162
Parties, 176, 178
without adult supervision, 67, 76,
185
drinking at, 210–11
Passivity
friendships and, 140–41
in school, 164–65, 167
Peers, 44, 65, 72, 130
academically oriented, 167
comparison to, 64
gifted students and, 165
learning about sex from, 170,
174
praise from, 157

during puberty, 131
ranking against, 132
See also Friends
Petting, 186
Phenylpropanolamine (PPA), 216
Physical fighting by siblings, 100
Physics, 149
Plastic surgery, 126–28
Politics, 70
Popularity, 44, 62, 133
school performance and, 158
Potassium, 117
Power, issues of, 35, 36
Poverty, cycle of, 30
Praise, 68
from peers, 157
Pregnancy, 27, 31, 192–95
acting out behavior and, 200
among African American girls, 22
and competitive mothers, 85
among Fast Trackers, 66
low self-esteem and, 15
preventing, 173
rate of, 171
smoking during, 207
Premenstrual syndrome (PMS), 56
Princeton University, 166
Privacy, 104
Private school, 168
Promiscuity, 187–88, 200
Prozac, 123
PSATs (Preliminary Scholastic
Aptitude Tests), 168, 169
Pubertal triangle, 92–93
Puberty, 14, 23, 25, 26, 46–59
acne and, 58
body odor and, 57–58
divorce during, 221, 222
eating disorders in response to,
120
fathers and, 48–49
growth spurt and, 49–50
mother-daughter bond during, 83
participation in sports during, 68
peer relationships during, 131

Puberty (*cont.*)
  physical signs of, 48
  preparing your daughter for, 47–
    48
  school performance and, 150,
    157–62
Pubic hair, 47, 51–52
Punishment, 210
  severe, 40
Purging, 117, 118

Racially mixed schools, 156
Radcliffe College, 166
Rage, relentless, 36
Rape, 26
  date, 172, 185, 190–92
Reading, 148
Recommended dietary allowance
    (RDA), 112
Rejection
  by friends, 134–35
  memory of, 37–38
Relationships, concern about, 23
Remarriage, 221, 223, 234
Resources, division among siblings
    of, 102, 103
Responsibility, 66
  sexual, 181
Rigidity, 36
Rivalry
  between mothers and daughters,
    85
  sibling, 35
Role models, 22, 81, 130, 232
  of followers, 142
  mothers as, 82
  negative, 61, 65, 91
Rooms, separate, 104
"Ruler of the roost" father, 96–97
Runner's high, 116

Safer sex, 15, 27, 173, 175, 181,
  184–85, 190

Safety, concerns about, 26
Sassy magazine, 112
SATs (Scholastic Aptitude Tests),
    28, 168, 169
School(s), 28–29, 69, 148–69
  aggressiveness in, 163–64
  boys as attention grabbers in, 150–
    151
  coed, 166–68
  gifted students in, 165
  lack of interest in, 159–60
  looks counting more than
    substance in, 110
  maintaining interest in, 162
  male and female subjects in, 151–
    153
  mediocre students in, 165–66
  older adolescents in, 168
  passivity in, 164–65
  puberty and, 157–62
  single sex, 166–68
  teasing at, 99
  transition from elementary to
    junior high, 153–57
Science, 14, 28, 69, 148–50
  and career options, 29, 161
  gifted students in, 165
  low grades in, 160
  as "male" subject, 151–53
Sebum, 58
Secretiveness, 115–16
  substance abuse and, 218
Sedentary lifestyle, 124
Self-confidence, maintaining, 149
Self-destructive behavior, 199–219
  See also Alcohol abuse; Drug
    abuse; Smoking
Self-esteem
  loss of, 21, 22, 155, 220
  low, 14, 15, 21, 28, 102, 149, 216
  and perception of own
    attractiveness, 109
Sense of self, poor, 14, 15, 109, 216
"Separate but equal" philosophy, 103
Seventeen magazine, 112

Sex, 27, 65–66, 77, 87, 170–96
  abstinence from, 175–76
  double standard of, 26–27
  drinking and, 209
  in early adolescence, 179–81
  eating disorders and, 120
  in late adolescence, 190–92
  in middle adolescence, 184–88
  need for knowledge about, 172
  risks of, 171–72
  and single parents, 233–34
  and values, 174–75
Sex-role stereotyping, 90
  in school, 150, 163
Sexually-transmitted diseases
    (STDs), 27, 171–73, 175
  See also AIDS
Shoplifting, 141, 199, 200
Siblings, 98–103
  conflicts between, 99–100
  daughter among sons, 102–3
  divorce and, 224
  eating disorders and, 119–20
  evenhanded approach among, 103
  fine on her own versus attention
      grabbers, 100
  in "good enough" home, 103–4
  problem girl versus perfect, 101–2
  rivalry among, 35
Single parents, 29–30
  dating by, 232–33
  sexuality of, 233–34
Sleep, 50
Smoking, 15, 30, 39, 199, 204–8
  contraceptive choices and, 206–7
  cosmetic concerns about, 206
  during pregnancy, 207
  health risks of, 205–6
  by parents, 87, 207–8
  social stigma of, 206
"Social liabilities," 133
Spatial skills, 151
Spontaneous sex, 173
Sports, *see* Athletics
Stage mother, 88–89

Stepfamilies, 234–35
Stepfamily Foundation, 235
Stimulants, 215
Stroke, 205
Substance abuse
  girls prone to, 216–17
  by parents, 217, 222
  preventing, 219
  treatment of, 218–19
  See also Alcohol abuse; Drug abuse
Suicide, 199, 200, 202–3
  homosexuality and, 196
  prevention of, 203–4
Superachievers, 120–21
Support groups, 229
  for eating disorders, 123
*Surgeon General's Report on Nutrition,
    The*, 112
Synagogue youth groups, 136, 146

Teachers, feedback from, 162
Teasing, 99
Telephone use, 143–44
Television, 16
Temper tantrums, 101
Tests
  scores on, 149, 168–69
  studying for, 161
Thrills
  looking for, 201
  vicarious, for parents, 217
"Today, I am . . ." phase, 69, 73
"Too empathetic" father, 95, 96
20/20 (television program), 175
Tyrant, father as, 97

Uncontrolled environments, 146
Underarm hair, 51–52
Uniqueness, expressing, 70
University of California at Los
    Angeles (UCLA), 152
Universities, single sex, 166
User Father, 227–28

Vaginal deodorants, 58
Values, 73–74
 family, 106
 of popular girls, 133
 and sex, 174–75
 and substance abuse, 216
Vandalism, 145
Vassar College, 166
Vegetarianism, 70, 113
Verbal skills, 148
Vicarious thrills, girls who provide
 parents with, 217
Violence
 drinking and, 209
 in school, 156
Vision, impaired, 117
Visitation agreements, 226
Vomiting, induced, 111, 117, 118

Wage gaps, 15
Wall Street Journal, The, 26
Weight
 obsession with, 24–25, 108–
 110
 realistic goals for, 125
 smoking to control, 205, 207
Welfare, 30
Withdrawal, paternal, 94
Women's movement, 21
Working mothers, 83–84
 divorced, 223, 225
Workplace, changes in, 28–29

Yeast infections, 58
Youth groups, church or synagogue,
 136, 146